ISAIAH

A PROPHET'S PROPHET

VOLUME 1

ISAIAH

A PROPHET'S PROPHET

VOLUME 1

CHAPTERS 1–31

ROBERT L. MILLER

CFI
AN IMPRINT OF CEDAR FORT, INC.
SPRINGVILLE, UTAH

ISBN 13: 978-1-4621-3901-9

Published by CFI, an imprint of Cedar Fort, Inc.
2373 W. 700 S., Springville, UT 84663
Distributed by Cedar Fort, Inc., www.cedarfort.com

Library of Congress Control Number: 2021947603

Cover design by Courtney Proby

Edited and typeset by Valene Wood

Printed in the United States of America

10 9 8 7 6 5 4 3 2 1

Printed on acid-free paper

Dedicated to

My wife and children

Louise, Derrik, Dallin,

Carson, Connor, and Clarissa

And my parents

Jerry and Gayle

Their love and support bless me every day.

Contents

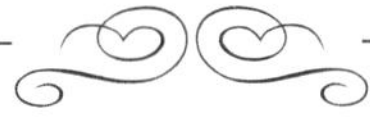

Author's Note

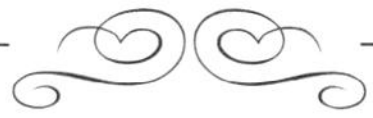

This work on Isaiah's teachings will help students of the scriptures increase their understanding of the words of Isaiah. His writings persuade us to believe in Christ, and they give hope to us in our day (see 1 Nephi 19:23–24). Through the words of modern-day prophets and apostles, we have added clarification, guidance, and encouragement to assist in this effort.

I am grateful to my family who studied the Book of Isaiah with me. We spent a year and a half studying Isaiah chapter by chapter. Their insights and corrections to this manuscript significantly strengthened and clarified what I wrote. I have tried to faithfully explain and interpret Isaiah's words in harmony with the teachings of The Church of Jesus Christ of Latter-day Saints. This reflects my understanding and should not be taken as an official statement of the Church, or that any official endorsement of this work is implied by the author. For the content of this work, I assume full responsibility.

Robert L. Miller, September 1, 2020

Introduction

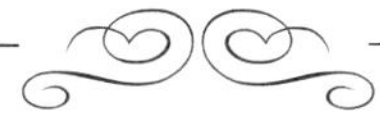

What Shakespeare is to English, Isaiah is to scripture.

Isaiah is a "Prophet's Prophet." Many prophets, including Christ, have quoted him. As a prophet, Isaiah's record speaks directly both to his own time as well as to the time that we live in. His writing style and use of words and phrases indicate his intelligence and guidance by the Spirit. Isaiah is a gifted writer and wrote and taught using the gift of prophecy to benefit all those who have a "heart to perceive, and eyes to see, and ears to hear" (Deut. 29:4).

Isaiah was commanded to record what he wrote. In Isaiah 8:16, he was told to "bind up" (Heb. tsârar—to wrap up, to safeguard from tampering) what he had testified of, and to "seal" (Heb. châtham—to attest as final, to close up) "the law" (teachings or doctrine) so that it could be available for ancient and modern disciples. Later in Isaiah 30:8, Isaiah was told to make sure that his writings were recorded "in a table," probably meaning to record them on a tablet of stone, wood, or metal so that these writings "may be for the time to come for ever and ever."

Relevance and Applicability of Isaiah

There is great relevance and applicability of Isaiah's words to us today. The Savior prophesied that their fulfillment will be in a day when the covenant that Heavenly Father made with the house of Israel is fulfilled (3 Nephi 20:11–12). Nephi, the Book of Mormon prophet, stated, ". . . in the days that the prophecies of Isaiah shall be fulfilled men shall know of a surety, at the times when they shall come to pass. Wherefore, they are of worth unto the children of men, and he that supposeth that they are not, unto them will I speak particularly, and confine the words unto mine own people; for I know that they shall be of great worth unto them in the last days; for in that day shall they understand them; wherefore, for their good have I written them" (2 Nephi 25:7–8).

The words of Isaiah are "directed to a sixth-century audience on the verge of a national crisis" (Smith, *American New Commentary*, 23). With an impending crisis on the horizon, Isaiah is consistently inspired to see our day and write about it. "Over fifty-five of the sixty-six chapters in the book of Isaiah predict the restored gospel in the last days, including the coming forth of the Book of Mormon (chapter 29); Joseph Smith as the prophet of the latter-day gathering and the Restoration, and as an ensign to the people (chapters 11, 29, and 49); missionaries going to all the world (chapters 18 and 60); establishment of the Church (2:2–3; 54:2); and other events of the last days and millennial era" (Nyman, *Isaiah and the Prophets*, 4–9).

Book of Mormon authors knew of Isaiah's emphasis on our day. As Mormon edited large quantities of records, he made sure to include a significant amount of Isaiah's writings. Of the sixty-six chapters of Isaiah, nineteen are quoted in their entirety in the Book of Mormon. There are several additional chapters that are partially quoted as well. "In total, there are 425 of the 1,292 verses of Isaiah that are quoted in the Book of Mormon. Of these 425 verses, 229 are quoted differently from those in the King James text, while 196 are identical" (Nyman, *Great Are the Words,* 283).

In revelations to the Prophet Joseph Smith, the Lord continued to apply the words of Isaiah to our day. "There are at least sixty-six quotations or paraphrases from the prophet Isaiah in the Doctrine and Covenants. Some of these are full verses, and some are only phrases. . . . Represented within the sixty-six passages are thirty-one different chapters of Isaiah" (Nyman, *Great Are the Words*, 289).

Oliver Cowdery referred to thirteen passages from Isaiah which the angel Moroni told Joseph Smith were being fulfilled in these latter days: Isaiah 1:7, 23–26; 2:1, 3–4; 4:5–6; 11:14, 16; 13:10, 13; 24:21; 28:21; and 29:11–14 (Cowdery, *Messenger and Advocate*, February 1835, 79–80; April 1835, 109–112).

"The Prophet Joseph Smith quotes or comments at least forty times concerning Isaiah. A study of these quotations and comments will show why the Savior said, 'Search these things diligently . . . for great are the words of Isaiah' (3 Ne. 23:1)" (Nyman, "Restoring 'Plain and Precious Parts'", 21).

Historical Background

Isaiah's call to be a prophet in chapter six came at the time of Uzziah's death (740 BC). He lived during the reign of these five kings:

King Uzziah	(792–740 BC)
King Jotham	(740–734 BC)
King Ahaz	(734–728 BC)
King Hezekiah	(728–697 BC)
King Manasseh	(697–642 BC)

(Compiled from King James Bible Dictionary, 638–639)

Some of the major nations in the Mediterranean and west Asia in Isaiah's time were Assyria, Syria, Babylon, Israel, and Judah. Very similar to Europe before World War I began, several of these nations were powerful and were intertwined with one another through diplomacy and alliances. These alliances shifted over time and the superpower of the time was Assyria. Assyria lay to the north-east of Israel (think modern day southeast Turkey and northern Iraq).

Dan Carlin compares Assyrians at this time to pre-WWI Germans "because the Germans have always had a reputation for being militarily tough, not just in the twentieth century, but throughout history. An oft-cited rationale proposed for this is that the area of modern Germany is surrounded by other powerful peoples and doesn't have a lot of natural frontiers, making it difficult to defend. From a social Darwinian perspective, you might say the only people who could survive in an area like that would be those who were tough and warlike. The same is often said about the Assyrians, because ancient Assyria was also ringed by powerful states and suffered a lack of natural frontiers, so the Assyrians had to be very tough, very centralized, very efficient, and very good warriors to survive" (Carlin, *The End is Always Near*, 72).

As the only superpower of the time, Assyria had the ability to plunder, conquer, and enslave other nations. Not only did they choose to do so, but they did it in a way that was cruel and destructive, then publicized the punishments they inflected on other nations. Their leaders appeared to be proud of what they did. They created great carvings in stone of what their armies did in war and the punishments their kings meted out to those who had rebelled against them. These carvings were prominently on display.

Understanding Assyria and its cruelty to other nations paints a large part of the background for geopolitical events of Isaiah's day. It helps modern-day readers to better understand the fears of kings and their people and why they react to and emphasize certain things. Assyria's plunder of other nations gives reason for many of their motives, actions, and even rebellions. And when a nation rebelled against Assyria, their Darth Vader and Death Star-like army was sent to take care of the plucky republic. For example, one Assyrian King, Ashurnasirpal II (883–859 BC and one of the most brutal of the Assyrian kings), punished a rebel city and boasted:

> I flayed as many nobles as had rebelled against me and draped their skins over the pile of corpses; some I spread out within the pile, some I erected on stakes upon the pile. . . . I flayed many right through my land and draped their skins over the walls.
>
> I felled 50 of their fighting men with the sword, burnt 200 captives from them, and defeated in battle on the plain 332 troops. With their blood I dyed the mountain red like red wool, and the rest of them the ravines and torrents of the mountain swallowed. I carried off captives and possessions from them. I cut off the heads of their fighters and built with the heads a tower before their city. I burnt their adolescent boys and girls.

Of another conflict, he recorded:

> In strife and conflict I besieged and conquered the city. I felled 3,000 of their fighting men with the sword. I captured many troops alive: I cut off of some their arms and hands; I cut off of others their noses, ears, and extremities. I gouged out the eyes of many troops. I made one pile of the living and one of the heads. I hung their heads on trees around the city. (Albert Kirk Grayson, Assyrian Royal Inscriptions, Part 2: From Tiglath-pileser I to Ashur-nasir-apli II (Wiesbaden, Germ.: Otto Harrassowitz, 1976), 126–127)

That gives a little idea of fears that a smaller nation like Israel would have for rebellion and why they might want to make an alliance with another nation(s). Assyria was seen by other nations as the evil empire. They could be compared to the Nazis in World War II. One of their preferred techniques to keep their subject peoples in line was a form of state terrorism.

Following the ascension to the throne by Tiglath-pileser III in 745 BCE, Assyria began to embark on its final (and greatest) phase of empire expansion. Fairly quickly Tiglath-pileser III's eyes turned to the territories to the south, to a strip of land that included Syria, Israel (or northern tribes), and Judah. Although not large, this small strip of land, bordered by the sea to the west and desert to the east, was an extremely valuable resource, both economically and militarily. Ownership of this land bridge meant control over the vital trade routes between the south (Egypt) and north (Assyria and beyond).

The Reigns of Uzziah and Jotham

Throughout King Uzziah's administration, Israel and Judah were wealthy and relatively powerful. Luxury had, however, brought about great social injustices, greed, envy, idleness, etc. The wealthy governing class took advantage of the poor through heavy taxation. Rejection of Jehovah and turning toward pagan gods became common. Isaiah's call came at this time of spiritual decline. Isaiah chapters 2–5 "fit well in the time of Uzziah and Jotham" (Smith, *New Commentary*, 28).

Reign of Ahaz

Isaiah chapters "7–11 and a few of the oracles against the nations in chapters 13–23 fit the reign of Ahaz (14:28–32)" (Smith, *New Commentary*, 28). During the reign of Ahaz, a major crisis occurred, the Syro-Ephraimite war (734 BC). Pekah, King of the northern kingdom of Israel, and Rezin, King of Syria, threatened to capture Jerusalem and replace Ahaz with a king of their own choosing for the purpose of forming a tripartite alliance, consisting of Syria, Israel, and Judah, against Assyria. Isaiah revealed the plot to Ahaz and prophesied that such an alliance would fail. The prophet tried in vain to convince Ahaz to place his trust in the Lord rather than in foreign alliances. Instead, Ahaz made an agreement with the Assyrian monarch, Tilgath pilezer II (Pul), and Judah became a vassal state, paying tribute to Assyria to escape the threat of Syria and Israel (2 Chron. 28:20–21).

During the reign of Ahaz, apostasy abounded. Ahaz supported the worship of Baal (2 Chron 28:1–4). Ahaz lacked faith and would not trust God.

Isaiah had encouraged Ahaz to believe and trust God (Isaiah 7:1–9) and was promised a victory if he would do so. In chapter 8, Isaiah lamented that the people of Judah had rejected the soft waters of Shiloh (Isaiah 8:6) but would instead receive the flood waters "strong and many" (Isaiah 8:7) of the Assyrian king. Ahaz's death is mentioned in Isaiah 14:28.

Reign of Hezekiah

Two key military events took place during Hezekiah's reign. About 713–711 BC, the Assyrian King Sargon II came west and defeated cities in the Philistine plain. "The second Assyrian incursion into Palestine was in response to king Hezekiah's refusal to pay his tribute to Sargon II (2 Kgs 18:7) and to Hezekiah's seizure of Assyrian territory in Philistia (2 Kgs 18:8). Sargon was unable to respond immediately to this act of rebellion because of trouble he was having with Babylon. . . . After Sennacherib put down the Babylonian rebellion, he attacked Sidon and then entered Palestine." Sennacherib defeated Egyptian forces in the plain of Eltekeh and then "turned his attention to key cities in Judah, such as Lachish, Libnah (37:8; 2 Kgs 19:8), and eventually, Jerusalem (Smith, *New Commentary*, 31).

Hezekiah made extensive preparations in Jerusalem to withstand Sennacherib's attack. He blocked off the spring of Gihon to protect the city's water source and dug a tunnel from the east side of the City of David to the west side where it emptied out at the Pool of Siloam (2 Chron. 32:3–5, 30). He also repaired and strengthened the city walls and did everything possible to prepare for an attack by the Assyrian army.

Hezekiah also strove to prepare the people of Judah spiritually. He enacted religious reforms, repaired the temple, and renewed their covenants with God (2 Chron. 29:3–11, 15–36). Hezekiah sought counsel from Isaiah (Isaiah 37) and Isaiah prophesied the defeat of the Assyrian army and the death of Sennacherib. The Assyrians invaded Judah and was nearly overwhelmed in 701 BC. Jerusalem was saved when the people followed Isaiah's counsel to trust in God. The Lord smote the Assyrian hosts and the survivors withdrew with heavy casualties (see Isaiah 37:36–38). This constituted perhaps the greatest political event in Isaiah's ministry.

Overview of Isaiah's Life

Isaiah was born about 770 BC and his father was named Amoz (Heb. *Uwma*—meaning "strong"). Isaiah's name means "Jehovah saves" or "the

Lord is salvation." Ancient traditions indicate he was related to the royal family of Judah. This allowed the prophet to have easy access to the kings of Israel throughout his ministry. He labored with the tribe of Judah, which included the tribe of Benjamin. Isaiah testified to the Jewish leaders and was known as a city prophet. The scriptures indicate his call to become a prophet came during the last year of King Uzziah's reign in 740 BC.

Isaiah spent the last two years of his life in the Bethlehem Mountains hiding from King Manasseh (Ascension 2:7–11). Isaiah's death is reported to have come by the hands of Manasseh (Babylonian Mishnah, Vol. 10, p. 702). Josephus stated that as soon as King Manasseh found Isaiah, he was placed in a hollow log and then sawed in half (Antiquities of Jews 10:3:1 and Ginsberg, Legends of the Jews 4: 279). An eastern tradition reports that he lived to one hundred and twenty.

Isaiah was married and had at least two children. His wife was called "the prophetess" in Isaiah 8:3. He must have been instructed by the Lord to name his children by the spirit of prophecy for their names were symbolic for the nations of Judah and Israel. His son Shearjashub had a symbolic name meaning "a remnant shall return." The Lord charges Isaiah and his son Shearjashub to go meet King Ahaz, king of Judah, and deliver him a message of confidence and a sharp warning for his lack of faith and unbelief. The other son was named "Maher-shalal-hash-baz," which illustrated the speed of how the Assyrian army will hasten to the spoil and hurry to the prey of Israel as they come upon Ephraim and Judah.

Doctrines to Watch for as You Read Isaiah

The greatest reason we study Isaiah is for the powerful doctrine that brings us closer to Christ. It helps us toward our eternal salvation. The doctrinal information that we should watch for as we read Isaiah comes in seven classifications.

> First, he teaches about the apostate conditions of Israel and surrounding nations during his lifetime, which Nephi indicates we can liken unto our own times in these last days "that it might be for our profit and learning" (1 Nephi 19:23). Second, he shows the hand of the Lord in the historical happenings of his time and the power of prophetic utterances of prophets of God. Third, he speaks of the coming forth of the Book of

> Mormon, of which few men fully understand what its impact has been, is now, and will be in the future in bringing souls unto Christ. Fourth, he foretells of the restoration of the Lord's church in these latter days. Fifth, he teaches of the latter-day gathering of Israel and her final triumph over evil and her glory. Sixth, he teaches of Christ and his atonement at his first coming. "Of the 425 separate verses of Isaiah which are quoted in the Book of Mormon, 391 say something about the attributes or mission of Jesus Christ" (Church News, June 30, 1990, p. 12). Seventh, he teaches of the second coming of Jesus Christ and of his millennial reign and glory with his faithful, obedient children. (Miller, *Isaiah in the Book of Mormon*, 3)

An Invitation to "Liken" Isaiah's Words to Our Life

We can study Isaiah to see how nations and their inhabitants faced their problems, sometimes failing and sometimes succeeding, and we can benefit from the lessons they learned (see Mormon 9:31). Nephi, explaining to his people why he quoted so freely from the great prophet Isaiah said,

> [T]hat I might more fully persuade them to believe in the Lord their Redeemer I did read unto them that which was written by the prophet Isaiah; for I did liken all scriptures unto us, that it might be for our profit and learning.
>
> . . . [H]ear ye the words of the prophet . . . and liken them unto yourselves, that ye may have hope." (1 Nephi 19:23–24)

Most authors who quote this verse emphasize the likening of scriptures to us and emphasize doing this with the words of Isaiah. Many times, the phrase "that ye may have hope" is left in the shadows. Nephi wrote these words and then chose a chapter of Isaiah that gives several reasons for hope in our lives today. Here are a just few reasons how and why God gives us hope from one chapter (1 Nephi 20):

We are strengthened through covenants (20:1).
God knows the future and knows us (20:2–3).
God will not cut us off (20:9).
Chooses and refines us in the "furnace of affliction" (20:10).
Hearkening to God brings a river of peace (20:18).

Hearkening to God brings waves of righteousness (20:18).
Today we can flee Babylon and sing the songs of redeeming joy (20:20).
God is able to do miracle in our lives (20:21).
God has "done all of this [for us], and greater also" (21:22).

The words of Isaiah are relevant and applicable to us today. They can bring us closer to Christ and bring us hope. When the Savior visited the Nephites, He gave a commandment to study the words of Isaiah. He said: "Yea, a commandment I give unto you that ye search these things diligently; for great are the words of Isaiah. For surely he spake as touching all things concerning my people which are of the house of Israel; therefore it must needs be that he must speak also to the Gentiles" (3 Nephi 23:1–2).

Enjoy your diligent study of the Book of Isaiah. May your study of Isaiah bring you peace, hope, and an assurance that Jesus is the Christ.

ISAIAH CHAPTER 1

The Sin of Apostasy upon Ancient Israel

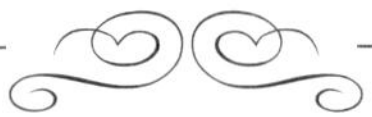

This chapter helps us understand the attitudes of the people of Israel and Judah and how they felt about their God. It shows how poorly they followed the prophets of God and lived His commandments. Chapter one of Isaiah provides a glimpse into the conditions of his time and some of the great concerns that he had for the Lord's people. Have you ever wondered what caused ancient Israel to fall so far into apostasy? This chapter provides some of the reasons for their downfall.

The first chapter is like a court scene with Israel being the defendant and Jehovah acting as both the plaintiff and the judge. Isaiah is an observer who sometimes is taking part in the dialog of the court. As a result, this chapter is often called the "Great Arraignment," the defendant Isaiah, as an observer and occasional interlocutor, and heaven and earth as the witnesses. After a prologue (Isa. 1:1) comes the court scene, which can be outlined as follows:

The Accusation—The Lord charges Israel of being guilty of sin and spiritual sickness (vs. 2–6).

"Immediate judgments: Physical and spiritual consequences are coming upon Israel because the people have not obeyed the Lord" (vs. 7–15).

"Promise of pardon: Conditions of cleansing, repentance, and blessing are presented (vs. 16–20).

"Final sentencing: The Lord will purge the wicked and redeem the righteous through apostasy, restoration, and judgment" (vs. 21–31). (Ludlow, 71)

Uzziah the King

1:1 The vision of Isaiah the son of Amoz, which he saw concerning Judah and Jerusalem in the days of Uzziah, Jotham, Ahaz, and Hezekiah, kings of Judah.

Background of the Man Isaiah

Isaiah was born about 770 BC and was the son of Amoz which means "strong." The name Isaiah (Heb. *hyevy*) means "Jehovah Saves" or "The Lord is Salvation." According to the Jewish authority Kimchi, Amoz, not to be confused with the prophet Amos, was "the brother of Amaziah, the father of Uzziah, . . . which would make Isaiah of royal lineage and a cousin of Uzziah," king of Judah. Isaiah lived under several kings of Judah. These were Uzziah (784–740 BC), Jotham (740–735 BC), Ahaz (735–715 BC), and Hezekiah (715–687 BC). Many scholars believe that Isaiah ministered between the years 740 and 700 BC (Parry, *Understanding Isaiah*, 8).

Isaiah was married and his wife was called (Heb. *haybn*) "The Prophetess." They had two sons (see 7:3, 8:3, and 8:18). Their two sons were named Shearjashub (Heb. *bwvy rav*) "The remnant shall return" and Mahershalalhashbaz (Heb. *zb vx llv rhm*) "He hastens the prey."

Tradition suggests that King Manasseh encased him in the trunk of a tree and sawed him in half (Josephus, Antiquities 10: 3 and Ginsberg, Legends of the Jews 4: 279.). An eastern tradition reports that he lived to one hundred and twenty.

Isaiah was called as a prophet in the same year that Uzziah died from leprosy.

> Then Uzziah was wroth, and had a censer in his hand to burn incense: and while he was wroth with the priests, the leprosy

> even rose up in his forehead before the priests in the house of the Lord, from beside the incense altar. (2 Chronicles 26:19)

Elder James E. Talmage explained what happened to Uzziah in his book *The Articles of Faith.*

> A striking instance of divine jealousy, which is righteous zeal, concerning priestly functions, is shown in the experience of Uzziah, king of Judah. He was placed upon the throne when but sixteen years old. As long as he sought the Lord he was greatly prospered, so that his name became a terror unto his enemies. But he allowed pride to grow in his heart, and indulged the delusion that in his kingship he was supreme. He entered the Temple and essayed to burn incense on the altar. Shocked at his blasphemous action, Azariah, the chief priest of the Temple, and fourscore priests with him, forbade the king, saying: "It appertaineth not unto thee, Uzziah, to burn incense unto the Lord, but to the priests the sons of Aaron, that are consecrated to burn incense: go out of the sanctuary; for thou hast trespassed." At this rebuke and condemnation from his subjects, though they were priests of the Lord, the king became angry; but immediately the scourge of leprosy fell upon him; the signs of the dread disease appeared in his forehead; and being now physically an unclean creature his presence tended the more to defile the holy place. So Azariah and his associate priests thrust the king out from the Temple; and he, a smitten thing, fled from the house of God never again to enter its sacred precincts. Concerning the rest of his punishment we read: "And Uzziah the king was a leper unto the day of his death, and dwelt in a several house, being a leper; for he was cut off from the house of the Lord" (Talmage, 185–186).

God's Children Rebelled against Him

1:2 Hear, O heavens, and give ear, O earth: for the Lord hath spoken, I have nourished and brought up children, and they have rebelled against me.

The beginning phrase of verse 2 echoes the words of Moses as he begins the great psalm that was his last mortal discourse: "Give ear, O ye heavens, and I will speak; and hear, O earth, the words of my mouth" (Deut. 32:1; compare Deut. 31:28). Moses's last sermon deals with God's greatness, His choice of Israel as His covenant people, Israel's rebellion, and God's final sovereignty over Israel and all nations. Isaiah expresses those same ideas and begins this chapter with a similar exhortation, indicating his familiarity with Moses's sermon. These words also serve as a reminder to Israel of the solemn covenants their ancestors made with the Lord before they entered the promised land. As in the past, willful disobedience to this covenant is sure to result in utter destruction (See Deut. 4:25–26).

A Loyal Animal Trusts Its Owner

1:3 The ox knoweth his owner, and the ass his master's crib: but Israel doth not know, my people doth not consider.

Consider (Heb. *bîyn*)—understand, to see to the heart of a matter or discern.

Crib—the stall where animals are fed.

Animals do not have the intelligence of man, but a loyal animal trusts its owner and knows where its food and lodging come from. If an ox or an ass knows where its home is and who its master is, then according to Isaiah this makes Israel dumber than both the ox and ass. Israel does not know Jesus Christ their master and will not obey His commandments, even though they have been rescued from bondage in Egypt by their Lord. They are unable to see to the heart of the matter.

Israel Is a Sinful Nation

In verse 4, the Lord ". . . elaborates upon Israel's corruption in a fourfold denouncement that describes four types of wickedness (sin, iniquity, evildoing, and depravity or corruption) among four groups (nation, people, brood or seed, and children). The description of the last group (depraved or corrupt children) demonstrates the seriousness of Israel's wickedness, for even her children are being taught to do evil" (Ludlow, 73).

1:4 Ah a sinful nation, a people laden with iniquity, a seed of evildoers, children that are corrupters: they have forsaken the Lord, they have provoked the Holy One of Israel unto anger, they are gone away backward.

Ah (Heb. *hoy*)—can be rendered simply as "ah!" although a more complete derivative would be "shame" or "alas."

"gone . . . backward"—literally, "estranged" (see Ps. 58:3).

Why are the nations of Israel and Judah so sinful? Isaiah tries to paint a general picture of their problems, and he will discuss each of them in more detail in his writings. They are a people laden with iniquity, a seed of evildoers, and their children are just like their parents. Why have they gone away backward? Isaiah tries to help us see that they are corrupters and have forsaken the Lord to the degree that they have provoked the Holy One of Israel to anger.

What does it mean to go "away backward?" This is done by individuals who make a covenant(s) with God and then choose to walk away from Him and the covenant that was made. A covenant binds you closer to God. Walking away from a covenant takes you away from God and you go "backward" in your relationship and spiritual progression. Those who may say that they are "stepping away" from the gospel for a while, or who indicate that they are "taking a break" from the Church are those who are "gone away backward."

Sin Overpowers Good Thinking and Sound Judgment of the Heart

1:5 Why should ye be stricken any more? ye will revolt more and more: the whole head is sick, and the whole heart faint.

In asking them the question, "why should ye be stricken any more?" God is asking them if it does any good for any of God's children to sin or to rebel. Isaiah paints a picture of a people who have no interest in God and living His commandments have no desire to change.

What is meant by the phase, "the whole head is sick, and the whole heart faint?" This does not just mean the king and government leaders are corrupt, the sickness goes through every grade of the society. John Taylor addressing this same issue said:

> Our systems, our policy, our legislation, our education, and philosophy, are all wrong, neither can we be particularly blamed, for these evils have been the growth of ages. Our fathers have left God, his guidance, control, and support, and we have been left to ourselves; and our present position is manifest proof of our incompetency to govern; and our past failures make it evident, that any future effort, with the same means, would be as useless. The world is diseased, and it requires a world's remedy. (Taylor, *The Government of God*)

> What is the true heart of any nation? It is the family. It is the family that provides the core strength to society in general. It is the family that teaches, nurtures and develops the individuals that make up society. If the heart or family is faint, the family is not teaching spiritual truths that will make families strong. For a family to be strong in our day, parents must teach their children to "love and serve one another, to observe the commandments of God, to follow the living prophets and to be law-abiding citizens wherever they live" (Proclamation on the Family). (Miller, 10)

Sores Represent Unchecked Open Rebellion

Isaiah desiring to show how deep Israel's revolt from their God has gone, says,

1:6 From the sole of the foot even unto the head there is no soundness in it; but wounds, and bruises, and putrifying sores: they have not been closed, neither bound up, neither mollified with ointment

Mollified (Heb. *rakak*)—softened.

Ointment (Heb. *shemen*)—olive oil. This oil is used in the temple in Isaiah's day.

Mollified with ointment—The use of this medicine consists chiefly in external applications. Nothing is taken internally.

The "sole of the foot," symbolizes the most common person in Israel while the "head" symbolizes the highest leaders in Jewish society. From the lower-class citizens to their dignified leaders, Israel had no resolve in themselves to develop any change of behavior unto that godly sorrow that leads to repentance.

Anciently, a wound was purified by "pouring in oil and wine" on the wound (see Luke 10:34). After the washing out and cleaning of the wound had taken place, a clean bandage was applied to the wound. Israel was not being compared to a person who had given attention to their wounds, but they were being referred to as not caring for them. Spiritually, their open wound become infected, discolored, and pussy. What is the spiritual meaning of all this? Why would anyone not take care of his putrefying sores which had been left undressed and ignored, neither bound up, nor mollified with ointment? Such action results in the wound becoming increasingly sore, pussy, and inflamed.

Their exposed sores represent their open sin and rebellion against God. They didn't seem to care who saw and knew of their wickedness. Their willful sinning had been unchecked, symbolized with wounds not closed up by the healing power of Jesus Christ's Atonement. Neither were their sins bound with a broken heart and a contrite spirit of sorrow of the repentant soul. A change of heart had not taken place and they were not repentant. No wonder they would not hear the words of Isaiah and make a mighty change and bind up their spiritual wounds through repentance in the atoning blood of Jesus Christ.

Remember that the Balm of Gilead is symbolic of the power to soothe and to heal and to make the wound whole, in other words to heal the sin-sick soul (Recreational Songs, The Church of Jesus Christ of Latter-day Saints, 1949, p. 130.) Yet Israel sought to "cure [their] guilt with self-justification, a quack medicine which only covers the symptoms; it will never cure the cause" (Packer, 10).

A Promise to Israel Because of Their Sin

Isaiah prophesies what the result will be of Israel's rebellion. He writes:

> 1:7 Your country is desolate, your cities are burned with fire: your land, strangers devour it in your presence, and it is desolate, as overthrown by strangers.

Why is the country of Israel to be desolate, with cities burned with fire and overthrown by strangers? History has born record that indeed, it was just as Isaiah taught: this great Assyrian army came upon them and gathered up all that could be moved and carried it off to Assyria and burned all the rest they could, leaving all cities in its path destroyed and desolate (see Isa. 37:36).

A Rotting, Decaying Society. Can Jerusalem Stand?

> 1:8 And the daughter of Zion is left as a cottage in a vineyard, as a lodge in a garden of cucumbers, as a besieged city.

Daughter—denotes the future, and in this context indicates that the future of Jerusalem will be one of decay.

The expression "cottage in the vineyard, as a lodge in a garden of cucumbers" refers to what happens after the harvest season. At the start of a harvest season, workers would go from their homes in a city or village to the neighboring field or orchard. To maximize the time that they could spend harvesting the crop, temporary shelters would be made of branches and leaves in a vineyard, or a garden. After the harvest, these huts or cottages quickly fall into decay. Any new occupant will be quickly exposed to the elements. This is a forecast of what Jerusalem

> will become; he now refers to the city as a temporary shelter for its inhabitants. Temporary assistance will be given them when the Lord will kill one hundred and eighty-five thousand Assyrian soldiers at the siege of Sennacherib; but the house of Judah should remember that without repentance Jerusalem is just temporarily rescued, for the savior made the following prophecy in reference to Jerusalem, "There shall not be left here one stone upon another, that shall not be thrown down" (Matthew 24:3). (Miller, 13)

Only a Remnant of Israel Left

1:9 Except the Lord of hosts had left unto us a very small remnant, we should have been as Sodom, and we should have been like unto Gomorrah.

What happened to the great wicked cities of Sodom and Gomorrah? They were totally destroyed and left without a sign of their existence. The Lord promises here that a remnant of Zion would be saved even though they chose evil over good. The apostle Paul quoted Isaiah 1:9 and 10:22 (see Rom. 9:27, 29) to demonstrate that God would allow a remnant of Israel to remain on the earth.

> Joseph Smith, in turn, provided an inspired commentary on these verses of Isaiah and Paul. Joseph concluded that "if it were not for the remnant which was left, then might men now be as Sodom and Gomorrah. (Parry, *Understanding Isaiah*, 13)

Will You Hear the Word of God Better than Those of the Past?

Verses 10–20 are arranged chiastically and emphasizes what the Lord requires. He invites us to cleanse ourselves through the Atonement of Christ and return to obedience.

A' The first summons: The Lord's displeasure (vs. 10–11)
 a1 The flouting of the law (vs. 10)
 a2 Ineffective religion (vs. 11)

B What the Lord has not asked: useless religion (vs. 12–15)
b1 No divine authorization (vs. 12)
b2 No divine acceptance (vs. 13–14)
b3 No divine response (vs. 15)
C What the Lord requires (vs. 16–17):
cl Towards God - cleansing (vs. 16abc)
c2 In personal life - reformation (vs. 16d–17b)
c3 In society - concern (vs. 17c–e)
A2 The second summons: The Lord's invitation (vs. 18–20)
a2 Effective cleansing (vs. 18)
a1 Return to obedience (vs. 19–20)

1:10 Hear the word of the Lord, ye rulers of Sodom; give ear unto the law of our God, ye people of Gomorrah.

In these last few verses, the Lord has compared the inhabitants of Jerusalem, its leaders, and its citizens, with the evil inhabitants of the cities of Sodom and Gomorrah. The first nine verses of this chapter paint a picture of this wickedness and indicate the reasons for the great fall of Israel, which started long before the time of Isaiah. In verses 10–15 Isaiah condemns Israel's apostate temple practices. Because their sacrifices are a mockery before God, He will not hearken to their prayers.

Sacrifices and Burnt Offerings

1:11 To what purpose is the multitude of your sacrifices unto me? saith the Lord: I am full of the burnt offerings of rams, and the fat of fed beasts; and I delight not in the blood of bullocks, or of lambs, or of he goats.

Full (Heb. *saba*)—to satisfy, to be weary of.

In this passage Isaiah teaches that although a multitude of sacrifices are being offered, the hearts of the children of Israel are not given with their offerings, and thus their sacrifices are in vain and have no power to draw on the salvation of the Atonement. The emptiness of such offerings, offensive to God,

> results in condemnation (1 Sam. 15:22). We are under the same condemnation when we observe the forms of our religion without yielding our hearts. (Parry, *Understanding Isaiah*, 15)

1:12 When ye come to appear before me, who hath required this at your hand, to tread my courts?

Tread (Heb. *ramac*)—to tromp, or to tromp through something.
Courts (Heb. *châtsêr*)—areas in which the worshippers were; none but priests entered the temple itself.

The imagery is that of the temple as a holy place where one is supposed to come spiritually prepared to be able to see the Lord (Psalms 24:6) but Israel is treating the temple grounds like some animal tromping through it that has no respect or any idea where he is, or what he is really doing. Alma will say the same thing in Alma 5:53, that they have trampled the Holy One of Israel.

Improve Your Prayers

1:13 Bring no more vain oblations; incense is an abomination unto me; the new moons and sabbaths, the calling of assemblies, I cannot away with; it is iniquity, even the solemn meeting.

Oblations (Heb. *min-khaw'*)—usually a bloodless and voluntary offering. In the old English sense, it meant an offering not of flesh, that is, of flour, fruits, oil, etc. (see Leviticus 2:1–13).

> Isaiah spoke of vain oblations meaning the ritualistic offering of sacrifices when the spirit and meaning of the ordinance and offering had been lost. Ezekiel foretold that oblations would again be offered by Israel in the day of gathering (Ezek. 20:33–44). (McConkie, *Mormon Doctrine*, 542)

Incense is often associated with prayer (see Rev. 8:3). The new moons refer to the monthly feasts that Israel had at the time of a new moon. The assemblies were times when God's people came together to worship. In each case, the intent of these three events was to remind and teach Israel of the coming sacrifice of Jesus Christ. In each event, "the offerings symbolized 'the entire surrender unto God, whether of the individual or of the congregation, and His acceptance thereof.'" It was a "sacrifice of devotion and service. Thus, day by day, it formed the regular morning and evening service in the Temple, while on the Sabbaths, new moons, and festivals additional burnt-offerings followed the ordinary worship. There the covenant people brought the covenant-sacrifice, and the multitude of offerings indicated, as it were, the fulness, richness, and joyousness of their self-surrender'" (McConkie, *The Mortal Messiah,* 135). The Law of Moses, including its Sabbaths, was a schoolmaster to bring us unto Christ.

1:14 Your new moons and your appointed feasts my soul hateth: they are a trouble unto me; I am weary to bear them.

The appointed feasts were the Passover, Offering of the Firstfruits, Festival of Weeks, Festival of Trumpets, Day of Atonement, and Feast of Tabernacles (see Lev. 23). They alone were fixed to certain times of the year. The Sabbath could also be considered an appointed time and a feast.

1:15 And when ye spread forth your hands, I will hide mine eyes from you: yea, when ye make many prayers, I will not hear: your hands are full of blood.

The imagery of spreading "forth your hands" is a "divine gesture [that] signifies prayer or supplication. Solomon, for instance, 'spread forth his hands toward heaven' (1 Kgs. 8:22) as he uttered the dedicatory prayer of the temple of Solomon. Other references to this temple practice include Ps. 28:2; 63:4; and 134:2" (Parry, *Understanding Isaiah*, 16).

1:16 Wash you, make you clean; put away the evil of your doings from before mine eyes; cease to do evil;

Wash (Heb. *râchats*)—to wash, to wash away. This word appears seventy-three times in the Old Testament, of which fifty-two refer to ceremonial cleansing (see Leviticus 15:5–28).

Clean (Heb. *zâkâh*)—to make clean before God.

The first fifteen verses list Israel's problems. Verses 16–20 proceed to list the solutions to these problems. In these verses the Lord gives nine imperatives to Israel: wash, clean, put away, cease, learn, seek, relieve, vindicate, and plead. These imperatives invite Israel to repent and cleanse themselves.

Isaiah places "wash you" and "make you clean" side by side without a connecting particle. "This means that the second phrase expresses the leading idea and the first qualifies it, hence 'make yourselves clean before the Lord by the cleansing ordinances he has provided'" (Motyer, 47). We are washed in Christ as we are baptized and made clean of our "evil doings" before God. In order to repent and cleanse ourselves, we must prepare ourselves for baptism by exercising faith in Christ and repenting of the "evil of your doings."

Good Works

1:17 Learn to do well; seek judgment, relieve the oppressed, judge the fatherless, plead for the widow.

Judge (Heb. *mishpâț*)—vindicate or render a judgment.

These phrases are all quotes from the Law of Moses (Deuteronomy 10:18; 14:29; 27:19) where the Lord begs of them to take care of the poor and the needy and the widowed and the fatherless.

Lord Will Forgive

1:18 Come now, and let us reason together, saith the Lord: though your sins be as scarlet, they shall be as white as snow; though they be red like crimson, they shall be as wool.

Scarlet was the color of Jesus Christ's robe when bearing our "sins" (Matthew 27:28). It was also the color of Rahab's thread (Joshua 2:18; compare Leviticus 14:4).

> The rabbins say that when the lot used to be taken, a scarlet fillet was bound on the scapegoat's head, and after the high priest had confessed his and the people's sins over it, the fillet became white: the miracle ceased, according to them, forty years before

> the destruction of Jerusalem, that is, exactly when Jesus Christ was crucified; a remarkable admission of adversaries. Hebrew for 'scarlet' radically means double-dyed; so the deep-fixed permanency of sin in the heart, which no mere tears can wash away. (Jamieson, *Commentary*)

In this verse Isaiah compares two colors to sin: Scarlet (bright red) and Crimson (dark red). The use of two colors suggests there are two types of sins. The first are bright—symbolic of being easily noticed. The second is dark—symbolic of being hidden. These noticeable or hidden sins may be seen by others, and sometimes they remain unseen even to ourselves.

A snowflake begins to form when an extremely cold water droplet freezes onto a small particle (like pollen or dust) in the atmosphere. This creates an ice crystal. As the ice crystal falls to the ground, water vapor freezes onto the primary crystal, building new crystals—the six arms of the snowflake. In comparing snow to repentance and the Atonement, Isaiah teaches that our "dirt" is covered up by the Atonement until it becomes beautiful and white.

This scripture was directed to a nation when it was first given. Joseph Fielding Smith points out the following promise:

> If you, a rebellious nation, will repent and turn again unto the Lord, your sins, "though as scarlet, they shall be as white as snow; though they be red like crimson, they shall be as wool." So, we see, this is not an individual promise, but one to a rebellious nation. No matter how many prophets the Lord sent to Israel and Judah, and how many times he pleaded with them, all through their history they were rebellious (Smith, *Answers to Gospel Questions*,180).

Isaiah compares the sins of a nation to being scarlet (Heb. *towla'*) in color. In Isaiah's time, scarlet dye was made from the dried body of the female scarlet worm called "coccus ilicis."

> When the female of the scarlet worm species was ready to give birth to her young, she would attach her body to the trunk of a tree, fixing herself so firmly and permanently that she would never leave again. The eggs deposited beneath her body were thus protected until the larvae were hatched and able to leave and enter their own life cycle. As the mother died, the crimson

> fluid stained her body and the surrounding wood. From the dead bodies of such female scarlet worms, the commercial scarlet dyes of antiquity were extracted. (Morris, 73.)

The great imagery associated with the scarlet worm foreshadows what Christ would do one day for a nation or an individual, if they would only attach themselves firmly and permanently to the atoning blood of Jesus Christ and never leave and return to their former sins. The Lord promises all those who will accept His Atonement unto repentance, that they will be forgiven.

How Do You Know That You Have Received a Remission of Your Sins?

President Henry B. Eyring taught how each of us could know that we have received a remission of our sins. He told of an experience that he had with a young man who had made some significant mistakes. He had exercised faith in Christ and repented of his sins and was preparing to be married in the temple. President Eyring had promised that this young man would know that the Lord had forgiven him, but the timing would be up to God. As the wedding day approached, the young man felt he had not yet received this witness. He desired to know that he was forgiven.

Soon after this interview, President Eyring found himself seeing Elder Spencer W. Kimball and the conversation turned to this young man's sincere desire to know that he had been forgiven. Elder Kimball did not give advice immediately but asked about the young man. He asked about his personal discipleship. Each question related to "little things, simple acts of obedience, of submission."

> And for each question I was surprised that my answer was always yes. Yes, he wasn't just at all his meetings: he was early; he was smiling; he was there not only with his whole heart, but with the broken heart of a little child, and he was every time the Lord asked anything of him. And after I had said yes to each of his questions, Elder Kimball looked at me, paused, and then very quietly said, "There is your revelation."
>
> . . . When I went back to the young man and told him what I then knew, he accepted it. But he may have simply had to take my word for it. You see, it's hard to feel that you are

sufficiently humble. If you did, you might not be. He went forward with his marriage. I've seen him since. To me he still looks as he did on the front bench before a priesthood meeting.

My guess is that he has retained a remission of his sins. I don't know if he knew then or if he knows now with the certainty he wanted, but I am sure of something. When that change of heart comes to me and to you, when we are cleansed and blameless before God, it will be because we have been made pure by the blood of Christ. And I know what I can and must do. I must be baptized by a servant of God holding the true priesthood, and I must have received the gift of the Holy Ghost by that same power, and then I must have exercised faith in the Savior long enough and carefully enough that his grace will be sufficient for me. And I know at least one way to know that is happening in your life, or in mine. You will have put yourself so often in the Master's service, bringing the cleansing companionship of the Holy Ghost, that you will be on the front row, early, whenever and wherever the Master calls. It will be gradual enough that you may not notice. You will be humble enough that you may be reluctant to believe it is happening. But those with spiritual discernment who love you will know. And the Savior and our Heavenly Father will know. And that is enough. (Eyring, "Come unto Christ")

Be Obedient or Die by the Sword

1:19 If ye be willing and obedient, ye shall eat the good of the land:

To Joseph Smith, the Lord said: "Behold, the Lord requireth the heart and a willing mind; and the willing and obedient shall eat the good of the land of Zion in these last days. And the rebellious shall be cut off out of the land of Zion, and shall be sent away, and shall not inherit the land" (Doctrine and Covenants 64:34–35).

1:20 But if ye refuse and rebel, ye shall be devoured with the sword: for the mouth of the Lord hath spoken it.

The second part of the promise in verse 19 is that if Israel is not faithful, but choose to rebel, then the outcome will be "the sword," or destruction by an invading army.

1:21 How is the faithful city become an harlot! it was full of judgment; righteousness lodged in it; but now murderers.

Verses 21–24 describe the apostasy of Israel. Victor Ludlow described it this way:

> The Israelite society has become so wicked that Jerusalem is compared to a harlot, quite a contrast from the "daughter of Zion" in verse 8. From verses 21 24, it is obvious that the people of Jerusalem do not heed Isaiah's admonition to repent. Consequently, they find themselves out of favor with God and subject to his wrath. Their sins include adultery, murder, graft (adulterating the silver with alloys), deception (watering the wine), rebellion, thievery, corruption (accepting bribes), and injustice (oppressing the needy). Small wonder, then, that they should be counted as the Lord's enemies and worthy of his vengeance (v. 24).
>
> One immediate fulfillment of this prophecy upon Israel was the invasion by Assyria and the forced resettlement of many Israelites in the far reaches of the Assyrian Empire. Also, according to Oliver Cowdery, the angel Moroni quoted these verses to Joseph Smith and told him that they referred to the Ten Tribes, who were scattered because of their apostasy. Moroni indicated that the next verses predict a future restoration of Israel (*Messenger and Advocate*, Apr. 1835, p. 110). (Ludlow, 79)

The word murders "may refer literally to murder or symbolically to those who guide individuals 'away unto destruction' (Alma 36:14; Matt. 10:28). Those who cause spiritual destruction are guilty of spiritual murder" (Parry, *Understanding Isaiah*, 20).

Israel Full of Mischief

The Lord continued to condemn Israel in their gross state of iniquity. He said:

1:22 Thy silver is become dross, thy wine mixed with water:

Water (Heb. *mayim*)—water or water of the feet; urine.

> Dross is the valueless waste material found on the surface of molten metal. Those who were once precious (like silver and wine) but have polluted themselves with the ways of the world are called dross. The Lord, through Ezekiel, said that "the house of Israel is to me become dross . . . they are even the dross of silver" (Ezek. 22:18; see Ps. 119:119; Alma 34:29). "Silver can contain some alloy and still be silver, but silver which has become dross has suffered total degeneration. Similarly, as soon as wine is touched with water no particle of it remains undiluted." Sin corrupts us as water dilutes wine and dross contaminates precious metal. (Parry, *Understanding Isaiah*, 20)

There is a slight possibility that the phrase "mixed with water" is a euphemism for "mixing with urine," since Hebrew has an expression "to throw water," which means "to urinate" (just as we use the phrase "to pass water" for the same idea).

1:23 Thy princes are rebellious, and companions of thieves; every one loveth gifts, and followeth after rewards; they judge not the fatherless, neither doth the cause of the widow come unto them.

Gifts (Heb. *shachad*)—a gift used in a bribe.

The princes are noblemen and should be examples. Yet they place themselves in a rebellious state above the laws and commandments of God and spend their time in the company of thieves that would encourage and help them to justify their actions. They succumb to bribes instead of providing righteous judgments and seek for personal rewards. They have forgotten the needs of the fatherless and turn away the widows and hear not the cries of the poor.

The Mighty One of Israel Avenges Enemies

1:24 Therefore saith the Lord, the Lord of hosts, the mighty One of Israel, Ah, I will ease me of mine adversaries, and avenge me of mine enemies:

Ah (Heb. *hôwy*)—woe, alas; a word indicating indignation.

Ease me (Heb. *nâcham*)—to be sorry, console oneself. i.e.—God's long tried patience will find relief in at last punishing the guilty (see Ezekiel 5:13).

A point comes even with the Lord when He says, I have had enough, and "I will ease me of mine adversaries, and avenge me of mine enemies." When will this take place? In a way, it is an ongoing process, yet it will climax at His Second Coming. The Lord will avenge His saints, for the Lord said: "Vengeance is mine; I will repay, saith the Lord" (Romans 12:19).

When political power had turned against Joseph Smith and he was a prisoner in Liberty Jail, his plea to the Lord was, "Let thine anger be kindled against our enemies" (D&C 121:5). How did a loving, patient Heavenly Father respond to Joseph? He said, in essence, "not yet." Then in a very tender way the Lord said, "My son, peace be unto thy soul; thine adversity and thine afflictions shall be but a small moment; And then, if thou endure it well, God shall exalt thee on high; thou shalt triumph over all thy foes" (D&C 121:7–8).

And then His counsel was: "And if thou shouldst be cast into the pit, or into the hands of murderers, and the sentence of death passed upon thee; if thou be cast into the deep; if the billowing surge conspire against thee; if fierce winds become thine enemy; if the heavens gather blackness, and all the elements combine to hedge up the way; and above all, if the very jaws of hell shall gape open the mouth wide after thee, know thou, my son, that all these things shall give thee experience, and shall be for thy good" (D&C 122:7).

Then God made a promise that if Joseph as a person would endure and be faithful, that "God shall exalt thee on high; thou shalt triumph over all thy foes" (v. 8), because the Lord will take vengeance upon the wicked Himself. It is for us to take care of the wickedness that is before us and serve God by serving our fellow men and God will one day avenge us upon our enemies, which are, we would hope in most cases, His enemies, as well. Sometimes in the heat of persecution and suffering one may wonder what good is going to come out of all this kind of trial and suffering to have such experiences be for our own good.

For those who turn the other cheek and love their neighbors as themselves, no matter how hard things seem to be, the Lord responds with this promise,

1:25 And I will turn my hand upon thee, and purely purge away thy dross, and take away all thy tin:

In biblical times (as now), metals were graded according to their degree of availability. Gold and silver were the most precious metals; tin, brass, lead, and iron were less precious (Ezek. 22:18–22; Dan. 2:31–42). "Tin in this context may represent mediocre individuals who are more righteous than those identified with dross but not as precious as those likened to gold or silver (1:22)" (Parry, *Understanding Isaiah*, 22). Isaiah's reference to "take away all thy tin" is symbolic of taking away the impurities of men by the Holy Ghost.

1:26 And I will restore thy judges as at the first, and thy counsellors as at the beginning: afterward thou shalt be called, The city of righteousness, the faithful city.

Verses 26–31 portend a future day. The Lord will refine His people so they may become pure and holy, and able to see His face and become acceptable before Him.

Zion Shall Be Redeemed

1:27 Zion shall be redeemed with judgment, and her converts with righteousness.

1:28 And the destruction of the transgressors and of the sinners shall be together, and they that forsake the Lord shall be consumed.

Destruction (Heb. *sheber*)—Literally, "breaking into shivers" (Revelation 2:27).

Transgressors (Heb. *pâsha'*)—those who seem to be those who act in violation of the law.

Sinners (Heb. *chaṭṭâ'*)—those who willfully are disobedient to the law.

Your Evil Actions Will One Day Condemn You

1:29 For they shall be ashamed of the oaks which ye have desired, and ye shall be confounded for the gardens that ye have chosen.

The "oaks" mentioned in verses 29 and 30 of the King James Version are usually identified as "terebinth" trees in modern translations (See footnote 29a). The terebinth is common in the eastern Mediterranean area and is used in landscaping either as a decorative windbreak or sunshield. It also yields a resinous sap from which turpentine is derived. Groves of terebinths were also used in pagan idol worship because, among other reasons, the pagans considered these evergreen trees to represent perpetual renewal and fertility. In general, the oaks and gardens symbolize the wickedness of the world.

Gardens of the mind and the heart provide the soil from which grows your actions, thoughts, and deeds. The oaks denote the evil you have desired and cultivated in your minds and hearts over the things of God. The Lord on one occasion said:

> For our words will condemn us, yea, all our works will condemn us; we shall not be found spotless; and our thoughts will also condemn us; and in this awful state we shall not dare to look up to our God; and we would fain be glad if we could command the rocks and the mountains to fall upon us to hide us from his presence. (Alma 12:14)

Results of Wickedness

When men no longer have the Spirit of the Lord to nourish them and water their testimonies, they will become as Isaiah said,

1:30 For ye shall be as an oak whose leaf fadeth, and as a garden that hath no water.

1:31 And the strong shall be as tow [inflammable fibers], and the maker of it as a spark, and they shall both burn together, and none shall quench them.

Isaiah prophecies that those who follow idols will become like the "oaks," or the object of their "desire" (Isa. 1:29). People become like the gods they worship; they never rise above their false god's level (Ps. 135:18). By following false gods and worshiping idols made by their own hands, the wicked will be as the mighty oak and garden without the spiritual water of Christ and His Atonement. Their substance is as the leaves of the oak and the garden that have no water and are drained of their spiritual power and understanding. Perhaps the leaves fading in color represent different levels of spiritual strength. If any of us become dried up from the spiritual strength of the Lord and forsake His gospel, spiritual death is sure.

ISAIAH CHAPTER 2

The Establishment of the Lord's House

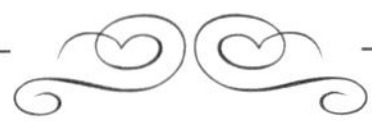

THIS CHAPTER IS QUOTED IN THE BOOK OF MORMON. IT IS QUOTED AFTER the Nephites have separated themselves from the Lamanites. This and subsequent chapters are read to the believing Nephites by Jacob as a part of his address. Jacob's address begins with 2 Nephi 6 recounting some important events of Jewish history. He speaks of Christ and His crucifixion and of the Jews being scattered along with the conditions that will take place before Christ returns the second time. Jacob concludes the first part of his speech by giving one of the greatest chapters in the Book of Mormon, which centers on the topic of the Atonement in 2 Nephi 9. After this chapter, he speaks of the crucifixion of the Christ and then quotes Isaiah chapter 2 encouraging his audience to "liken them unto you and unto all men" (2 Nephi 11:8). This chapter opens with a view of the House of the Lord, located in the tops of the mountains.

2:1 The word that Isaiah the son of Amoz saw concerning Judah and Jerusalem.

2:2 And it shall come to pass in the last days, that the mountain of the Lord's house shall be established in the top of the mountains, and shall be exalted above the hills; and all nations shall flow unto it.

The word "that" in verse 2, italicized by the King James scholars because they were unsure of the correct translation, is rendered "when" in the Book of Mormon and the JST.

In reference to verse two, President Harold B. Lee said, "With the coming of the pioneers to establish the Church in the tops of the mountains, our early leaders declared this to be the beginning of the fulfillment of that prophecy" ("The Way to Eternal Life," *Ensign*, Nov. 1971, 15).

In the general conference of October 2000, President Gordon B. Hinckley testified: "I believe that prophecy applies to the historic and wonderful Salt Lake Temple. But I believe also that it is related to this magnificent hall. For it is from this pulpit that the law of God shall go forth, together with the word and testimony of the Lord" ("This Great Millennial Year"). On top of this conference center, one can walk out into what would seem to be a park, a garden grove of trees, flowers, and waterfalls where one can go to meditate. For some, it might give a feeling of reverence of a high place of worship, perhaps, in a small sense, a feeling of an outside temple. President Hinckley added: "We have not built a temple with trees and fishponds on the roof. But on this edifice, we have many trees and running water. Brigham Young may have foreseen this structure very near the temple" ("To All the World in Testimony," April 2000 general conference).

> This prophecy speaks to us in our day. The gathering of Israel, temples, and temple service are the principal themes of the first part of this chapter. We will "flow" upwards to the temple mountain, learn of God's ways (in the temple), and walk in God's paths (in the temple). In addition, temple service and worship (2:2–3) are directly connected to worldwide peace and prosperity (2:4); that is, temple attendance (2:2) results in peace (2:4), a desire to learn of God (2:3), and a willingness to walk in his light (2:5). Micah presents the same prophecy in his writings (Micah 4:1–3).
>
> Joseph Smith summed up the connection between the gathering of Israel and temple service: "The object of gathering the Jews, or the people of God in any age of the world . . . was to build unto the Lord a house whereby He could reveal unto His people the ordinances of His house and the glories of His

kingdom, and teach the people the way of salvation" [History of the Church, 5:423] (Parry, *Understanding Isaiah*, 24).

2:3 And many people shall go and say, Come ye, and let us go up to the mountain of the Lord, to the house of the God of Jacob; and he will teach us of his ways, and we will walk in his paths: for out of Zion shall go forth the law, and the word of the Lord from Jerusalem.

Elder Bruce R. McConkie commented on the phrase, "out of Zion shall go forth the law, and the word of the Lord from Jerusalem" when he wrote that, "One shall be the seat of government, the other the spiritual capital of the world." (*The Mortal Messiah*, 1:95)

President Harold B. Lee adds some additional light. He had for years wondered what was meant by the expression, "out of Zion shall go forth the law." It wasn't until he heard President George Albert Smith's inspired dedicatory prayer on the Idaho Falls Temple that he understood. President Smith said:

> Note what they said, "We thank thee that thou hast revealed to us that those who gave us our constitutional form of government were men wise in thy sight and that thou didst raise them up for the very purpose of putting forth that sacred document [as revealed in Doctrine and Covenants, section 101] . . .
>
> "We pray that kings and rulers and the peoples of all nations under heaven may be persuaded of the blessings enjoyed by the people of this land by reason of their freedom and under thy guidance and be constrained to adopt similar governmental systems, thus to fulfill the ancient prophecy of Isaiah and Micah that '. . . out of Zion shall go forth the law and the word of the Lord from Jerusalem.'" ("The Way to Eternal Life," *Ensign*, November 1971, 15)

Joseph Smith taught the order in which this will occur. He said:

> The Lord will begin by revealing the house of Israel among the Gentiles. And those who have gone from the ordinances of God shall return unto the keeping of all the law and observing his

> judgments and statutes to do them. Then shall the law of the Lord go forth from Zion and the word of the Lord to the priests, and through them from Jerusalem. (*Discourse of Joseph Smith*, 21 March 1841, recorded by Martha Jane Coray; WJS, 67).

2:4 And he shall judge among the nations, and shall rebuke many people: and they shall beat their swords into plowshares, and their spears into pruninghooks: nation shall not lift up sword against nation, neither shall they learn war any more.

After the Lord has judged the nations with all kinds of judgments and rebukes the evils of men who would not repent, He will bring forth a day as Elder Bruce R. McConkie describes when:

> There will be peace on earth; wars will be unknown and unheard of crime and evil and carnality will vanish away; and the Son of Righteousness shall replace evil with good, for he, as "The Prince of Peace," and the Creator of Righteousness, shall reign "upon the throne of David." (Isa. 9:6–7)
>
> There will be no murders; even if an evil Cain should seek the life of a righteous Abel, he could not slay him. During the Millennium there will be no death because, for one reason, there will be no blood to spill upon the ground. There will be no robbing, nor stealing, nor kidnapping, nor treachery, nor immorality, nor lasciviousness, nor any manner of evil. What would our society be like if these sins and all their ilk were abolished, if there were no prisons for the criminals, no reformatories for the recalcitrant, no lands of banishment for the treasonous? Where there is peace, there is neither crime nor war.
>
> And in that day men "shall beat their swords into plowshares, and their spears into pruninghooks: nation shall not lift up sword against nation, neither shall they learn war any more." (Isa. 8:4.) "He maketh wars to cease unto the end of the earth." (Ps. 46:9.) "The whole earth is at rest, and is quiet: they break forth into singing." (Isa. 14:7.) "And the work of righteousness shall be peace; and the effect of righteousness quietness and assurance for ever. And my people," saith the Lord, "shall dwell

in a peaceable habitation, and in sure dwellings, and in quiet resting places." (Isa. 32:17–18.). (McConkie, *The Millennial Messiah*, 654–655)

A plowshare is the cutting blade of a plow; a pruning hook is a tool with a hooked blade that is used for pruning plants. Swords, spears, plowshares, and pruning hooks all have blades; plowshares and pruning hooks are useful and conducive to the work ethic and eventual prosperity, therefore representing instruments of peace and prosperity. (Parry, *Understanding Isaiah*, 28)

2:5 O house of Jacob, come ye, and let us walk in the light of the Lord.

2 Nephi 12:5 O house of Jacob, come ye and let us walk in the light of the Lord; yea, come, for ye have all gone astray, every one to his wicked ways.

Beginning in verse 5, Isaiah's attention shifts from the future back to his people. He rebukes them for their pride and idolatry and warns of the sure judgment of the Lord. While reading Isaiah's rebuke, notice that some words such as "gold," "silver," "idols," "proud," "humbled," "rocks," and "holes" are often repeated. Also, recognize that three major themes are repeatedly stressed: the people's worldliness, the Lord's vengeance, and the wicked's humility and fear (See Ludlow, 89–90).

2:6 Therefore thou hast forsaken thy people the house of Jacob, because they be replenished from the east, and are soothsayers like the Philistines, and they please themselves in the children of strangers.

2 Nephi 12:6 Therefore, O Lord, thou hast forsaken thy people the house of Jacob, because they be replenished from the east, and hearken unto the soothsayers like the Philistines, and they please themselves in the children of strangers.

Soothsayers (Heb. *ânan*)—practiced soothsaying or spiritism, magic or witchcraft.

Please (Heb. *caphaq*)—clap hands or strike a deal.

One meaning of the phrase "clasp hands . . . children of strangers" is to "participate and make covenants in apostate temple systems with those who are not affiliated with the true Israelite temple. The Hebrew word for strangers has reference to characters who are 'foreign' or 'alien' to the house of Israel. A command from the Law of Moses warned the Israelites, 'Thou shalt make no covenant with them strangers; such as the Amorites, Hittites, Perizzites, Canaanites, Hivites, and Jebusites, nor with their gods' (Ex. 23:32). The phrase also refers to God's command that Israelites not intermarry with those who do not belong to covenant Israel (Deut. 7:1–4)" (Parry, *Understanding Isaiah*, 29).

In verse six, Isaiah identifies three ways the sons and daughters of the house of Jacob had forsaken the Lord. We can learn vicariously from ancient Israel so that we do not follow their example and repeat their sins.

The first is that they choose to "be replenished from the east." This denotes that ancient Israel was attracted to the glitter of the larger cities of the eastern nations and sought to follow after their evil practices. They were titillated by the excitements and romances that the larger cites had to offer. The second reason that led Israel to forsake their God was that they would "hearken unto soothsayers." These are false prophets who claimed to be able to foretell the future. The third reason Isaiah gives why Israel had forsaken their God is that "they please themselves in the children of strangers." This denotes their make free exchange among those who know not the God of Israel and had no interest in their eternal welfare. Israel enjoyed the good times with their new friends while turning their back on their God and their worship, selling their birthright for the glitter of a dirty world. Elder Spencer W. Kimball applied this to us today as he stated:

> Not so different are we today! We want the glamour and frothiness of the world, not always realizing the penalties of our folly. The non-member next door has a boat—we want a boat even though, in many instances, it means the abandonment of Sabbath activities and the breaking of the Lord's holy day. Our contemporaries have pagan weddings—we must adopt their

every style and pattern, even though it glamorizes the world and loses sight of the solemnity of true marriage.

Our neighbors and fellow workers use tobacco—we must use tobacco. We cannot stand to be different! Others drink their cocktails and indulge in their social drinking—"we must also have a king like unto other nations!" Styles are created by the vulgar and money-mad and run from one extreme to the other to outdate present wardrobes and create business for merchants. We cannot be different. We would rather die than be not up to date. If the dress is knee length, we must go a little above the knee. If shorts are short, we must have the shortest. [If] sweaters are tight, we must have the tightest; if bathing suits are skimpy, we must have the skimpiest. "We must have a king like unto other nations!"

The Lord says he will have a peculiar people but we do not wish to be peculiar. If the style is monopolistic dancing, we will dance with no one but the partner with whom we came. If intimate fondling is the pattern of the crowd, we will fondle. "We must have a king like unto other nations!" The world has a queen in every industry, business, factory, school, and social group. She must dress immodestly, display her figure and appear in public places to further the financial interests of business, entertainment, and social groups. We must have a queen around which to center our activities. Ours, also, must have a beautiful face, a little talent, and a well-formed body for public exhibition. We can do little else for "we must have a queen like unto other nations!" When, oh when, will our Latter-day Saints stand firm on their own feet, establish their own standards, follow proper patterns and live their own glorious lives in accordance with Gospel inspired patterns, aping no one who has not a better program! Certainly good time and happy lives and clean fun are not dependent upon the glamorous, the pompous, the extremes." ("Like All the Nations," *Church News*, 15 October 1960, 14)

2:7 Their land also is full of silver and gold, neither is there any end of their treasures; their land is also full of horses, neither is there any end of their chariots:

The Lord had blessed Israel's monetary resources with gold and silver and with all the purchasing power that comes from a strong economy. Horses and chariots denote the greatness of their military power. Even in the area of national security, they were blessed. However, the problem came when they set their hearts on these riches. The seed of greed is nourished by the lust for more wealth. The more the greedy have, the more they must have!

President Brigham Young feared that the Latter-day Saints would succumb to the same spirit of materialism as ancient Israel. So less than two years after the Saint's arrival in the Salt Lake Valley, he stated:

> The worst fear that I have about this people is that they will get rich in this country, forget God and His people, wax fat, and kick themselves out of the Church and go to hell. This people will stand mobbing, robbing, poverty, and all manner of persecution, and be true. But my greater fear for them is that they cannot stand wealth; and yet they have to be tried with riches, for they will become the richest people on this earth. (Young, as reported in Brown, 122–23)

2:8 Their land also is full of idols; they worship the work of their own hands, that which their own fingers have made:

The phrase "land . . . full of idols" may refer to public idolatry while "own hands" and "own fingers" may refer to private forms of idolatry.

The idols in the land were indeed plentiful, as they are today. Israel was deeply involved in the worship of that which they made with their own hands. Let us not forget that today's "[m]odern idols or false gods can take such forms as clothes, homes, businesses, machines, automobiles, pleasure boats, and numerous other material deflectors from the path of godhood" (*The Teachings of Presidents of the Church: Spencer W. Kimball*, 146).

It makes no difference if the item in question is not shaped out of stone and wood. A false idol is anything that we place importance on which takes us away from Christ.

2:9 And the mean man boweth down, and the great man humbleth himself: therefore forgive them not.

> 2 Nephi 12:9 And the mean man boweth not down, and the great man humbleth himself not, therefore, forgive them not.

The mean man who would not bow down represents the average person who is trying to walk the fence in their behaviors. They avoid getting too involved in the "cares of the world" but simple acts of service like their ministering assignments seldom get done. Their works are not really good nor really evil, but they are full of what President Benson called "the universal sin—pride." They are just coasting along through life and will not humble themselves to pray and seek counsel from the Lord.

The great man is the one who has already established himself in the accolades of the social ladder and is so caught up in themselves that they too will not humble themselves enough to turn to the Lord. For this the Lord says He will "forgive them not."

The Day of Jehovah, Christ's Second Coming—Verses 10–22

2:10 Enter into the rock, and hide thee in the dust, for fear of the Lord, and for the glory of his majesty.

> 2 Nephi 12:10 O ye wicked ones, enter into the rock, and hide thee in the dust; for the fear of the Lord and the glory of his majesty shall smite thee.

The phrase "for fear of the Lord" literally means "from the face of the terror of the Lord." The Jerusalem Bible translates this verse to read—"at the sight of the terror" of the Lord. The wicked will simply want to hide from the presence of Christ at His Second Coming.

2:11 The lofty looks of man shall be humbled, and the haughtiness of men shall be bowed down, and the Lord alone shall be exalted in that day.

Lofty (Heb. *gabhûwth*)—haughty. The phrase "lofty looks" is literally translated "eyes of pride" (see Psalms 18:27).

2:12 For the day of the Lord of hosts shall be upon every one that is proud and lofty, and upon every one that is lifted up; and he shall be brought low:

Verses 12–16 emphasize the status symbols of ancient times. The "cedars of Lebanon" symbols of strength, splendor, and glory (v. 13) provided beautiful, fragrant wood for major Israelite buildings such as Solomon's Temple. (IDB 1:545.) The "oaks of Bashan" (v. 13) came from the wooded areas east of the Sea of Galilee and were an important local source of hardwood, often a rare commodity in Palestine. The high mountains with their surrounding hills (v. 14) and the high towers with their surrounding walls (v. 15) represent man's false trust in natural and man-made defenses. The "ships of the sea" (v. 16) represent the people's commercial enterprises, especially the "ships of Tarshish," which were noted for their ability to travel long distances, their strength as war vessels, and their large storage capacity as commercial carriers. (IB 5:186; IDB 4:333, 517 18.) The "beautiful craft" (NAS) or "pleasant pictures" (KJV, v. 16) were apparently the pleasure crafts or ships in which the wealthy traveled throughout the Mediterranean. Isaiah prophesies that the Lord will abase all these superficial symbols of wealth and power. (Ludlow, 91)

2:13 And upon all the cedars of Lebanon, that are high and lifted up, and upon all the oaks of Bashan,

Bashan = "fruitful"—district east of the Jordan known for its fertility which was given to the half-tribe of Manasseh. It was famous for its oak that made the oars for Tyre. It was also the center of wheat and cattle.

Trees represent people. Green trees are the righteous (Psalms 1:3; D&C 135:6) and dry trees are the wicked (Luke 23:31; 3 Nephi 14:17–18). The

Cedar and oak trees are considered in the Middle East the most impressive of all trees. Why will the Lord inflict such destruction on all the "cedars of Lebanon" and "upon all the oaks of Bashan"? Symbolically, the scriptures indicate that these trees represent the proud and lofty men of the world. When the scriptures speak of the destruction of these respective trees, this denotes the fall of all the proud and the high and mighty of all nations of the earth that would not obey God's commandments and come unto Him.

2:14 And upon all the high mountains, and upon all the hills that are lifted up,

2 Nephi 12:14 And upon all the high mountains, and upon all the hills, and upon all the nations which are lifted up, and upon every people.

2:15 And upon every high tower, and upon every fenced wall,

2 Nephi 12:15 And upon every high tower, and upon every fenced wall;

2:16 And upon all the ships of Tarshish, and upon all pleasant pictures.

2 Nephi 12:16 And upon all the ships of the sea, and upon all the ships of Tarshish, and upon all pleasant pictures.

Tarshish = "yellow jasper"—A far off and sometimes idealized port. Ships of Tarshish came to connote the large seagoing ships of the time and became a phrase for richly laden and far-voyaging vessels. The judgment shall be on all that minister to man's luxury (compare Rev. 18:17–19).

"Pleasant pictures" were the pleasure or cruise ships that the wealthy used (see Ludlow, 91). The Vulgate translation is perhaps better for this phrase —"All that is beautiful to the sight"; not only paintings but all luxurious ornaments.

The Book of Mormon adds five phrases in these few verses, four of which stress the universality of the judgment that will come upon "all nations" and "every people," even the high and lofty ones (the proud) as represented by tall trees, mountains, and towers (vs. 12 15). The fifth edition in verse 16 is also found in the early Greek version of the Old Testament, the Septuagint or LXX. (See BD "Septuagint.") The sixteenth verse in 2 Nephi 12 consists of three phrases, two of which are found in both the Septuagint and the Hebrew Masoretic text (which the KJV followed; see BD "Masoretic text"). However, the same two phrases are not in both the Greek and Hebrew texts. The structure of the three versions can be shown as follows:

Three phrases of verse 16	in KJV	in Septuagint	in B of M
And upon all the ships of the sea	-	+	+
And upon all the ships of Tarshish	+	-	+
And upon all pleasant ships	+	+	+

Thus, it appears that the Book of Mormon contains the most complete retention of the original structure of this verse. Since the prophet Joseph Smith did not know Greek, and since there is no evidence that he had access to a copy of the Septuagint when he completed his Book of Mormon translation in 1829, this addition supports the fact that Joseph Smith translated the Isaiah portion in the Book of Mormon from a more authentic ancient text. (Ludlow, 90–91)

2:17 And the loftiness of man shall be bowed down, and the haughtiness of men shall be made low: and the Lord alone shall be exalted in that day.

2:18 And the idols he shall utterly abolish.

2:19 And they shall go into the holes of the rocks, and into the caves of the earth, for fear of the Lord, and for the glory of his majesty, when he ariseth to shake terribly the earth.

2:20 In that day a man shall cast his idols of silver, and his idols of gold, which they made each one for himself to worship, to the moles and to the bats;

2:21 To go into the clefts of the rocks, and into the tops of the ragged rocks, for fear of the Lord, and for the glory of his majesty, when he ariseth to shake terribly the earth.

2:22 Cease ye from man, whose breath is in his nostrils: for wherein is he to be accounted of?

In verses 17–22, the Lord reminds us to cease going around with wicked men that one day will have to account for each breath that the Lord gave them. The telestial people will not be able to be lifted up to meet Christ when He comes, their sins will weigh them down. They will try with frantic efforts to hide their idols which they made in the clefts of ragged rocks or in caves just so God will not see them; as if He had not already seen them (see D&C 101:23–24).

> The imagery of verse 20 is striking: the people will throw their gold and silver idols to moles and bats, animals who are blind from living so long in darkness. The irony of this is that people who understood the material value of the precious metals, and should also have seen the spiritual impotence of the idols, will throw these precious items to animals who will not be able to see them at all. (Ludlow, 92)

God's Kingdom Compared to Man's Kingdom

One of the themes that Isaiah will bring out in his writing is introduced in this chapter. Isaiah wants you to understand the tremendous difference between God's kingdom and its effects on all of its inhabitants and with Man's kingdom. God's kingdom brings peace, trust, joy, and humility. The kingdom of man encourages idolatry, sin, pride, and despair. Taking God out of a nation's politics will leave a nation spiritually devastated and Isaiah prophesies that it will end in the nation's destruction. Smith wrote of this comparison and summarized it as follows:

God's Kingdom	Man's Kingdom
2:1–4 People come to hear God's law	5:24; 10:1–2 People reject God's law
2:4 End of war	5:28; 7:1; 10:6 Wars between nations
2:18–20 People reject gold and idols	2:7–8 Land full of gold and idols
2:11,17; 5:16; 12:4 God alone exalted	2:7–16 People and possessions exalted
2:11, 17; 5:15; 10:12 People humbled	2:11, 17; 3:16; 5:15; 9:8; 10:12 People proud
7:9; 8:17; 10:20; 12:2 Trusting God	2:22; 7:12; 10:13 Trusting man
4:2–3 Zion will be holy and cleansed	3:9; 5:8–24; 6:5; 8:6, 19 Zion sinful
6:3; 8:13 God is holy	6:5, 9–10 Man is not holy
9:1–2; 10:17 God is light	8:22–9:1 Earth is in darkness
9:3; 12:3, 6 Joy	5:8–24; 8:22; 10:1, 5 Woe and gloom
9:6–7; 11:4–5 Just and righteous king	7:12; 9:14–17; 10:12 Wicked kings
11:3; 8:13; 12:2 Fear of God	5:12; 7:2; 8:12 No fear of God; fear of man
11:9; 12:4–5 Will know the Lord	5:19; 6:9 Do not know God

(Smith, *American Commentary*, 123–124)

ISAIAH CHAPTER 3

Say to the Righteous—"It Will Be Well with You"

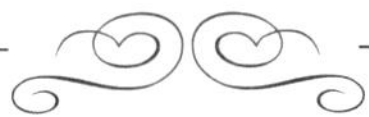

This chapter is quoted in the Book of Mormon in 2 Nephi 13. In the first twelve verses of this chapter, Isaiah prophesies anarchy and ruin for Jerusalem and Judah.

3:1 For, behold, the Lord, the Lord of hosts, doth take away from Jerusalem and from Judah the stay and the staff, the whole stay of bread, and the whole stay of water,

Lord of hosts—The word host is a military term referring to a group of soldiers. Lord of hosts is a God of an army.

Isaiah prophesies that anarchy and ruin will come upon the inhabitants of Jerusalem and Judah because of the sinful nature of their inhabitants, whose speech and actions are against the Lord, and whose sins are likened to the sins committed in Sodom before its destruction (3:8–9). Anarchy may also come because of the Lord's removing the supply of bread and water (famine or drought), or by the loss of righteous leadership in the region, for God, we are told, will remove the region's luminaries (3:2–3), and children, babes, and women will become the rulers

> (3:4, 12). These prophecies seem to have a double application, referring to judgments against ancient Judah as well as against the wicked in the last days. (Parry, *Understanding Isaiah*, 37)

The words "stay" and "staff" are the same words in Hebrew. One is masculine and the other is feminine. *Mash'en* masc. is translated "stay," and *Mash'enah* fem. is translated "staff." Both words mean support such as a crutch to lean on or it is that which you use to support yourself. By using both forms, Isaiah seems to suggest complete destruction —spiritual, social, and physical. Thus, the prophet's language and imagery carry many implications beyond the threat of physical famine.

Bread/water:

> These are perhaps representative of all forms of physical nourishment, but they also have spiritual connotations in reference to the Lord, who is metaphorically the bread of life (John 6:33, 48) and the living water (John 4:6 14; 7:37 38). Certainly, God removes his presence from us when we become wicked, just as bread and water will be removed from Judah and Jerusalem for their iniquity (3:8–9). Thus, this prophecy foresees both physical and spiritual famine. (Parry, *Understanding Isaiah*, 38)

3:2 The mighty man, and the man of war, the judge, and the prophet, and the prudent, and the ancient,

Prudent (Heb. *qâçam*)—soothsayer (see also Deut. 18:10–14); thus it will mean, the diviners, on whom they rely, shall in that day fail.

> Isaiah lists eleven types of people as a way to represent all who have achieved community honor and status, whether religious (prophets), civic (judges), political (men of war), artistic (craftsmen and orators), or in wisdom (older men). The nation will be left without military might (mighty man, man of war, captain of fifty), spiritual guidance (prophets), wise men (ancients), justice (judges), and artisans (skilled craftsmen). All these will be removed from Jerusalem. (Parry, *Understanding Isaiah*, 39)

It should be noted that neither the king nor priests are mentioned. The reason why may correspond with what is explained in 2 Chronicles 26:16–21. In these verses, King Uzziah had been "separated from society for several years because of his leprosy, and that a group of at least eighty priests faithfully served God" (Smith, *American Commentary*, 146).

3:3 The captain of fifty, and the honourable man, and the counsellor, and the cunning artificer, and the eloquent orator.

Cunning—skillful.

The phrase "eloquent orator" sometimes is translated as "skilled in whispering," that is, incantation (see Psalm 58:5).

3:4 And I will give children to be their princes, and babes shall rule over them.

Babes (Heb. *ta'□lûwl*)—capricious or delirious.

In 722 BC, Nebuchadnezzar "carried away all Jerusalem, and all the princes, and all the mighty men of valour, even ten thousand captives, and all the craftsmen and smiths: none remained, save the poorest sort of people of the land" (2 Kgs. 24:14). With the leaders of society killed or taken into captivity, only the poor, weak masses remained. Therefore, the warning in verse 4 that "capricious children" or "babes" (KJV) shall rule over Israel most likely refers to people with childish understanding who will unsuccessfully face the challenge of bringing order to anarchy. They will be childish in nature with its associated immaturity and selfishness.

3:5 And the people shall be oppressed, every one by another, and every one by his neighbour: the child shall behave himself proudly against the ancient, and the base against the honourable.

Base (Heb. *qâlâh*)—literally "the one who ought to be thought nothing of."

There will be great divisiveness in their society and neighbors will oppress their neighbors. There is no consideration to those who merit honor, but the selfishness of pride pits those who esteem themselves highly against those who esteem themselves even higher.

3:6 When a man shall take hold of his brother of the house of his father, saying, Thou hast clothing, be thou our ruler, and let this ruin be under thy hand:

2 Nephi 13:6 . . . let not this ruin be under thy hand—

In a time of societal and political upheaval, no one honorable has a desire for leadership. "No one will desire to rule the people because of the great ruin that has come upon Judah and Jerusalem. Yet the people will ask the man with clothing to lead them; perhaps his clothing indicates wealth or preparedness" (Parry, *Understanding Isaiah*, 39). People are afraid that no matter what they do, they are ruined. They despair and hope there is someone who will lead them into prosperity with no mention of being led into spirituality.

3:7 In that day shall he swear, saying, I will not be an healer; for in my house is neither bread nor clothing: make me not a ruler of the people.

Swear (Heb. *nâsâ'*)—"to lift up or to bear up;" namely, the lifting of their hand; the gesture used in a solemn attestation.

> These verses (6–7) are important because they reemphasize both the social breakdown of the patriarchal order and the extreme physical poverty of the state. That the man mentioned here should "lay hold of his brother in his father's house" indicates, first of all, that the father has disappeared and left the family in upheaval, for the son (by custom, the eldest) refuses to fulfill the duty that is his by lineage. The cloak, or *simlah*, which is the brother's so-called claim to power, is not a rich robe but is itself a sign of extreme poverty. In other words, the petitioner is saying, "You have at least some sort of cloak and the provisions necessary for physical sustenance, food and clothing." Without either physical or social "stays," it is no wonder that the brother declines a position for which he might otherwise be ambitious. (Ludlow, 103)

3:8 For Jerusalem is ruined, and Judah is fallen: because their tongue and their doings are against the Lord, to provoke the eyes of his glory.

3:9 The shew of their countenance doth witness against them; and they declare their sin as Sodom, they hide it not. Woe unto their soul! for they have rewarded evil unto themselves.

Show (Heb. *hakkârâh*)—that which may be known by their countenances.

A better translation of the phrase "rewarded evil unto themselves" is provided by the New International Version: "They have brought disaster upon themselves."

At times, consequences of sin may appear to be very subtle to the sinner. We may even convince ourselves . . . that no one will be able to detect our sins and that they are well concealed. But always to our Heavenly Father and often to spiritually sensitive leaders, parents, and friends, our sins are glaringly apparent.

While attending a youth fireside with Elder Richard G. Scott, I noticed five youths scattered among the congregation whose countenances or body language almost screamed that something was spiritually amiss in their lives. After the meeting, when I mentioned the five youths to Elder Scott, he simply replied, "There were eight."

Isaiah prophesied, "Their countenance doth witness against them, and doth declare their sin to be even as Sodom, and they cannot hide it" (2 Nephi 13:9; see also Isaiah 3:9). (Jones, "Overcoming the Stench of Sin")

3:10 Say ye to the righteous, that it shall be well with him: for they shall eat the fruit of their doings.

The righteous are not promised that they will escape the difficulties of life. The promise to them is that it will "be well with him." This promise is an eternal promise that the righteous will receive the "fruit of their doings." God will reward the righteous in His kingdom.

3:11 Woe unto the wicked! it shall be ill with him: for the reward of his hands shall be given him.

Hands (Heb. *yawd*)—open hands indicating power, means, direction, conduct. Hands are the instrument of actions (see Ecclesiastes 8:12, 13).

The same promise is made to the wicked. They too will be rewarded for the actions of "his hands." They are responsible for what they do and if they are wicked they will receive "woe," which means "misery."

3:12 As for my people, children are their oppressors, and women rule over them. O my people, they which lead thee cause thee to err, and destroy the way of thy paths.

Oppressors (Heb. *nâgas*)—to press or drive. Literally means "exactors."

Those who ought to be protectors drive the people like you would drive cattle or sheep. There is no care for them, but only for themselves. Their leaders are exactors and are as unqualified to rule as ""children" would be.

3:13 The Lord standeth up to plead, and standeth to judge the people.

3:14 The Lord will enter into judgment with the ancients of his people, and the princes thereof: for ye have eaten up the vineyard; the spoil of the poor is in your houses.

The terms "elders" and "princes" represent the leadership in the vineyard, or in the house of Israel (5:7; Ps. 80:8–14). They are shepherds who consume or take away and have given nothing back in return (see Ezekiel 34).

3:15 What mean ye that ye beat my people to pieces, and grind the faces of the poor? saith the Lord God of hosts.

The phrases "beat my people" and "grind the faces of the poor" "may refer to actual physical punishment or to economic hardships due to insufferably high taxes and duties, levies, or assessments imposed on the poor; it may also refer to attitude, for we are also condemned for the state of our hearts" (Parry, *Understanding Isaiah*, 43).

We hope to have people in leadership positions "that [inspire] a confidence that shows the way ahead—where the strong are marshaled to give liberally of their leadership, of their means, of their talents; where the weak are urged to maximum effort in providing for themselves; where emergency needs can be met in a way that fosters brotherhood, instead of a deadening process that is described, scripturally, as to 'grind the faces of the poor.' (Isaiah 3:15)" (Lee, Harold B., "Watch, That Ye May Be Ready).

3:16 Moreover the Lord saith, Because the daughters of Zion are haughty, and walk with stretched forth necks and wanton eyes, walking and mincing as they go, and making a tinkling with their feet:

Daughters are the future of Zion and the phrase "daughter of Zion" moves us into the future from Isaiah's time to our day. This term refers to the inhabitants of Jerusalem and Judah (see Lam. 1:6–8; 2:8; Zech. 9:9; 2 Ne. 8:25).

> What then is the meaning of the plural daughters of Zion? There are several possible interpretations. If the phrase daughter of Zion represents Jerusalem, then perhaps the plural daughters refers to Jerusalem at the time of Isaiah as well as Jerusalem in the last days. The plural daughters of Zion may also refer to ancient Jerusalem (and the Southern Kingdom of Judah) and to Samaria (and the Northern Kingdom of Israel). The phrase may be literal, referring to actual women, or it may point to women as symbols of pride and sin in the last days. Note the women's clothing described in 3:18–24 and the actual women that seem to be identified in 4:1. This interpretation parallels Isaiah's condemnation of male pride (2:10–22) and the sick nature of the inhabitants of Jerusalem (1:5–6, 21–23). (Parry, *Understanding Isaiah*, 43)

The phrase "stretched forth necks" is an ancient idiom describing haughtiness or pride in self and scorn toward others (see Young, *Book of Isaiah*, 1:162). It is symbolic of walking in darkness.

> This expression portrays women who look sideways to see if others notice their beauty as they prance along the way or as they look upwards with high heads in a proud manner. For the children of Israel in all eras, the expression denotes a people

> who pay idolatrous heed to others rather than to God above. (Parry, *Understanding Isaiah*, 43)

The women wore costly ornamental chains connecting rings about the ankles that minced and tinkled as they walked. These chains were often adorned with bells (see Keil and Delitzsch, *Commentary*, 7:1:143). This was worn to attract attention. They want to be noticed. Elder Jeffery R Holland spoke to this saying that "women as well as men can be predatory" (Holland, "Of Souls, Symbols, and Sacraments").

> Isaiah, one of the great prophets of early times, saw our day, and he described the conditions that would prevail among the 'daughters of Zion' in these latter days. ... Now, in this modern day, Isaiah's prophecy has been and is being fulfilled. ... The standards expressed by the General Authorities of the Church are that women, as well as men, should dress modestly. They are taught proper deportment and modesty at all times. It is, in my judgment, a sad reflection on the 'daughters of Zion' when they dress immodestly. Moreover, this remark pertains to the men as well as to the women. The Lord gave commandments to ancient Israel that both men and women should cover their bodies and observe the law of chastity at all times. (Smith, *Answers to Gospel Questions*, 5:172–174.)

3:17 Therefore the Lord will smite with a scab the crown of the head of the daughters of Zion, and the Lord will discover their secret parts.

The phrase "smite with a scab" literally means to "make bald," namely by disease. Their head will have no covering of hair. The Hebrew word for atonement means "covering." This could also refer to not having the "covering" of the Atonement.

The result of their pride is that the Lord will "discover their secret parts," or He will put the haughty to shame.

3:18 In that day the Lord will take away the bravery of their tinkling ornaments about their feet, and their cauls, and their round tires like the moon,

"In that day" or in the day when the Lord will humble the proud in Zion, He will take away that which caused them to be "brave." God is not condemning specific clothing or jewelry, but He is clearly teaching that if something influences you to be proud and gives you "bravery" to sin, then God will cause that to be taken away from you.

The "cauls . . . round tires like the moon" were ornamental jewelry in the shape of suns and moons according to the fashions of that day (see Young, *Book of Isaiah*, 1:165). These were also amulets that were worn by the pagans.

The timing of the fulfillment of the last few verses of chapter 3 is not certain but it is likely that it in part refers to the last days. The first verse of chapter 4 is tied to the last few verses of this chapter in the Joseph Smith Translation. When the angel Moroni visited Joseph Smith in September 1823, he quoted part of chapter 4 and said that those verses (5–6) would soon be fulfilled (see *Messenger and Advocate*, Apr. 1835, 110). Regardless, it does seem that Isaiah has made a transition to a latter-day context in verse 16 and these verses will apply to those that are prideful in the last days (see Ludlow, 108).

3:19 The chains, and the bracelets, and the mufflers,

Chains (Heb. *netiyphah*)—ornaments.
Mufflers (Heb. *raâ€˘alah*)—veils.

3:20 The bonnets, and the ornaments of the legs, and the headbands, and the tablets, and the earrings,

Bonnets (Heb. *pa'er*)—turbans.
Ornaments of the legs (Heb. *tseâ˘adah*)—stepping chains or ankle bracelets.
Tablets (Heb. nephesh *bayith*)—perfume boxes.
Earrings (Heb. *lachash*)—charms or amulets.

3:21 The rings, and nose jewels,

Nose jewels (Heb. *aph nexem*)—nose rings.

3:22 The changeable suits of apparel, and the mantles, and the wimples, and the crisping pins,

Changeable suits of apparel (Heb. *machălâtsâh*)—clothing for festivals only.

Mantle (Heb. *ma'□ṭâphâh*)—overcloak.

Wimples (Heb. *miṭpachath*)—a type of shawl or veil worn over the head.

Crisping pins (Heb. *chariyt*)—erroneously rendered as hair curling implements. The Hebrew suggests a bag, like modern purses or handbags.

3:23 The glasses, and the fine linen, and the hoods, and the veils.

Glasses (Heb. *gillayown*)—most authorities translate as a metal mirror, although some suggest transparent clothing.

Hoods (Heb. *tsânîyph*)—turbans, head cover wrapped by hand.

In the next few verses (24–26), it show us that an emphasis on one's own beauty, pride, and fashion becomes a tragedy, a disaster, and will end in slavery.

3:24 And it shall come to pass, that instead of sweet smell there shall be stink; and instead of a girdle a rent; and instead of well set hair baldness; and instead of a stomacher a girding of sackcloth; and burning instead of beauty.

Stomacher (Heb. *pethiygiyl*)—rich or expensive robe.

Fashion and beauty are now replaced with stink and "rent." The stink might possibly be from festering wounds (see Psalms 38:5) or arising from ulcers (see Zechariah 14:12). The girdle in verse 24 was the sash used to fasten the outer clothing. The "rent" or torn cloth which was to replace it was the rope used to bind slaves.

> Self-imposed baldness (3:24), sitting on the ground (3:26), and sackcloth (3:24) are all symbols of mourning, mentioned in connection with the terms lament and mourn in 3:26. Clearly, the context of 3:24–26 is mourning caused by God's judgments

> on Judah and Jerusalem as well as upon the world in the last days. (Parry, 44).

In the end, instead of being beautiful, the marks of "burning" are placed on the daughters of Zion. The "burning" refers to the branding that often accompanied one's being made a slave.

Keil and Delitzsch translated this verse: "And instead of balmy scent there will be moldiness, and instead of the sash, a rope, and instead of artistic ringlets a baldness, and instead of the dress cloak a frock of sackcloth, branding instead of beauty" (*Commentary*, 7:1:147).

3:25 Thy men shall fall by the sword, and thy mighty in the war.

3:26 And her gates shall lament and mourn; and she being desolate shall sit upon the ground.

What awaits the prideful is forced humility. They are to sit upon the ground. This act is a visible symbol of those who deeply mourn or have nothing else to sit on. They are in a state of desperation and deprivation.

ISAIAH CHAPTER 4

The Refuge and Protection of Zion

4:1 And in that day seven women shall take hold of one man, saying, We will eat our own bread, and wear our own apparel: only let us be called by thy name, to take away our reproach.

The Hebrew versions of the Old Testament always place this verse as the last verse of chapter 3 and so does the Joseph Smith Translation of the Bible. The placement of this verse at the end of chapter three changes the context from millennial to premillennial. Current editions of the Book of Mormon place the verse in a millennial context (chapter four). However, the current chapter and verse breakdown was not part of the original manuscript. If one examines the printer's manuscript of the Book of Mormon, the verse comes in the middle of a rather lengthy run-on sentence that connects chapters 3 and 4 of Isaiah. What is clear from this verse is that there will be a time where there will be a lack of men everywhere. The number seven is symbolic of completeness and indicates that there will be a desire among women to be associated with a man. This should not be interpreted as a vision of plural marriage in the future. Plural marriage is only authorized by God at times through a living prophet through revelation (see Doctrine and Covenants 132, especially verses 34–51, 61–63).

The events spoken of in this verse are connected with our day or the last days. Wilford Woodruff had a dream which also placed this verse in a premillennial time. He dreamed:

> I had been reading the revelations . . . when a strange stupor came over me and I recognized that I was in the Tabernacle at Ogden. I arose to speak and said . . . I will answer you right here what is coming to pass shortly. . . . I then looked in all directions . . . and I found the same mourning in every place throughout the Land. It seemed as though I was above the earth, looking down to it as I passed along on my way east and I saw the roads full of people principally women with just what they could carry in bundles on their backs. . . . It was remarkable to me that there were so few men among them. . . . Wherever I went I saw . . . scenes of horror and desolation rapine and death . . . death and destruction everywhere. I cannot paint in words the horror that seemed to encompass me around. It was beyond description or thought of man to conceive. I supposed that this was the End but I was here given to understand, that the same horrors were being enacted all over the country. . . . Then a voice said "Now shall come to pass that which was spoken by Isaiah the Prophet "That seven women shall take hold of one man saying &C." (Journal of Wilford Woodruff, 15 June 1878)

The Survivors: Those Who Escape the Judgments of God Are Cleansed (4:2–6)

4:2 In that day shall the branch of the Lord be beautiful and glorious, and the fruit of the earth shall be excellent and comely for them that are escaped of Israel.

In this verse, Isaiah refers "to two parallel acts of God that will transform Zion" (Smith, *American Commentary*, 156). The first of these acts is to transform the "branch of the Lord," or those who have escaped the destruction spoken of in Isaiah 2:6–4:1. This transformation makes the people of Israel become "beautiful and glorious" in God's eyes. This transformation will replace the pride and sins of the past with holiness (see Isaiah 4:3). The transformation of becoming holy is generally connected to the temple.

> The temple theme is also present in the four explicit references to Zion or mount Zion. The temple, always an integral part of Zion, is located at its center. Further, Zion's inhabitants are pure in heart and worthy to enter the temple and participate in its ordinances. It is significant that the survivors of God's judgments (3:13 4:1) will be a temple oriented people, for it is their temple orientation that will help them escape his judgments. Isa. 4:6 states that the Lord's true servants will find safety and refuge in Zion, an idea repeated in D&C 45:66 70. The command to us in this dispensation is, "Stand ye in holy places, and be not moved, until the day of the Lord come; for behold, it cometh quickly (D&C 87:8; 45:32). (Parry, *Understanding Isaiah*, 46–47)

The second transformation that God orchestrates is that the poor soil of the land becomes fertile. The "fruit of the earth" will become "excellent and comely." It is interesting to note that centuries ago John Calvin saw in this verse a promise that "a New Church shall arise" created by Jesus Christ himself (Calvin, "Commentary on the Bible, 1840–47," 1:152–53).

4:3 And it shall come to pass, that he that is left in Zion, and he that remaineth in Jerusalem, shall be called holy, even every one that is written among the living in Jerusalem:

> Written—in the book of life (See Php 4:3; Re 3:5; 17:8). Primarily, in the register kept of Israel's families and tribes.
>
> Living—not "blotted out" from the registry, as dead; but written there as among the "escaped of Israel" (Dan 12:1; Ezek 13:9).

Those who have been raised up to meet the Savior in the clouds and will come down with Him to help Him cleanse the earth will live with Him in His holy cities, New Jerusalem and Jerusalem. They who live with Him will be called holy. The Prophet Joseph Smith taught that Zion or the New Jerusalem would be called the holy city, the first of Zion's communities built in preparation for the Millennium. The center of New Jerusalem will be located at Independence, Jackson County, Missouri (D&C 57:1 3; 101:20).

4:4 When the Lord shall have washed away the filth of the daughters of Zion, and shall have purged the blood of Jerusalem from the midst thereof by the spirit of judgment, and by the spirit of burning.

The Lord restates that He will cleanse the "filth of the daughters of Zion" from the earth that only the righteous will be left to inhabit the cities of New Jerusalem and Jerusalem. He will do this "by the spirit of judgment, and by the spirit of burning." There must be a cleaning process that takes place before the Lord can provide us with the promised blessings (see D&C 88: 85–98). President Ezra Taft Benson explained, "We must cleanse the inner vessel (see Alma 60:23), beginning first with ourselves, then with our families, and finally with the Church" (Benson, "Cleansing the Inner Vessel").

4:5 And the Lord will create upon every dwelling place of mount Zion, and upon her assemblies, a cloud and smoke by day, and the shining of a flaming fire by night: for upon all the glory shall be a defence.

Defence (Heb. *chuppâ*)—canopy or a protective covering.

Dwelling place (Heb. *mâkôwn*)—a habitation. This word is used 10 times in the Old Testament and in each case it refers to the place where the Glory of God dwells (see Ex 15:17; and 1 Kings 8:13, translated "the place" and 1 Kings 8:39, translated dwelling "place" and 1 Kings 8:43 translated: dwelling "place", and 1 Kings 8:49 translated: dwelling "place"; and 2 Chron 6:30 translated: dwelling "place"; and Ps 89:14 translated: "habitation" of your throne; and Ps 97:1 translated: "habitation" of his throne; and Isa 4:5 translated: "establishment" but KJV "dwelling place"; and in Isa 18:4 translated "dwelling place" Dan 8:11 translated: "place" of his sanctuary) (See Miller, *Commentary on Isaiah*).

Note: Verses five and six of this chapter were quoted by the Angel Moroni to Joseph Smith. Moroni said that these verses were soon to be fulfilled (*Messenger and Advocate*, April 1835, 110).

The visual elements of a "cloud," "smoke," and "fire" are elements "that often accompany a theophany or God's presence in the temple. For instance, God appeared at the Sinai sanctuary (Ex. 15:17) and was accompanied by a cloud, smoke, fire (Ex. 19:9, 18), and similar elements associated with Solomon's temple (1 Kgs. 8:10) and the temple in heaven (6:4; Rev. 15:8). The cloud symbolizes the Lord's glory (D&C 84:2 5). The people of the latter-day Zion will be so righteous that they will all enjoy such blessings" (Parry, *Understanding Isaiah*, 49).

Isaiah indicates that Zion will become a defense or protection to its inhabitants from spiritual harm just like an individual is protected from physical harm by a canopy or protective covering. This protection is available to all who abide in Zion.

Here is how you could read this verse applying the symbolism to us in our day. "And the Lord [Jesus Christ] will create upon every dwelling place [home] of mount Zion [Church], and upon her assemblies [wards and stakes], a cloud and smoke [the visible presence and protection of God] by day, and the shining of a flaming fire [presence and protection of God] by night: for upon all the glory shall be a defence [to each saint in Zion]. And there shall be a tabernacle [temple] for a shadow in the daytime from the heat [a place of comfort], and for a place of refuge, and for a covert [protection] from storm [personal difficulties] and from rain.

Are our homes a place where God could dwell? Is your bedroom a place where you feel the Spirit? Does it provide a defense against the heat of the adversary? If Christ were to come to your homes, would you be comfortable in inviting Him in to stay for a while?

4:6 And there shall be a tabernacle for a shadow in the daytime from the heat, and for a place of refuge, and for a covert from storm and from rain.

Tabernacle—portable temple.

These two verses give the Saints a great promise of the Lord's protective power over His cities during the Millennium. It will be similar to the protection and help that the people of Moses enjoyed during their travels in the wilderness coming out of Egypt. The Lord will, in this millennial day, provide "a tabernacle for a shadow in the daytime from the heat, and for a place of refuge, and a covert from storm and from rain."

The Lord's people will see wonderful events take place in the Millennium and have seen in our own day many wonderful happenings. Take, for example, what occurred in my own family after an unusual activity of endowment work that was done by the Hale family in the Logan temple. The temple was "filled with light on Friday and Saturday nights, and the whole outside of the building shone with a pale pink glow. Hundreds of people saw it and marveled at the sight, for there were no electric lights at the time" (Jonathan H. Hale History, Blackfoot, Idaho).

The Lord will give the faithful His personal umbrella of protection in New Jerusalem, and these things that we have experienced in our lifetime thus far will be dimmed by the greatness of the Lord's power yet to be shown us. The Lord said of the supernatural light shining in His city of New Jerusalem, "And the city had no need of the sun, neither of the moon, to shine in it: for the glory of God did lighten it, and the Lamb is the light thereof" (Revelation 21:23).

This will serve as a powerful testimony to the Saints and a great witness to the world of God's influence and presence with His holy children whom He calls Saints. This prophecy as described has not yet occurred since the day that Isaiah uttered this prophecy, and the promise is still yet to be seen by God's faithful in these latter days.

ISAIAH CHAPTER 5

The Parable of the Vineyard and Seven Indictments of Israel

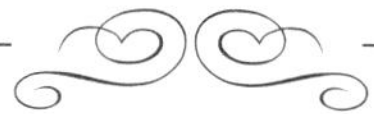

Chapter 5 begins with imagery of peace and success. The vineyard is established and fruitful and likely reflects the prosperous years of Uzziah and Jeroboam II (see Smith, *American Commentary*, 164). The vineyard produced wild fruit, which leads Isaiah to compare this fruit to Israel and give eight reasons why Israel is comparable to this wild fruit. There is also a harbinger of a powerful force about to descend on Israel but also a promise of an ensign and a gathering.

The Parable of the Vineyard

This chapter starts with a parable dealing with the house of Israel, the men of Judah, and the Lord Jesus Christ's birth into mortality through the house of David. Isaiah wrote as if his voice were the voice of God. Isaiah is delivering the Lord's message, not just his personal philosophy.

5:1 Now will I sing to my wellbeloved a song of my beloved touching his vineyard. My wellbeloved hath a vineyard in a very fruitful hill:

Very fruitful hill—literally in Hebrew "a horn, the son of oil"

Why sing this message? Songs can be more powerful than just words depending on the level of their personalization and emotion. We can convey a more powerful emotion through songs. Our hymns are a special type of song that can increase the power of spiritual messages as they enter into our hearts. Isaiah now sings a song about a very personal subject—the Master's vineyard.

In the first two verses, Isaiah describes the preparations of his friend for the vineyard. "The master of the vineyard follows five steps to ensure a productive harvest: (1) choice of fertile soil, (2) cultivation of the soil, (3) selection of good stock, (4) protection of the crop, and (5) preparation for harvesting and storing the crop. His extreme care is evidenced even more in the original language. In Hebrew, the hill chosen for the vineyard is literally translated as "a horn, the son of oil," indicating that the vineyard would be located on the summit of a very fertile hill. Special grapevines (*soreq*) were used instead of the more common variety (*gephen*). The *soreq* grapes produce a red wine famous for its bouquet and taste.

> Other indications of the vineyard master's efforts include the clearing out of stones and the building of walls and a watchtower. He obviously anticipates a plentiful harvest because he also "hews" a winepress or vat in the middle of the vineyard. Such a wine vat consists of two basins or pits carved out of the rocks. The upper pit, where the grapes are trodden out, is shallow and large enough to accommodate the workers. A trench carries the pressed out juices to a lower, deeper pit, where the wine accumulates until it is stored in clay jars or skin bags. The construction of this type of press is usually undertaken by wealthy landowners or by those who press grapes for many farmers. Thus, the fact that the master of this vineyard builds a vat in the middle of his own field indicates that he expects his harvest alone to justify its construction. To his disappointment, however, his vines yield only wild, sour grapes. (Ludlow, 112).

Preparations Made for the Vineyard

5:2 And he fenced it, and gathered out the stones thereof, and planted it with the choicest vine, and built a tower in the midst of it, and also made a winepress therein: and he looked that it should bring forth grapes, and it brought forth wild grapes.

Grapes—represent the righteous fruits expected from the vineyard. These grapes are sweet to the taste. Wild grapes represent wickedness and are bitter.

Fenced the Vineyard

The fence symbolizes the protection of the Lord for the house of Israel. The archaic definition of the word fenced means to "defend or ward off: protection." The degree of protection that we have in our lives depends on our willingness to follow the direction of God. The strength of the fence or our spiritual protection increases as we:

Are Obedient to the Commandments of God

If we obey holy laws from God, we will take upon ourselves "the whole armour of God" and receive greater guidance and greater protection against the wiles of the devil (See Eph. 6:11–18). Obedience ensures us of the guidance and protection of the Holy Spirit.

Study the Scriptures

When the Lord was facing Satan by Himself, He drew upon scriptures for protection. President Ezra Taft Benson promised if we would read the Book of Mormon we will "find great power, great comfort, and great protection" (Benson, "The Book of Mormon—Keystone of Our Religion"). Bible stories will give us power and protection as we remember them, for the Bible states that God "is a shield unto them that put their trust in him" (Proverbs 30:5).

Are Protected by the Ministering of Angels

John A. Widtsoe said, "Undoubtedly angels often guard us from accidents and harm, from temptation and sin. They may properly be spoken of as guardian angels. Many people have borne and may bear testimony to the guidance and protection that they have received from sources beyond their natural vision. Without the help that we receive from the constant presence of the Holy Spirit, and from possible holy angels, the difficulties of life would be greatly multiplied" (*Improvement Era*, April 1944, 225).

Hearken to Apostles and Prophets

Mark E. Petersen said:

> These apostles and prophets, the revelators of God, were to act as a protection for the people against false prophets and false teachings. Therefore, if somebody secretly comes to you claiming to have had a secret revelation and trying to lead you astray, all you have to do is remember that this person is not an apostle. If you want to know what the word of God is, go to the Council of the Twelve or the First Presidency. They are the foundation of the Church; they will keep you on the right track so that you will not need to worry. (Petersen, "A Man Must Be Called of God")

Strengthen the Family

The family can be a wonderful source of moral strength, physical and emotional health, along with protection against adversity. The holding of regular family home evenings is a shield and protection against the evils of our day

Seek Truth

Joseph F. Smith said:

> The most needful inspiration for young men is the Spirit of God. All your efforts, brethren, should be directed towards the possession and the inculcation of the spirit of the Gospel which is true knowledge. True knowledge bears the right kind of fruit; but knowledge alone does not, for many men have knowledge enough to be saints, but instead are wicked sinners. Lucifer himself knows the truth, he possesses knowledge, but he lacks the essential principle with it—the spirit of truth. He is devoid of the spirit although he has the knowledge, and, for that reason, he remains the fallen Son of the Morning.
>
> Of what use is it that we know the truth, if we lack its spirit? Our knowledge, in this event, becomes a condemnation

> to us, failing to bear fruit. It is not sufficient that we know the truth, but we must be humble and with this knowledge possess the spirit to actuate us to good deeds. Baptism, as well as all other outward ordinances, without the spirit accompanying, is useless. We remain but baptized sinners.
>
> It is the duty of the young men of Israel to seek first the Kingdom of God and his righteousness, and leave other things to follow; to seek the spirit of truth so as to possess the knowledge of God, which giveth them a desire for purity, light, truth; and a spirit to despise evil and to turn away from all that is not of God. (Smith, "Fruits of the Spirit")

Seek the Guidance of the Holy Ghost

There is an ample shield against the power of Satan and his hosts. This protection lies in the "power of discernment" through the gift of the Holy Ghost (see D&C 46:23) by personal revelation to those who strive to obey the commandments of the Lord and to follow the counsel of the living prophets.

Attend the Temple

Temples are spiritual sanctuaries. President James E. Faust said, "Those who attend the temples can find protection against Satan and his desire to destroy them and their families" (Faust, "Opening the Windows of Heaven"). Elder Joseph B. Wirthlin said, "Regular temple work can provide spiritual strength. It can be an anchor in daily life, a source of guidance, protection, security, peace, and revelation. No work is more spiritual than temple work" (Wirthlin, "Seeking the Good").

Repent

Repentance and righteousness bring divine protection.

Taking the Sacrament Worthily

Each Sabbath we can partake of the sacrament, which involves regular repentance and covenant making to keep ourselves clean and "unspotted from the world." It is an inspired plan for protection against immorality, rebellion, the breakdown of family structure and values, and other spiritual dangers that threaten us.

Church Attendance

> Young people of the Church should, for their own protection, welfare, and happiness, as also for the happiness, relief from great anxiety, and satisfaction of their parents, identify themselves with the local Church organization in the place where they are resident and take part in Church activities. (Clark, 135)

Keep the Sabbath Day Holy

Elder James E. Faust taught, "In this day of increasing access to and preoccupation with materialism, there is a sure protection for ourselves and our children against the plagues of our day. The key to that sure protection surprisingly can be found in Sabbath observance: 'And that thou mayest more fully keep thyself unspotted from the world, thou shalt go to the house of prayer and offer up thy sacraments upon my holy day' (D&C 59:9)" (Faust, "The Lord's Day").

Pray Night and Morning

> Prayer protects families. Let us all revive our individual and family prayers. Prayer is an armor of protection against temptation, and I promise you that if you will teach your children to pray, fervently and full of faith, many of your problems are solved before they begin. (*The Teachings of Spencer W. Kimball*, 117)

> Prayer is a request for further light, protection or whatever else is desired. Prayer is the first and greatest means of reading God's messages, for by intense prayer man gradually places himself in tune with the infinite so far as his request is concerned. Those who do not ask, naturally do not establish an understanding relationship with the unseen world, and no message appears. The Being of higher intelligence, to whom the request is directed, may or may not grant the prayer, but some answer will be given. Prayer has been said to be "the soul's sincere desire." Only when it is such will the fullest answer be obtained, and it is doubtful if such a prayer is ever refused. No prayer is unheard. The place and time of prayer are of less

importance. Morning, noon and night, prayer is always fitting. However, it is well to be orderly, and to beget habits of prayer, and certain hours of the day should therefore be set aside for prayer, both in private and in the family. Frequent and regular prayer helps to remind man of his dependence on a Being of a higher intelligence in accomplishing the great work of his heart. A man should pray always; his heart should be full of prayer; he should walk in prayer. Answers will then be heard as God pleases. Seldom is a man greater than his private prayers. (Widtsoe, *A Rational Theology*, 76–77)

The Lord Gathered the Stones from the Vineyard

Farmers often spend hours and days getting stones out of their fields so they will not break up his machinery, and so his crops can grow and not be smothered by the rocks. As the Lord prepares the earth for the growth of His gospel, He too takes great efforts to prepare the hearts of His children to receive His gospel truths and teachings. The stones come in different shapes and sizes, with each having the capability of limiting spiritual growth, and taking away their ability to discern between truth and error along with their inner strength to resist temptation. It's the Lord's desire for each of us to gather the undesirable rocks out of our lives. These rocks symbolize the effects of sin and even though we work to get these rocks out, Satan continually attempts to bring them right back into the vineyard. We must determine if each rock will be a stumbling block or a steppingstone and if we will recognize their potential danger and remove them before they become pitfalls for our families and us.

With these stones left lying around, we experience heartaches, sorrow, death, sins, weakness, disasters, physical illness, pain, mental anguish, unjust criticism, loneliness, or rejection—and the list goes on. As we develop faith and thicken our fencing fabric against Satan, and happily help rid the vineyard of sin and stumbling stones; we are better able to handle these challenges and know that each stone is a steppingstone toward perfection. With faith strengthened and our ability to identify stones increasing, our fence's fabric will be thicker and more protective. By using our agency wisely and making good choices, the valiant will find these challenges make progression and development possible.

The Lord Built a Tower in His Vineyard

The tower can be compared to a temple (see D&C 101:46).

The Lord Made a Winepress in the Vineyard

This winepress was built as a permanent structure in the middle of the vineyard and showed the hopes that the harvest of the vineyard would justify the presence of the winepress. This type of winepress has an upper and lower area. The grapes were placed in the press and then trodden underfoot in the upper area, and the juice is collected in the vat in the lower area.

Wild Grapes

The expectation is to have grapes that would produce great wine. Instead, the grapes are sour and unusable in the winemaking process. The Lord of the vineyard invested a lot of time and effort with the expectation of a great harvest.

Judge between the Lord of the Vineyard and His Earth

5:3 And now, O inhabitants of Jerusalem, and men of Judah, judge, I pray you, betwixt me and my vineyard.

There comes a time for each of us in the vineyard to be judged according to our fruits. Isaiah asks the men of Judah, and symbolically all of the house of Israel to judge between themselves and the Lord Jehovah and His vineyard. After all that the Lord has done for us, what are we producing? Is the fruit of our lives, or what we are doing and becoming, sweet or is it wild and bitter?

What More Could I Have Done?

The Lord continues in a reflective sort of way, such as a concerned parent would do and asks the question:

5:4 What could have been done more to my vineyard, that I have not done in it? wherefore, when I looked that it should bring forth grapes, brought it forth wild grapes?

What more could God do for the earth? God has given mankind of this earth prophets, apostles, covenants, ordinances, even His firstborn son Jesus Christ.

The Earth Will Fall into Apostasy

The Lord tells us four things that He will do to His non-productive vineyard. He said:

5:5 And now go to; I will tell you what I will do to my vineyard: I will take away the hedge thereof, and it shall be eaten up; and break down the wall thereof, and it shall be trodden down:

5:6 And I will lay it waste: it shall not be pruned, nor digged; but there shall come up briers and thorns: I will also command the clouds that they rain no rain upon it.

First, the Lord promises to take away the hedge which symbolizes the fence or protection that surrounds the vineyard. They must now "make it" totally on their own, for His protection will not be theirs any longer. Second, the Lord will lay it (the vineyard) waste. It will be neglected, ignored, and will decay. Third, He will not prune or cultivate the land and He will let the vineyard become a mass of briers and thorns. Fourth, the Lord will command the clouds that they shall not rain upon the land. There will be a termination of living water in Israel. The Spirit of God will no longer rain down on their heads to guide, comfort, and bless them.

Lord Gives Explanation of His Parable

5:7 For the vineyard of the Lord of hosts is the house of Israel, and the men of Judah his pleasant plant: and he looked for judgment, but behold oppression; for righteousness, but behold a cry.

> God wanted his people to be just and righteous, but instead he found bloodshed and cries of distress. Isaiah's use of Hebrew terms in this verse demonstrates his brilliant and elegant literary style. Note the similarity between the Hebrew words for judgment (*mishepat*) and bloodshed (*misepach*),

righteousness (*tsedaqah*) and cry (*tse'aqah*). Hence Isaiah's message is clear: the people chose *misepach* (bloodshed) instead of *mishepat* (judgment), *tse'aqah* (crying) rather than *tsedaqah* (righteousness). (Parry, *Understanding Isaiah*, 53–54)

Indictments against Israel

Isaiah's parable is followed by seven counts of indictments against the tribes of Israel, including Judah, in verses 8–25. This paragraph repeats words and themes that tie into the parable of the vineyard. "The verbal roots "know" *(yāda)* and "do" (*āśâ*) appear in 5:2 ("do" twice), 5:4 ("do" three times), 5:5 ("know" and "do"), 5:10 ("do" twice), 5:12 ("do"), 5:13 ("know"), and 5:19 ("do" and "know")" (Smith, *American Commentary*, 170). Isaiah emphasizes that Israel must come to know God's will and do it. Failure to learn God's will results in captivity (see verse 13).

Indictment Number One Is Greed

5:8 Woe unto them that join house to house, that lay field to field, till there be no place, that they may be placed alone in the midst of the earth!

5:9 In mine ears said the Lord of hosts, Of a truth many houses shall be desolate, even great and fair, without inhabitant.

These verses seem to give a warning against all those who are rich and use their money to greedily buy land that they have no need of, other than to be sure no one else has it. The prophet Micah said, "And they covet fields, and take them by violence; and houses, and take them away: so they oppress a man and his house, even a man and his heritage" (Micah 2:2).

Robert D. Hales said, "We make poor and irrational decisions if our decision is motivated by greediness: greed for monetary gain; greed that results in a conflict of interest; desire for power, titles, and recognition of men" (Hales, "Making Righteous Choices at the Crossroads of Life").

The Result of Greed

Isaiah foretells the outcome of such actions of greed upon the earth; the result is less productivity of the land. Isaiah gives us an account of the resulting process of greed. He said,

> 5:10 Yea, ten acres of vineyard shall yield one bath, and the seed of an homer shall yield an ephah.

What does this mean that "Ten acres of vineyard shall yield one bath?" Ezekiel stated that a bath is a Hebrew liquid measure, the tenth part of a homer (Ezek. 45:14). One-tenth of a homer contained 8 gallons and 3 quarts of our measure. Thus if "ten acres of vineyard shall yield one bath" this denotes the great unproductiveness of the land. How great the unproductiveness is seen by comparing this vineyard's production with that of a typical vineyard. A typical acre of a vineyard produces between 1.5 and 2 tons of grapes each year. Two tons of grapes will produce about 320 gallons of wine. So this ten-acre vineyard should be producing about 3,200 gallons of wine, but it is producing less than 9 gallons. It is producing only 1/356th of what it should be producing. Indeed, this is a great concern for the Lord, when so many in the land were in great need of the land to be productive.

Isaiah speaks of "the seed of a homer shall yield an ephah," what is meant by this? The seed of a homer is about six and one-half bushels. This quantity of seed yields only "an ephah" which is only one-tenth of a homer or 0.65 of a bushel (see Ex. 16:36; 1 Sam. 17:17; Zech. 5:6 and Bible Dictionary). The word "ephah" is Egyptian in origin, meaning measure. In this case, the farmer should expect a great increase when harvest time arrives but obtains only one-tenth of what he planted. Once again, Isaiah reemphasizes one of the consequences of Israel's wickedness of greed in the great unproductiveness of the land.

Indictment Number Two Is Focus on Passion for Pleasure

> 5:11 Woe unto them that rise up early in the morning, that they may follow strong drink; that continue until night, till wine inflame them!

5:12 And the harp, and the viol, the tabret, and pipe, and wine, are in their feasts: but they regard not the work of the Lord, neither consider the operation of his hands.

Those who rise up early in the morning to drink alcohol and continue until night are focused on a life of pleasure. Verse twelve alludes to those who listen to their music while sitting around drinking their "strong drink" and talking about things of the world. In so doing, they ignore or regard not the work of the Lord and consider not the operation of His hands, which should be the most important consideration of this earth. "Sadly, this intoxicating behavior has dulled their observation of what God was doing in their world. . . . As Oswalt states, 'When the passion for pleasure has become uppermost in a person's life, passion for God and his truth and his ways are squeezed out'" (Smith, *American Commentary*, 174).

Results of a Focus on Passion for Pleasure

5:13 Therefore my people are gone into captivity, because they have no knowledge: and their honourable men are famished, and their multitude dried up with thirst.

Knowledge from God gives power, and without knowledge, people go into social, spiritual, emotional, and intellectual captivity. This lack of knowledge can limit one's "perception of God's hand and purposes in this world, which they do not comprehend. [Someone's] lack of knowledge is not just due to ignorance but is also due to their lack of a meaningful relationship with God" (Smith, *American Commentary*, 175). Without God's knowledge, a person may feel they thirst for greater things, but never will be able to quench that thirst. They may hunger for hope and assurance but never connect to the Source of all hope.

A lack of knowledge leads to decreased motivation to learn from spiritual problems and make lasting changes. In our lives, we need to understand that the grace of God transforms us and changes us to become more like Christ. With the knowledge of God, it becomes "impossible for a man to be saved in ignorance" (D&C 131:6). Thus a man is saved no faster than he can receive knowledge.

Second Result of Alcoholism, "Merrymaking," and Spiritual Famine

5:14 Therefore hell hath enlarged herself, and opened her mouth without measure: and their glory, and their multitude, and their pomp, and he that rejoiceth, shall descend into it.

"Hell hath enlarged herself"—The term hell (Hebrew *sheol*) in this verse refers to the world of spirits. Hell opens her mouth wide enough to receive all who are pompous and wicked, as well as their pomp and glory; both the wicked and their evil traits will be cast down to hell. This "opened mouth" image that is connected to hell continues the symbolism of feasting ("strong drink," "wine," "feasts") and famine ("famished," "dried up with thirst"). The wicked open their mouths as they eat, drink, and are merry, while at the same time hell opens her mouth to swallow them. In the end, hell's mouth, not the mouths of the wicked, will be filled (Parry, *Understanding Isaiah*, 57). "Isaiah's imagery seems to personify death as a hungry monster, but he could be playing off the well-known ancient myth that pictured death as a monster swallowing its helpless victims" (Smith, *American Commentary*, 175).

5:15 And the mean man shall be brought down, and the mighty man shall be humbled, and the eyes of the lofty shall be humbled:

5:16 But the Lord of hosts shall be exalted in judgment, and God that is holy shall be sanctified in righteousness.

"Sanctified in righteousness"—"The New International Version presents a better reading of this phrase: "God will show himself holy by his righteousness" (Parry, *Understanding Isaiah*, 57). As people are humbled by God, and as they stand in judgment by Him, they will know that God has always kept His word. In every circumstance and time, He has done the right thing, at the right time, in the right way in an effort to help us and still allow us to keep our agency.

5:17 Then shall the lambs feed after their manner, and the waste places of the fat ones shall strangers eat.

Lambs/goats. Lambs and goats roam freely where prosperous people once lived.

Fat ones = Prosperous people.

Isaiah takes time here in verses 14–17 to make a teaching interlude and to discuss the results of those who choose to rejoice in evil. Hell will take in all those who have not qualified to be with the Lord. The Lord mentions who they are; He speaks of all those who are mean or average who have thought they would slide into heaven by just the grace of the Lord and not by any works of their own. The mighty powerful man who is always pushing his weight around, and the eyes of the lofty or proud whose eyes are always on lofty things of the world rather than on things of God. Satan has always been enticing men to involve themselves in such things that will separate them from the Spirit of God and permit him to drag them down to hell.

Indictment Number Three Is Gross Pride and High-Mindedness

5:18 Woe unto them that draw iniquity with cords of vanity, and sin as it were with a cart rope:

The prideful fasten their sins around them as with strong cords, fastened with tight knots. The sins of the wicked are fastened just like one would tie down a cart with rope. The wicked seem to have no desire for loosening the cords of their sins through the Atonement of Christ. They are so tightly bound to their evil ways that they have lost their desire to repent.

Indictment Number Four Is Sign Seekers

5:19 That say, Let him make speed, and hasten his work, that we may see it: and let the counsel of the Holy One of Israel draw nigh and come, that we may know it!

They say, "let the Lord show us that we may see." These people desire signs if they are expected to believe and change their behavior. These people are generally sign seekers not because they would believe, but because they do not wish to do so. They taunt the ministers of the Lord, demanding a sign as proof of authority and truthfulness. The Savior stated that it is, "an evil and adulterous generation [that] seeketh after a sign" (Matthew 12:39). This seems to be universally the case. Elder Bruce R. McConkie explained it this way: "Some sins cannot be separated; they are inseparably welded together. There never was a sign seeker who was not an adulterer, just as there never was an adulterer who was not also a liar. Once Lucifer gets a firm hold over one human weakness, he also applies his power to kindred weaknesses" (McConkie, *Doctrinal New Testament Commentary*, 1:277–78).

> The Prophet Joseph Smith said, "When I was preaching in Philadelphia, a Quaker called out for a sign. I told him to be still. After the sermon, he again asked for a sign. I told the congregation the man was an adulterer; that a wicked and adulterous generation seeketh after a sign; and that the Lord had said to me in a revelation, that any man who wanted a sign was an adulterous person. 'It is true,' cried one, 'for I caught him in the very act,' which the man afterwards confessed when he was baptized." (Smith, *History of the Church*, 5:268)

The Lord has stated, "He that seeketh signs shall see signs, but not unto salvation" (D&C 63:7). And again, he "showeth no signs, only in wrath unto their condemnation" (D&C 63:11).

Indictment Number Five Is Deception

Elder Spencer W. Kimball of this upcoming verse said, "Infidelity is one of the great sins of our generation. The movies, the books, the magazine stories all seem to glamorize the faithlessness of husbands and wives. Nothing is holy, not even marriage vows. The unfaithful woman is the heroine and is justified, and the hero is so built up that he can do no wrong" (Conference Report, Oct. 1962, 56). Elder Kimball continued: "It reminds me of Isaiah who said:

5:20 Woe unto them that call evil good, and good evil; that put darkness for light, and light for darkness; that put bitter for sweet, and sweet for bitter!

> An increasingly wicked world today not only perceives evil as good, but also harbors anger and resentment toward righteous people and principles. Elder William Grant Bangerter of the Seventy, now an emeritus General Authority, summarized this situation as follows: "In doing these wicked things [adultery, indulgence in pornography] they [who participate] suggest that

> it is not so bad anymore. Since so much of the world accepts these actions, if we resist them or speak out against them, we will be scoffed at. We will be called prudish, Victorian, puritan, and self-righteous, as if *we* had become the sinners." (Williams, "A Shield against Evil"; Elder Bangerter quote from "Coming through the Mists," *Ensign*, May 1984, 27)

Many in the world say it is okay to do evil because it is good for business. Some are so deceptive in their lack of honesty that they would take that which is shaped like an apple, such as an onion perhaps, and coat it with caramel, and try to pass it off as a caramel apple if it made them more money. Their business tactics are unethical. Would it take more than one bite in the caramel onion to know you have been deceived? Sad is the politician who runs on a platform that he or she never intends to honor. Many feel deception is a part of the game, and thereby find ways to justify sin. Yet sin is still sin, no matter how it is disguised. Evil will always be evil and good will always be good.

Satan enjoys hiding truth in his false advertising schemes, for example, let's use the Lord's indictment of Israel being involved in "alcoholism" to look at how Satan works. There are some microorganisms that produce toxic substances called "micro organic pathogens." These pathogens are harmful to life and contain yeast that is capable of producing a toxin called "ethyl alcohol." This substance is detoxified by our liver as are most toxins we consume. It is ethyl alcohol which over time that causes cirrhosis of the liver. The liver then ceases to function. Satan is no dummy; he knows that through calling an evil good that he can get men to buy a poisonous toxin and enjoy it as they slowly kill themselves. To do this, Satan uses clever names to camouflage his evil intent. The containers are attractive. The advertisements portray wickedness as being glamorous, desirous, and popular.

President N. Eldon Tanner told a story of a young man who came from a family of wealth and position in their community. He was an exceptional student, and his future was very promising. But somewhere along the way, he obtained the attitude of wanting to do things "his way." President Tanner said:

> Although warned of the dangers which lay ahead, he continued in the forbidden paths, experimenting with alcohol, drugs, and the gay life. Eventually he left his home and family, traveled across the country, took up residence in a community comprised

> of nomads, or wanderers, we might say. They were accountable to no one; they were free to come and go as they pleased; they had no responsibilities and seemingly were leading the kind of carefree lives that they thought they wanted.
>
> There is a sad ending to nearly every story I have heard about those who drift away from the straight and narrow path. Such a tragedy ended the life of the young man to whom I refer. Under the influence of drugs and alcohol, and motorcycling with his companions late one night, he plunged through the rails of a bridge over a murky river and was killed. In agreement with some facetious pact he had supposedly made with his friends, they, without consulting his parents, conducted his funeral service, cremated the body, and strewed the ashes over the spot where he died.
>
> Imagine the grief of his parents and his loved ones who were not able even to claim his body for proper burial. Just think of the many, many parents and family members who grieve daily over the absence of one of their number who has chosen to wander and waste his life in pursuit of he knows not what. (Tanner, "Why Is My Boy Wandering Tonight?")

Unscrupulous men and women will do anything to make a dollar. They are generally far away from their destructive influences. They destroy by crying that evil is good, and good is evil. They call darkness light, and light they call darkness.

Indictment Number Six Is against an Intellectual Wannabe

5:21 Woe unto them that are wise in their own eyes, and prudent in their own sight!

Isaiah refers here to people who believe they at times know more than God, or perhaps better than God. They are intellectuals whose pride often leads to cynicism. They believe their opinion is more discerning than the prophets of God. Their pride leads them to sneer and scoff at that which they do not understand, or do not want to understand (in Conference Report, October 1966, 5). Many of these intellectuals in this present enlightened age think they have outgrown the basic and fundamental principles that the Savior and His holy prophets have stressed throughout the ages of time.

President Spencer W. Kimball advised: "We must oppose the so-called intellectuals who reason that they have all the answers, and we must contend mightily with those whose lust for power and worldly gain destroy their sense of right and wrong" (in Conference Report, April 1979, 7). We must keep a constant vigil among us to beware of false Christs and false Christianity which is springing up among some of the so-called intellectuals of the Church. Be not deceived, a time will come when the Lord will reveal all that which pertains to this earth to those who have been faithful. (See D&C 101:32–34.)

Indictment Number Seven Is That Wicked Men Justify Sin to Get Gain

5:22 Woe unto them that are mighty to drink wine, and men of strength to mingle strong drink:

> Mighty to drink wine is a phrase describing the lifestyle of those who reject God and think that they themselves are gods in the world. (Parry, *Understanding Isaiah*, 58)

5:23 Which justify the wicked for reward, and take away the righteousness of the righteous from him!

There are many on the earth that "justify the wicked for reward." Some are seemingly declared "not guilty" by virtue of their position, popularity, or wealth. We hear of others who are innocent who are found guilty because of their lack of financial means to adequately represent themselves and then years later are exonerated and released from prison. Those who "take away the righteousness of the righteous" are those who would deny justice and righteous, impartial judgment. This phrase is related to those who call "evil good and good evil" in that they mislead or seduce righteous people into sin.

By studying Isaiah we can be more observant of the darkness that enveloped the minds of the children of Israel, with all sorts of evil deeds. We can better understand why blessings were withheld and why the judgments of God came down upon them. Yet, can we see that we must be better than they or the same consequences will fall upon us as a nation? No nation is exempt from following the commandments of God. For those who do not, the Lord promises these consequences:

5:24 Therefore as the fire devoureth the stubble, and the flame consumeth the chaff, so their root shall be as rottenness, and their blossom shall go up as dust: because they have cast away the law of the Lord of hosts, and despised the word of the Holy One of Israel.

The "root" has reference to one's parentage and the "blossoms" to offspring. The unrepentant wicked will not enjoy family ties in the eternities (Job 18:16) (See Parry, *Understanding Isaiah*, 58). When the Lord comes to destroy the wicked, He will "devoureth the stubble." The hot flames will consume the stubble, which are the wicked people of the earth (Isa. 9:18). He will do this because they have not rooted their faith in the gospel of Jesus Christ, and their deeds are evil. They will have "cast away the law of the Lord of Hosts, and despised the word of the Holy One of Israel."

5:25 Therefore is the anger of the Lord kindled against his people, and he hath stretched forth his hand against them, and hath smitten them: and the hills did tremble, and their carcases were torn in the midst of the streets. For all this his anger is not turned away, but his hand is stretched out still.

"His hand is stretched out still." Even though God is angry with His people because of their wickedness, He still stretches out His hand to deliver them from destruction. There are many ways that God has done this. The next few verses prophesy one very important way that God will help to save His people in the last days. In the last days, He will lift up an ensign to the nations.

Lift Up an Ensign to the Nations

5:26 And he will lift up an ensign to the nations from far, and will hiss unto them from the end of the earth: and, behold, they shall come with speed swiftly:

An ensign serves as a rallying standard, a standard that inspires and enlightens. It is The Church of Jesus Christ of Latter-day Saints. Isaiah foretells that the Lord will establish His church as an ensign to the nations of the world. Far away from Isaiah and Jerusalem, on April 6, 1830, in the house of Peter Whitmer, Sr., in Fayette, New York, Joseph Smith organized the Church of Christ in these last days. The Saints were driven from there to the Rocky Mountains and on the morning of July 25, 1847, Brigham Young, Wilford Woodruff, and a handful of their associates hiked from their campground up the hill of a domeshaped peak. That peak today is called Ensign Peak and refers to Isaiah's words found in Isaiah 5:26.

As these brethren looked south over the mostly barren Salt Lake Valley, Elder Wilford Woodruff took out a bandanna handkerchief from his pocket and waved it as an ensign or a standard to the nations. They felt that from this place, the word of God would speedily go forth to the ends of the earth, and the people of the world would gather there.

President Gordon B. Hinckley commented on this event and said:

> How foolish, someone might have said, had he heard these men that July morning of 1847. They did not look like statesmen with great dreams. They did not look like rulers pouring over maps and planning an empire. They were exiles, driven from their fair city on the Mississippi into this desert region of the West. But they were possessed of a vision drawn from the scriptures and words of revelation.
>
> I marvel at the foresight of that little group. It was both audacious and bold. It was almost unbelievable. Here they were, almost a thousand miles from the nearest settlement to the east and almost eight hundred miles from the Pacific Coast. They were in an untried climate. The soil was different from that of the black loam of Illinois and Iowa, where they had most recently lived. They had never raised a crop here. They had never experienced a winter. They had not built a structure of any kind. These prophets, dressed in old, travelworn clothes, standing in boots they had worn for more than a thousand miles from Nauvoo to this valley, spoke of a millennial vision. They spoke out of a prophetic view of the marvelous destiny of this cause. They came down from the peak that day and went

> to work to bring reality to their dream. (Hinckley, "An Ensign to the Nations")

Travel—to Take the Ensign to the Nations

From there the Lord has sent His gospel to be taught to the ends of the earth. Isaiah foretold that the time would come when the church missionaries shall come to their field of labor by the quickest mode of transportation that could be had. Years ago in the early church, it took missionaries three months to get to Europe. Now, they can get there in several hours. And when they get there, they are fresh and ready to serve.

The journey will be so nice in the airplanes that:

> 5:27 None shall be weary nor stumble among them; none shall slumber nor sleep; neither shall the girdle of their loins be loosed, nor the latchet of their shoes be broken:

> 5:28 Whose arrows are sharp, and all their bows bent, their horses' hoofs shall be counted like flint, and their wheels like a whirlwind:

> 5:29 Their roaring shall be like a lion, they shall roar like young lions: yea, they shall roar, and lay hold of the prey, and shall carry it away safe, and none shall deliver it.

The arrows being sharpened refer to the excellent training that the missionaries will have received at the Missionary Training Centers that will prepare them to have their "bows bent" and ready to teach mankind the gospel of Jesus Christ as His ambassadors. A bow is not strung unless one is ready to begin the hunt. This is the case as the missionaries come out into the world, ready to teach about the Son of God, Jesus Christ, to the inhabitants of the world.

Elder LeGrand Richards said:

> Since there were no such things as trains and airplanes in that day, Isaiah could hardly have mentioned them by name, but he seems to have described them in unmistakable words. How better could "their horses' hoofs be counted like flint, and their wheels like a whirlwind" than in the modern train? "Their roaring . . . be like a lion" than in the roar of the airplane? Trains and airplanes do not

> stop for night. Therefore, was not Isaiah justified in saying: "none shall slumber nor sleep; neither shall the girdle of their loins be loosed, nor the latchet of their shoes be broken"? With this manner of transportation the Lord can really "hiss unto them from the end of the earth" that "they shall come with speed swiftly." (*A Marvelous Work and a Wonder*, 230)

All of these methods of transportation have been developed for a mode of speedy travel to get the Lord's servants out to the nations of the world in the fastest way possible. This allows Israel to be more effectively taught and gathered.

It would appear that the coming forth of the railroad, airplane, telegraph, telephone, television, microwaves, silicon chips, discs, and satellite systems are part of the fulfillment of what Isaiah saw in vision hundreds of years ago. What a time saver it is to travel or call on the phone in the modern age in which we live. Just think, the distance one can travel by railroad in two or three days today took the pioneers some ninety to a hundred days to travel in covered wagons. And now it takes just a few hours by jet airplanes, and we arrive refreshed, and ready to go.

Missionaries Will Bring Home the Prey

5:30 And in that day they shall roar against them like the roaring of the sea: and if one look unto the land, behold darkness and sorrow, and the light is darkened in the heavens thereof.

The Lord's messengers are like young lions, youthful and energetic, holding authority from God to bring truth seekers into God's kingdom. They are to teach and take away the "prey" of Satan, the arch-deceiver. The prey refers to those who accept the gospel of Christ and who are given membership into His church through baptisms. He will then give them the companionship of a member of the Godhood, the Holy Ghost. This gift will develop with them and give them direction and hope in living His commandments, as they seek eternal life.

ISAIAH CHAPTER 6

The Calling of a Prophet

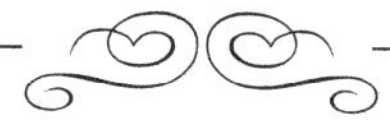

Isaiah's Vision and Call to The Ministry

In the previous five chapters, Isaiah had given us an understanding of the situation that he entered into when he became the prophet. In this chapter, Isaiah sees the Lord and is called to be a prophet. Isaiah's vision of the Lord likely took place in 740 BC (the year that King Uzziah died). Both John the Revelator and Nephi testified that the Lord whom Isaiah saw was the premortal Jesus Christ (see John 12:41; 2 Nephi 11:2–3). In this vision, Isaiah also sees the heavenly or celestial temple, or more specifically, the throne room or holy of holies located in this temple. Isaiah must have been at least age thirty when this call came, for it was the age when the sons of Aaron and even the Savior received His call (See Smith, *Doctrines of Salvation*, 86; Woodruff, *Collected Discourses*, 1 September 1889).

6:1 In the year that king Uzziah died I saw also the Lord sitting upon a throne, high and lifted up, and his train filled the temple.

The last year of Uzziah's life was around 740 BC.

> [Uzziah had] entered the Temple and essayed to burn incense on the altar. Shocked at his blasphemous action, Azariah, the chief priest of the Temple, and fourscore priests with him, forbade the king, saying: "It appertaineth not unto thee,

> Uzziah, to burn incense unto the Lord, but to the priests the sons of Aaron, that are consecrated to burn incense: go out of the sanctuary; for thou hast trespassed." At this rebuke and condemnation from his subjects, though they were priests of the Lord, the king became angry; but immediately the scourge of leprosy fell upon him; the signs of the dread disease appeared in his forehead; and being now physically an unclean creature his presence tended the more to defile the holy place. So Azariah and his associate priests thrust the king out from the Temple; and he, a smitten thing, fled from the house of God never again to enter its sacred precincts. (Talmage, 185–186)

Isaiah saw the "Lord sitting upon a throne, high and lifted up, and his train filled the temple." A train is a long piece of material attached to the back of a formal robe (or dress) that trails along the ground. The Lord's train is symbolic of His glory that filled the temple. There are many similarities to other people seeing God in the times before Isaiah lived, and many more recorded after (See Gen. 16:9–13, 28:13–15; Exodus 24:9–11; 34:5–10; I Kings 22:19; Ether 3:4–16).

There is no doubt that Isaiah was acting in the role of a prophet before this vision and seemingly official call to be a prophet. Joseph Smith taught us that this vision was not a part of Isiah's first call to serve God but connected to Isaiah having his calling and election made sure (*Teachings of Presidents: Joseph Smith*, 150–151).

In Latter-day Saint theology, we accept Isaiah at his word that he did see the Lord. We also accept that other prophets in the Old Testament, Book of Mormon, and Doctrine and Covenants wrote what they saw and experienced. There have been other modern-day visitations from the Lord to prophets and others. Besides the recorded visitations of the Lord to Joseph Smith, I will share two others that show the personal love of the Savior to His children. These experiences have helped build our faith. The first is taken from Elder Melvin J. Ballard as he shared his intimate experience with Jesus Christ. The second is the experience and the recorded testimony of Zebedee Coltrin at the school of the prophets. Both experiences carry with them great power to deepen our testimonies and can help us in understanding what Isaiah saw when he received his call from the Lord.

Elder Melvin J. Ballard Sees the Savior

> Away on the Fort Peck reservation where I was doing missionary work with some of our brethren, laboring among the Indians, seeking the Lord for light to decide certain matters pertaining to our work there, and receiving a witness from Him that we were doing things according to His will, I found myself one evening in the dreams of the night in that sacred building, the temple. After a season of prayer and rejoicing I was informed that I should have the privilege of entering into one of those rooms to meet a glorious Personage, and, as I entered the door, I saw, seated on a raised platform, the most glorious Being my eyes have ever beheld or that I ever conceived existed in all the eternal worlds. As I approached to be introduced, he arose and stepped toward me with extended arms, and he smiled as he softly spoke my name. If I shall live to be a million years old, I shall never forget that smile. He took me into his arms and kissed me, pressed me to his bosom, and blessed me, until the marrow of my bones seemed to melt! When he had finished, I fell at his feet, and, as I bathed them with my tears and kisses, I saw the prints of the nails in the feet of the Redeemer of the world. The feeling that I had in the presence of Him who hath all things in His hands, to have His love, His affection, and His blessing was such that if I ever can receive that of which I had but a foretaste, I would give all that I am, all that I ever hope to be to feel what I then felt! (Ballard, 138–139)

The Father and the Son Are Seen by Members of the School of the Prophets

Zebedee Coltrin tells of this wonderful appearance of both God the Father and His son to those present at the school of the prophets. The following comes from his minutes of this event, he recorded:

> At one of these meetings after the organization of the school, (the school being organized on the 23rd of January, 1833) when we were all together, Joseph having given instructions, and while engaged in silent prayer, kneeling, with our hands uplifted each one praying in silence, no one whispered above

his breath, a personage walked through the room from east to west, and Joseph asked if we saw him. I saw him and suppose the others did and Joseph answered "that is Jesus, the Son of God, our elder brother." Afterward Joseph told us to resume our former position in prayer, which we did. Another person came through; he was surrounded as with a flame of fire. [I] experienced a sensation that it might destroy the tabernacle as it was of consuming fire of great brightness. The Prophet Joseph said this was the Father of our Lord Jesus Christ. I saw Him.

[When asked about the kind of clothing the Father had on, Brother Coltrin said:] I did not discover his clothing for he was surrounded as with a flame of fire, which was so brilliant that I could not discover anything else but his person. I saw his hands, his legs, his feet, his eyes, nose, mouth, head and body in the shape and form of a perfect man. He sat in a chair as a man would sit in a chair, but this appearance was so grand and overwhelming that it seemed I should melt down in his presence, and the sensation was so powerful that it thrilled through my whole system and I felt it in the marrow of my bones. The Prophet Joseph said: "Brethren, now you are prepared to be the apostles of Jesus Christ, for you have seen both the Father and the Son and know that they exist and that they are two separate personages." (Coltrin, "Statement," 56–58)

Seraphim

6:2 Above it stood the seraphims: each one had six wings; with twain he covered his face, and with twain he covered his feet, and with twain he did fly.

The term "Seraphim" in Hebrew is plural, and the King James Version of the Bible reads "seraphims." The Book of Mormon corrects this error. The singular word for seraphim is seraph. Seraphim literally means "burning ones" (Smith, *American Commentary*, 188) or ones that can dwell in everlasting burnings, in the presence of God.

The seraph's wings are symbolic. With two he covered his face, for he was in the presence of the Lord. With two he covered his feet denoting that he was on holy ground and follows the Middle East custom of showing respect. With two wings they could fly denoting the power to move (See D&C 77:4).

President Charles W. Penrose spoke on who and what are angels, he said:

> Angels are God's messengers, whether used in that capacity as unembodied spirits, selected according to their capacities for the work required, or as disembodied spirits, or as translated men, or as resurrected beings. They are agents of Deity of different degrees of intelligence, power and authority, under the direction of higher dignitaries, and subject to law and order in their respective spheres. Elijah, who appeared with Moses on the mount of transfiguration, was a translated man; Moses at that time was either a translated man or a spirit ministering to the Savior; both acted in the capacity of angels (Luke 9:28–33). (Penrose, "Who and What Are the Angels?")

Bruce R. McConkie, speaking of seraphim said:

> Seraphs are angels who reside in the presence of God, giving continual glory, honor, and adoration to him. "Praise ye him, all his angels: praise ye him, all his hosts." (Ps. 148:2.) It is clear that seraphs include the unembodied spirits of pre-existence, for our Lord "looked upon the wide expanse of eternity, and all the seraphic hosts of heaven, before the world was made." (D&C 38:1.) Whether the name seraphs also applies to perfected and resurrected angels is not clear. While petitioning on behalf of the saints, the Prophet prayed that "we may mingle our voices with those bright, shining seraphs around thy throne, with acclamations of praise, singing Hosanna to God and the Lamb!" (*D&C 109:79). (Mormon Doctrine,* 702)

Isaiah saw these seraphim in vision and heard them cry one to another:

6:3 And one cried unto another, and said, Holy, holy, holy, is the Lord of hosts: the whole earth is full of his glory.

The number three is symbolic of unity, completeness, or of being whole. When the angels repeat the word holy three times, they are emphasizing the fullness or complete holiness that is an attribute of God. This is the second of three times in this chapter where the glory of God is described as filling something. The first is in verse one where His train (symbolic of God's glory) fills the temple. Here God's glory fills the whole earth. In the next verse, the earthly temple will be filled with smoke and is also a symbol of the glory of God (see Rev. 15:8). God's glory is complete and is in His celestial temple, in His creations (like the earth), and in His earthly temples.

What do the seraphim mean when they say that "the whole earth is full of his glory"? Some scholars ask, "How can the seraphs claim that the sinful and rebellious world where Isaiah was ministering if full of God's glory?" (see Smith, *American Commentary*, 190). The Hebrew in this verse focuses on the "whole earth" and could be translated "the fulness of the whole earth is His glory." That translation fits better into Isaiah's teachings.

The Elements Even Know the Voice of the Lord

6:4 And the posts of the door moved at the voice of him that cried, and the house was filled with smoke.

Posts of the door—this refers to the foundations of the temple.

The doorposts moved back and forth in a trembling motion. The footnote in Isaiah reads, "Foundations of the thresholds trembled" (Isaiah 6:4). The temple filled up with smoke and this symbolically shows the presence and glory of God (Revelation 15:8). When the children of Israel were camping under the shadows of the Sinai Mountain, they became frightened by the fire and smoke which they saw. They didn't understand that this was the same cloud they had followed out of Egypt, which had given them shade by day and a pillar of fire by night. Now that they were to come unto the Lord their God, He showed them His power and they saw that "mount Sinai was altogether on a smoke, because the Lord descended upon it in fire" (Exodus 19:18). The smoke and fire were a sign of His glory.

Isaiah's Personal Concern of Worthiness

6:5 Then said I, Woe is me! for I am undone; because I am a man of unclean lips, and I dwell in the midst of a people of unclean lips: for mine eyes have seen the King, the Lord of hosts.

Isaiah was not expecting such an experience in the temple on that occasion and was concerned of his unworthiness to be in the presence of the Lord. He knew the wickedness of people he lived around, which caused him to express that he was "undone." This was something like saying, whoops I am in trouble, because I have "unclean lips" and have seen the Lord. It was a natural, humble feeling of Isaiah as he thought that he was not clean enough to behold the Lord. But it is the Lord who judges our personal worthiness and actions, and determines to whom He will appear. Isaiah would never have had this experience in the temple, had the Lord not judged him worthy, despite his living in a very wicked city.

Cleansing Power of the Atonement

6:6 Then flew one of the seraphims unto me, having a live coal in his hand, which he had taken with the tongs from off the altar:

Even though seraphim are described as "fiery beings," one of them needed the tongs to take a live coal from the altar. The coal is symbolic of the power to cleanse or forgive and comes from the altar in the temple. On this altar a perpetual fire was lit (see Lev. 6:12–13) and here a sacrifice was placed as a substitute for or symbol of Jesus Christ. Only Christ can forgive and even a heavenly being could not give this personally to Isaiah. A mediator (symbol of the tongs) was needed.

6:7 And he laid it upon my mouth, and said, Lo, this hath touched thy lips; and thine iniquity is taken away, and thy sin purged.

The symbolism of the "live coal" being placed on Isaiah's lips reconfirmed to him the cleansing power of the Atonement and his worthiness to stand in God's presence. The word "purged" in Hebrew (*kaphar*) literally means "covered," "covered over," or to "make atonement for."

> On our part, to give full efficacy to his atonement and to claim for ourselves the cleansing power of his blood, we must believe in him and in his Father, repent of our sins, covenant in the waters of baptism to love and serve them all our days, and then receive the gift of the Holy Ghost. (McConkie, "The Mystery of Mormonism")

Whom Shall God Send to the Wicked House of Judah?

6:8 Also I heard the voice of the Lord, saying, Whom shall I send, and who will go for us? Then said I, Here am I; send me.

Isaiah chapters 1–5 gave us an overview of the spiritual state of the people in Isaiah's day. In verse eight of this chapter the Lord asks Isaiah whom they should send to call Judah to repentance and teach them the ways of the Lord. Isaiah could have looked down to the ground trying to avoid eye contact or simply said, "I don't have a clue, who would want this job to call wicked Israel to repentance?" Yet here Isaiah is depicted as one like the Savior who was willing to do the will of the Father in all things asked of him. He quickly and humbly accepts the call to be the prophet of the Lord. Should it be any different today how we receive a call from the Lord, no matter what the call pertains to? The position we are called is not the important thing, but how we serve and exercise our faith in that calling. And if we have done our very best until we are released is what makes us a chosen servant.

The "us" in the phrase "who will go for us?" is often overlooked as being plural in nature. One of those referred to would be Jesus Christ and John indicates that this is the case in John 12:41. The second time this is quoted in the New Testament, the author of Acts records that the Holy Ghost also spoke these same words in Acts 28:25. Hence, this refers to Christ, and to the Holy Ghost. A prophet is sent to deliver a message from Christ and will be witnessed to by the Holy Ghost.

Symbolism of Verses One through Eight

Verses one through eight uses symbolism to teach truths to Isaiah. We can apply this symbolism to us in our day.

Symbol in Isaiah 6:	Symbolic of:	How it can be symbolic to us:
Throne	God is a King and Judge	We will stand before God to be judged.
Train/Smoke	Glory of God	We can and will behold His glory.
Seraphim	Heavenly beings assist	Heavenly beings will assist us. Their role is to bring us to God and help in applying the cleansing power of the Atonement.
Foundation of Temple	God is our foundation	Temples brings us to closer to our spiritual foundation—God.
Unclean lips	Personal unworthiness	We too have personal sins.
Live coal	Process of purification	We can be purified too through the Atonement of Christ.
Isaiah	He is a type of Christ	We can go where God wants us to go and say "Here am I, send me."

Jesus Uses the Prophet Isaiah (Esias) to Help Us Understand

Here the Lord is instructing His prophet Isaiah to go and teach His people who are not willing to receive counsel,

> 6:9 And he said, Go, and tell this people, Hear ye indeed, but understand not; and see ye indeed, but perceive not.

Jesus quotes from Isaiah (called Esaias in Matthew 13 and Luke 4:17) in the middle of His parable of the sower, because "the disciples came, and said unto him, Why speakest thou unto them in parables?" Jesus answered them and said, "Speak I to them in parables: because they seeing see not; and hearing they hear not, neither do they understand" (Matthew 13:10, 13). Jesus is explaining that the house of Israel was in fulfillment at that time of Isaiah's prophesy. Christ again quotes Isaiah saying in a little clearer text the same as in 2 Nephi 16:9, which reads, "By hearing ye shall hear, and shall not understand; and seeing ye shall see, and shall not perceive" (Matthew 13:14). To hear the truth and see the reality of its concepts takes the Holy Ghost. The lack of understanding Isaiah refers to in this verse is not very clear. Isaiah said of the people of Israel,

6:10 Make the heart of this people fat, and make their ears heavy, and shut their eyes; lest they see with their eyes, and hear with their ears, and understand with their heart, and convert, and be healed.

Note how the Savior quotes and clarifies this verse when He taught, "For this people's heart is waxed gross, and their ears are dull of hearing, and their eyes they have closed; lest at any time they should see with their eyes, and hear with their ears, and should understand with their heart, and should be converted, and I should heal them" (Matthew 13:15). This could be restated by saying that if a person opens their heart, listens to God's word, and sees His Hand in our lives then understanding will come to the heart through the Holy Ghost and they will be converted and healed. This verse is arranged in a chiastic structure (heart, ears, eyes, eyes, ears, heart) and emphasizes their total or complete inability to understand.

Note the definition of the word "lest" in Isaiah 6:10. The Merriam-Webster dictionary defines the word "lest" to mean "for fear that." Israel felt that if they did not consistently remain obstinate in their sin, "they should see with their eyes, and hear with their ears, and should understand with their heart, and should be converted," which means they would have to change and soften their hearts that the Lord "should heal them."

I have often wondered why anyone would not want to become healed. When I am sick, bruised, or emotionally wounded, I look forward to the healing process even though it often requires patience on my part as I go through the healing process. The diminishing of one's spiritual sight, spiritual hearing, and spiritual feeling invites an entrenchment into sin. "There is a self-hardening in evil . . . sin from its very nature bears its own punishment. . . . An evil act in itself is the result of self-determination proceeding from a man's own will" (Keil, 7:1:201). An individual cannot resist or reject the truth without eventually becoming spiritually hardened (see Smith, *History of the Church*, 4:264). Isaiah's indictment of the kingdom of Judah was cited again in the New Testament to show that the people of that time were no different. Today the decibels of decadence actively sound to decrease our spiritual hearing, the images of popular culture flash to blind us, and the Googlization of knowledge emphasized the rapidity of knowledge access at the expense of understanding with our hearts. The cure is simple. We must see our need to be healed and then look for and listen to the Holy Spirit as it brings truth to our heart and our understanding leads to true conversion to the gospel of Jesus Christ.

How Long Must I Serve?

> 6:11 Then said I, Lord, how long? And he answered, Until the cities be wasted without inhabitant, and the houses without man, and the land be utterly desolate,

This is really a great question that many of us have asked ourselves at one time or another in some of our more challenging callings. Maybe we have asked this question about personal ministry—how long must I endure doing this? And the answer comes crystal clear into our spiritual ears, at least until the day you die and then it probably goes on in the next life. Remember it's not where, or how long we serve, but with what dedication, faith, and determination you serve. The Lord has told us to love and serve our neighbors as ourselves. For Isaiah, this is primarily fulfilled at the time of the Babylonian captivity, and more fully at the dispersion under the Roman Titus.

Coming Forth of the Ten Tribes of Israel

> 6:12 And the Lord have removed men far away, and there be a great forsaking in the midst of the land.

The northern ten tribes and Judah both have been removed from their homes and taken as the spoil of war into Assyria and the Jews all over the world. Why? Because of their sins and because they did not follow the prophets.

> 6:13 But yet in it shall be a tenth, and it shall return, and shall be eaten: as a teil tree, and as an oak, whose substance is in them, when they cast their leaves: so the holy seed shall be the substance thereof.

Teil tree (Heb. *'elah*)—terebinth tree

Eaten (Heb. *ba'ar*)—also means burned

Substance (Heb. *matstsebeth*)— also means tree stump

Tenth—Only a small remnant of Israel will remain after the destruction spoken of in 6:11–12.

When the ten tribes were captured by Assyria, they were taken up into the northern country and then were lost to historical whereabouts. The ten tribes are compared to a teil tree which "stands isolated and weird—like in some bare ravine or on a hill-side" (Tristram, 581). This describes the ten tribes, they are isolated and stand alone "far away" from Israel with their whereabouts unknown. Scattered Israel will return home even though like the teil leaves, they have fallen and have been scattered but the tree has the power to bring forth new ones. The teil tree's sap (which represents God) remains within the stump of the trunk and can still give it (the ten tribes of Israel) strength and substance to return to its full beauty. The Lord promised that they (the ten tribes) will, at the right time, cast forth new leaves drawn from the substance of the "holy seed," which is the Lord Jesus Christ, and the Jews will return to Jerusalem and the ten tribes will go to Zion, the New Jerusalem.

ISAIAH CHAPTER 7

Prophesies Concerning Israel and Judah

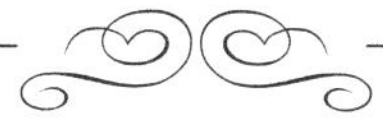

Isaiah chapter 7 transitions from Isaiah's call (chapter 6) to focusing on Israel and Judah. In 734 BC the kingdom of Judah was under a severe threat. Rezin, king of Syria, and Pekah, king of Israel, had formed an alliance and wanted Ahaz, king of Judah, to join them against Assyria. Ahaz refused and they decided to attack Judah. Pekah's army slew 120,000 men of Judah and took 200,000 captives in one day (See 2 Chronicles 28:6–15). Although the alliance eventually released the Judean captives, it appeared that Judah would soon fall. Reports of further enemy success in the north caused Ahaz to fear greatly for the safety of Jerusalem. He was inspecting the city's water supply in the Kidron Valley when Isaiah came to him with a message of comfort. Isaiah will emphasize the issue facing the nation was not the creation of a defensive alliance but was whether the Lord could be relied on to do what He had promised.

This chapter begins with an emphasis on what the Lord can and will do. In looking at the chiastic structure of the first seventeen verses, we can see that the center of the chiasmas, or focus of these verses, is what happens when we do not believe in the Lord, nor will we ask the Lord to help us in our times of need.

A1 The hour of David threatened (vs. 1–2)
B1 Isaiah's son: the plans of the northern powers (vs. 3–6)
C1 The Lord's word of assurance (vs. 7–9)
D The response of unbelief (vs. 10–12)
C2 The Lord's sign of judgment (vs. 13–15)
B2 The virgin's son: the destruction of the northern powers (vs. 16)
A2 The house of David destroyed (vs. 17)
(see Motyer, 80–81)

WAR AGAINST JERUSALEM

7:1 And it came to pass in the days of Ahaz the son of Jotham, the son of Uzziah, king of Judah, that Rezin the king of Syria, and Pekah the son of Remaliah, king of Israel, went up toward Jerusalem to war against it, but could not prevail against it.

Ahaz is the son of Jotham and grandson of Uzziah. He is described as a wicked king in 2 Kings 16:1–4 and 2 Chronicles 28:1–4 and was the king of Judah. The division between the northern tribes and Judah had been widening for some time. At the death of King Solomon (about 968 BC), his son Rehoboam succeeded him. The northern tribes of Israel were upset over Solomon's heavy taxation. After Soloman's death, Rehoboam was invited by the northern tribes' council to come to Shechem to receive their conditions for them to support him as king of Israel.

It was customary for the people to come to the capital of Jerusalem to ratify a new king. However, this was not the case with Rehoboam becoming king. The tribal leaders preferred to have him come to them and receive their grievances on their home turf before they ratified his succession to the throne. This council informed Rehoboam that they would only support his claim to the throne if he would reduce the taxes that his father had placed upon them. It may have still been fresh in their minds that Ahijah, the prophet from Shiloh, had prophesied of an upcoming division of the kingdom of Israel to the northern tribes before Solomon's death. He stated that the Lord would give the northern ten tribes to Jeroboam, who was from the tribe of Ephraim, to rule over (see 1 Kings 11:28–40). So they felt justified in giving the new king their demands.

Rehoboam demonstrated his total lack of concern for the people. Instead of decreasing the taxes, he increased them, which inflamed emotions from a silent insurrection to a full-fledged rebellion. When Adoran, the tax collector, was collecting taxes in the northern area of the kingdom, he was killed in a tax revolt and the king barely escaped with his life.

When Rehoboam rejected the advice of the elder's council, the council promptly withdrew their support of him as their king and formed a separate kingdom. Jeroboam, a decedent of Ephraim, was made king of the Ten Tribes, which fulfilled the words of the prophet Ahijah. This revolt seemed to have the blessings of the prophet Ahijah. It did not take much time for Jeroboam to let his pride get the best of him. He became jealous of his subjects needing to go to the holy city of Jerusalem to worship.

To discourage them from going to Jerusalem, he had two golden calves built for the people to worship. One at Bethel and another at Dan in an attempt to satisfy the people's need to go to Jerusalem, but this act caused a severe rebuke of the new king by the prophet Ahijah (1 Kings 14:6–16). These calf images were fashioned and supposedly were images of Jehovah. They were presented to the tribes as a symbol of the Northern tribes newly obtained freedom from Judah. Jeroboam added some of his own worship ceremony along with the false idols for his people to worship. The Levite priests, knowing that these new ceremonies were not of the Lord, refused to conduct them. To circumvent this, Jeroboam just called his own priests, like wicked King Noah in the Book of Mormon (Mosiah 11:1–7).

Eventually, Jeroboam no longer permitted the people to go to Jerusalem to worship. The apostasy of the northern nation was now complete as Jeroboam encouraged his people to worship false Gods in place of the true living God of Israel. As a result, Ahijah prophesied that the king's house would become extinct because Jeroboam encouraged idolatry (1 Kings 14:6–16). The next 19 kings that followed Jeroboam would be affected by the evils and false worship developed by King Jeroboam and his pride.

These sinful events lead the ten tribes of Israel to threaten war on their southern neighbor, Judah. So, Ephraim, the larger of the two nations, not being confident that they can conquer Judah alone, made a confederacy with Syria with the sole purpose of going to battle against Judah as described in verse one. This occurred between 734 BC to 732 BC (see Smith, *American Commentary*, 200).

The early stages of the war are described in 2 Chronicles 28 and "indicate that God gave Ahaz into the hand of Syria (indicating Syrian leadership in this plan), thereby allowing them to defeat Judah's army in battle and take prisoners (2 Chr. 28:5). Israel's army also inflicted heavy casualties on Judah, killing 120,000 troops, the king's son, and the person who was second in command to the king (2 Chr 28:6–8). Nevertheless, the two armies of Syria and Israel were never able to defeat the city of Jerusalem" (Smith, *American Commentary*, 206).

Ephraim Makes a Confederacy with Syria

This is Isaiah's first prophecy to Judah,

7:2 And it was told the house of David, saying, Syria is confederate with Ephraim. And his heart was moved, and the heart of his people, as the trees of the wood are moved with the wind.

Fear traveled like wildfire that Syria and Ephraim had united their forces together against Judah and were pushing their way toward Jerusalem. Each day as outlying cities fell, more and more of the people in the path of this oncoming army were fleeing toward the capital city of Jerusalem for refuge. As they came into the city, each had a tale to tell, and their fears would add to the fear of the trouble they were in for from the oncoming enemy army. Rumors were flying back and forth in every direction within the city of Jerusalem, like trees swaying back and forth in the wind. Of course, this caused great fear and panic among all the people. As the armies pushed their way toward Jerusalem, Ahaz and his people were in a state of panic.

Isaiah Commanded to Council Ahaz

7:3 Then said the Lord unto Isaiah, Go forth now to meet Ahaz, thou, and Shear-jashub thy son, at the end of the conduit of the upper pool in the highway of the fuller's field;

Shear-jashub = "a remnant shall return"

Fuller—The word "full" is from the Anglo Saxon *fullian*, meaning "to whiten." To full is to press or scour cloth in a mill. This art is one of great antiquity.

The upper pool is located today about 700 yards from the Jaffa Gate and is on the highway leading to the fullers' field. It was in a position near water for washing of the cloth previous to drying and bleaching and was probably alongside the aqueduct. These are two interesting images in this verse: fuller "to make white" and the spring. The fuller makes the ordinary cloth white (pure), and the spring provides water essential for life in Jerusalem. In other words, there is a source that can purify us and lead us to life eternal.

In this verse, the Lord had Isaiah go as a prophet and visit King Ahaz to calm his fears concerning the oncoming army. He was also to warn Ahaz of the danger of seeking assistance from Assyria in gaining the upper hand on Ephraim and Syria.

The Lord commanded Isaiah to take his son Shear-jashub with him to meet King Ahaz. The prophet was instructed where he needed to go to locate the king. The meaning of his son's name would bring additional importance to the audience, "the remnant shall return." His name is a promise stating that the Lord will not leave His people to be utterly destroyed. His name also forbodes disaster and that only a remnant will survive. Isaiah and his son found Ahaz in the precise location the Lord had indicated, up at the "conduit of the upper pool in the highway of the fuller's field." It is not known what Ahaz was doing at the upper pool, some have suggested maybe he was inspecting the city's water supply, based on his fears of the approach of the invading armies.

Smoking Firebrands

The Lord's instructions for the prophet were to say to Ahaz:

7:4 And say unto him, Take heed, and be quiet; fear not, neither be fainthearted for the two tails of these smoking firebrands, for the fierce anger of Rezin with Syria, and of the son of Remaliah.

Smoking (Heb. *˜ashen*)—as about to go out; not blazing.

Ahaz should have become a leader and an example to the people. The Lord said he was to remain calm and reassure the people that the Lord would come to their aid and had already doused the fire in the oncoming army to continue the fight. They were now just "smoking firebrands." The "two tails of these smoking firebrands" referred to the attacking two armies and their kings. Their forces are spent and are like a smoldering ember. They have little or no will to fight.

Isaiah's encouragement to Ahaz was to "be careful, keep calm and don't be afraid, do not lose heart" (Smith, *American Commentary,* 208). Even though Ahaz was a wicked man, God gave him encouragement. The phrase "take heed, and be quiet" (Heb. *Shamar shaqat*) "can be used to give an admonition, exhortation, or to express a distinct assurance" (Smith, 208). There is an assurance in the Lord's encouragement to look to God when things appear to be very bad. Ahaz needed to be "calm" and rational and not give in to his fears. "These exhortations called Ahaz not to look at this war through the perspective of human eyes but from God's perspective. . . . Surprisingly, Isaiah does not condemn Ahaz for worshipping other gods or any of the other things mentioned in 2 Kgs. 16:1–4, nor does he interpret this war as a punishment from God as in 2 Chr. 28:5. Isaiah focused on God's instructions for him to guide and direct Ahaz to the place where he could trust God with his kingdom" (Smith, 209).

The Advancing Army Shall Not Stand

Isaiah speaks of Ephraim and Syria discussing war against Judah:

7:5 Because Syria, Ephraim, and the son of Remaliah, have taken evil counsel against thee, saying,

7:6 Let us go up against Judah, and vex it, and let us make a breach therein for us, and set a king in the midst of it, even the son of Tabeal:

Breach (Heb. *baqa`*)—cleave it asunder

Tabeal—"God is good." He was a man whose son was either in the army of Pekah or the army of Rezin and whom Pekah and Rezin proposed to make the king of Israel.

7:7 Thus saith the Lord God, It shall not stand, neither shall it come to pass

The ambitions of the advancing armies of Ephraim and Syria were greater than their ability to accomplish their desire, especially when the Lord took sides with Israel. There were sacred promises made by the Lord that the Savior of the World would be born through the loins of King David, through the nation of Judah (see Gen.49:10). Do you think the Lord would have a now unknown foreign king—the son of Tabeal—be in the way of that promise? The Lord is in control. In His own hands are the destinies of the armies, nations, and of all men. He has the power to govern and control them. His angels are ready and waiting to go forth and reap down the wicked who are on the earth. Ahaz was told to have faith in the Lord and the Lord would not fail him, "it shall not stand, neither shall it come to pass." Sometimes, like Ahaz, we are asked to be careful to do nothing and thereby rely on the promises that the Lord has made to us.

Isaiah's First Prophecy—Concerning Syria

7:8 For the head of Syria is Damascus, and the head of Damascus is Rezin; and within threescore and five years shall Ephraim be broken, that it be not a people.

7:9 And the head of Ephraim is Samaria, and the head of Samaria is Remaliah's son. If ye will not believe, surely ye shall not be established.

Ahaz's inability to believe the words of the Lord's prophet caused him to turn his trust toward the visible armies of the Assyrians and away from the powerful arm of the God of Israel. Isaiah tries to persuade Ahaz to just give it a little time and trust the Lord, for the armies have no more power to push forward, and that Syria will remain as a nation, with King Rezin as its king and Damascus as its capital. Isaiah prophecies that within sixty-five years that Ephraim, who was at the head of the idol worshiping in the northern ten tribes of Israel, would no longer be a nation. This all would result because of sin. He also points out to King Ahaz that if he doesn't start trusting the Lord, he would not be established in his own kingdom. The

NIV Bible translates it this way: "If you do not stand firm in your faith, you will not stand at all."

Ahaz's lack of faith in the Lord was due to the fact he was not living in harmony with the teachings of the prophets. At this time, Ahaz had sent ambassadors to Assyria to obtain help in Judah's hour of need. He could have called his ambassadors back from their journey to solicit help from Assyria, but he did not. He put his nation, and all nations around him, in harm's way by disregarding the advice of the Lord's prophet.

Ahaz, You May Have a Sign

In verses ten through seventeen Isaiah attempts to first move Ahaz to faith (vs. 10–12). When this fails, he denounces Ahaz as a traitor and lets him know that a greater destruction awaits for him and his people (vs. 13–17).

7:10 Moreover the Lord spake again unto Ahaz, saying,

7:11 Ask thee a sign of the Lord thy God; ask it either in the depth, or in the height above.

The Lord loves us so much He is always trying to help us build our faith in Him. The Lord permitted the prophet to invite Ahaz to build his faith by asking for a sign "either in the depth, or in the height above." This is okay if a prophet invites us to ask for a sign as a faith promoting experience. However, Ahaz shows his arrogance by giving the prophet his rendition of a memorized scripture of what appears to be found in Deuteronomy 6:16, "Ye shall not tempt the Lord your God."

The word sign is written in Hebrew with the Aleph (the first letter), then the vav which is a hook tying it to the tav which is the last letter. Therefore, when the Savior in Hebrew would say, "I am Aleph and Tav," the beginning and the end. He is saying, "I am the sign."

7:12 But Ahaz said, I will not ask, neither will I tempt the Lord.

Tempt (Heb. *nacah*)—put to the proof, implying trust.

When he said this, he must have thought he was very clever. This was his way of refusing to develop his faith and maybe an attempt to put the prophet in what he thought was his place—after all, he was the king. The king's wickedness will be seen over and over again, even to the point that he will, during his reign, offer up his own son to a heathen sacrifice. He destroyed the brazen sea that Moses had assembled and made him a new altar. He then changed the order of sacrifices in the temple. Ahaz's true reason for declining was his resolve not to do God's will, but to negotiate with Assyria, and persevere in his idolatry (see 2 Kings 16). Isaiah was not happy with the insulting attitude of the king in refusing a sign, so he made the following statement:

7:13 And he said, Hear ye now, O house of David; Is it a small thing for you to weary men, but will ye weary my God also?

Isaiah was not so concerned for himself being abused, but was upset that Ahaz wearied the Lord.

Isaiah's Second Prophecy—The Immanuel Prophecy

7:14 Therefore the Lord himself shall give you a sign; Behold, a virgin shall conceive, and bear a son, and shall call his name Immanuel.

Since Ahaz would not ask for a sign, the prophet gave him one anyway, and the sign was one dealing with the birth of Jesus Christ. This second prophecy was a reminder from the Lord that the house of David (Judah) would play a vital role in the fulfillment of the promise that the Messiah would be born through the loins of David (Genesis 49:10). In the Hebrew, a definite article precedes the term translated as "virgin" or "young woman," "*ha'almah*" or literally "the virgin" indicating that she is the virgin and not just a virgin or any young woman. This prophecy stands as a warning to the Jewish nation. It doesn't matter if Ahaz or any other Jewish king was evil and had no faith, God will still bring forth the Savior of the World through the house of David. This would be done as prophesied. He would be born through a divine conception of "the virgin." For God will come, and as the word "Immanuel" means that He, "God will be with us."

7:15 Butter and honey shall he eat, that he may know to refuse the evil, and choose the good.

Butter and honey are symbols of humble circumstances as also mentioned in verses 21–22 of this chapter. The ancients used honey instead of sugar (Ps. 119:103; Prov. 24:13). With this consideration, Christ will be born of humble circumstances, and He will know to refuse the evil and choose the good, the only perfect person born on the earth.

Third Prophecy—The Loss of Both Kings

Judah abhorred Syria and Ephraim for declaring war on her. The promise is that both conspiring nations will lose their king because of this action. Isaiah then gives Ahaz a third prophecy which may be considered an extension of the second prophecy. He said:

7:16 For before the child shall know to refuse the evil, and choose the good, the land that thou abhorrest shall be forsaken of both her kings.

How old is a child before he shall know good from evil? In ancient Hebrew culture, at about three years of age moral consciousness begins (compare Isa 8:4; De. 1:39; Jon. 4:11). History shows that within three years this prophecy was fulfilled. Pekah, king of Israel, was killed under the conspiracy of Hoshea (2 Kings 15:30). Rezin, the king of Syria, was killed by the hands of the Assyrians when they conquered Syria and took over their land in response to Ahaz's call for help (2 Kings 16:9).

Isaiah's Fourth Prophecy—Bad Days Ahead for the House of Israel (735–720 BC)

7:17 The Lord shall bring upon thee, and upon thy people, and upon thy father's house, days that have not come, from the day that Ephraim departed from Judah; even the king of Assyria.

7:18 And it shall come to pass in that day, that the Lord shall hiss for the fly that is in the uttermost part of the rivers of Egypt, and for the bee that is in the land of Assyria.

King Ahaz felt the need to request help from the king of Assyria and did not necessarily care if the prophet Isaiah knew about it. Through inspiration, the prophet Isaiah prophesies that if Ahaz requests help from Assyria, the

Assyrian king would double cross him and will not stop after conquering Syria and Ephraim, but would advance upon the nation of Judah as well. The Assyrian's will bring such great destruction to their land that they will basically take everything that is not nailed down. If they thought things were bad when Ephraim and the northern ten tribes parted ways with them, they have not a clue how bad it will be when Assyria breaks its oaths and come upon Judah, while they are in the area.

Isaiah stated that the land which is so productive and well developed for agriculture will be left plundered and uncultivated after the Assyrian assault. The fly is a symbol for Egypt. When the Nile floods, swarms of flies invade the land. The hill districts of Assyria are full of bees making the bee an appropriate symbol for Assyria.

The process of this conquest is described starting in verse 18 and continues into chapter eight. An overview of this process is:
The completeness of the conquest (vs. 18–20)
The results of the conquest (vs. 21–25)
The course of the conquest (8:1–8)

Isaiah next speaks of the greatness of the Assyrian army when he says,

7:19 And they shall come, and shall rest all of them in the desolate valleys, and in the holes of the rocks, and upon all thorns, and upon all bushes.

Desolate (Heb. *battâh*)—meaning to break in pieces; desolation.

This verse is indicating that when the Assyrian army comes, they will destroy all that is in their path. The army will swarm the populated valleys, the secret places of hiding (holes of the rocks), as well as the inaccessible places of the land. There will be no escape from this enemy.

7:20 In the same day shall the Lord shave with a razor that is hired, namely, by them beyond the river, by the king of Assyria, the head, and the hair of the feet: and it shall also consume the beard.

The razor indicates a change of focus from the land to the individuals living in the land. The humiliation of their future slavery is represented by the razor cutting off their hair from the head to the foot. The Assyrians cut off all the hair from their captives for three reasons: humiliation, sanitation, and isolation (from non-slaves). The hair of the feet (hidden hair) symbolizes the indignities that will be heaped on the conquered (Motyer, 89). The hair of feet along with the beard symbolizes totality, or the completeness of the indignities that they will suffer.

Throughout history, the Lord has used the wicked to destroy the wicked. In Isaiah's prophesy, the Lord will use the wicked king of Assyria to humble and to punish Israel for her false worship of idols, and for their attack on Judah their brethren. Even Judah will not escape from the Assyrian army, because many cities of Judah will be taken, until the Assyrian army is stopped by the Lord at the city of Jerusalem.

The Consequences of War

7:21 And it shall come to pass in that day, that a man shall nourish a young cow, and two sheep;

7:22 And it shall come to pass, for the abundance of milk that they shall give he shall eat butter: for butter and honey shall every one eat that is left in the land.

Nourish (Heb. *chayah*)—to keep alive, or to sustain life

The seriousness of the devastation in the land is expressed in verses 22–25. People will be able to retain only a fraction of their original herds and flocks (vs. 22), yet the population will be so decimated that the limited livestock will provide plentiful milk and curds to the survivors

An abundance of honey comes from the large land areas that are left uncultivated and quickly turn to wildflowers, weeds, and other blossom producing plants. These two verses also indicate that there will be very little let over to sustain life as a result of the invasion. There will be a heavy dependence on animal husbandry that will come as a result of the land not being actively farmed. The people will subsist on these animals and on food that is found naturally in the land like honey.

7:23 And it shall come to pass in that day, that every place shall be, where there were a thousand vines at a thousand silverlings, it shall even be for briers and thorns.

7:24 With arrows and with bows shall men come thither; because all the land shall become briers and thorns.

7:25 And on all hills that shall be digged with the mattock, there shall not come thither the fear of briers and thorns: but it shall be for the sending forth of oxen, and for the treading of lesser cattle.

The Assyrians will leave the land so wasted that where once lush and productive vineyards were, now would be only thorns and briers. These vineyards had in the past produced a "thousand silverlings" in wealth from the grape crops. Now the vineyards are a place to graze a few cows, oxen, and sheep. These once beautiful vineyards, now lay desolate in the hot sun. They are a tangled mess of unpruned briers and thorns only good for hunters who will seek food from small animals. Some may be lucky enough to find some edible roots with their hoe, which is called a mattock.

All that which Assyria could take and carry off to their homeland would become their spoils of war. There would not be much left in the lands of Israel and Judah. It did not have to be that way. Just think, this could all have been avoided if Ahaz had trusted God, listened to his prophets, and not hired the Assyrian army against the direct council of the prophet Isaiah. This serves as a reminder to us always to follow the prophets of God in every age.

ISAIAH CHAPTER 8

The Power of Christ and His Prophets

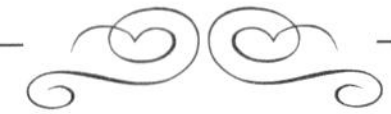

There is a law often stated in the scriptures which governs testimony and the appointment of witnesses. One such reference is, "at the mouth of two witnesses, or at the mouth of three witnesses, shall the matter be established" (Deuteronomy 19:15). In this chapter, Isaiah will focus on the captivity of the ten tribes and will also present three images of Christ for us to consider: water, temple, and light.

Faithful Witnesses Taken before the King

8:1 Moreover the Lord said unto me, Take thee a great roll, and write in it with a man's pen concerning Maher-shalal-hash-baz.

"Man's pen" meaning in ordinary characters which the humblest can read (Habakkuk 2:2). In Hebrew, *enosh* means a "common man," is contrasted with the upper ranks. The date of this prophecy concerning the capture of the northern kingdom by "the king of Assyria" can be determined quite closely because the newly born son (Mahershalal-hash-baz, "to speed to the spoil") would not even be old enough to speak before the captivity was to take place. This capture of the ten tribes comprising the kingdom of Israel is usually dated 722 BC.

8:2 And I took unto me faithful witnesses to record, Uriah the priest, and Zechariah the son of Jeberechiah.

8:3 And I went unto the prophetess; and she conceived, and bare a son. Then said the Lord to me, Call his name Maher-shalal-hash-baz.

Isaiah is directed to go again and visit Ahaz and take with him a pen and a "great roll," which would be better translated as "large placard" (Motyer, 90) and gives the idea that Isaiah should write this message as public and as noticeable as possible. He should give his son the name of Maher-shalal-hash-baz which will send a message to the king that the Assyrian army will come upon Syria, Ephraim, and even upon several of the cities of Judah. It will even reach the capital city of Jerusalem with great "speed to rob and swift to plunder," which is the meaning of his son's name. This is an object lesson to teach the king that the words of the prophets will be fulfilled. Such testimony, according to the law, must be given before at least two faithful witnesses. "Uriah the priest, and Zechariah the son of Jeberechiah" were two such men, besides Isaiah and his son. The testimony was recorded with a man's pen on a scroll to testify for all time that Israel had been warned of pending danger. Future events could at this point be altered if the king would follow the Lord's prophet and exercise his faith to call back his entourage seeking help from the Assyrians.

Why Was the Assyrian Army Something to Fear?

> The most vital part of the Assyrian government was its army. Warfare was a science to the leaders of Assyria. Infantry, chariots, cavalry (introduced by Ashurnasirpal to aid the infantry and chariots), sappers, armor made from iron, siege machines, and battering rams were all developed or perfected by the Assyrians. Strategy and tactics were also well understood by the Assyrian officers. (Durant, 1:270–71)

It is interesting that the very thing that made the Assyrian army so great also inflicted weaknesses inside her finely oiled war machine. Will Durant noted, "the qualities of body and character that had helped to make the Assyrian armies invincible were weakened by the very victories that they won; in each victory it was the strongest and bravest who died, while the infirm and cautious survived to multiply their kind; it was a dysgenic [biologically defective] process that perhaps made for civilization by weeding out the more brutal types, but undermined the biological basis upon which Assyria had risen to power. The extent of her conquests had helped to weaken her; not only had they depopulated her fields to feed insatiate Mars [the God of war], but they had brought into Assyria, as captives, millions of destitute aliens who bred with the fertility of the hopeless, destroyed all national unity of character and blood, and became by their growing numbers a hostile and disintegrating force in the very midst of the conquerors. More and more the army itself was filled by these men of other lands, while semi-barbarous marauders harassed every border, and exhausted the resources of the country in an endless defense of its unnatural frontiers." (Durant, 1:283; See also *Old Testament Manual, 1 Kings-Malachi*, 114)

Timetable for Assyrian Invasion

The prophet foretells the timetable for when the Assyrian army would be coming when he said,

> 8:4 For before the child shall have knowledge to cry, My father, and my mother, the riches of Damascus and the spoil of Samaria shall be taken away before the king of Assyria.

It normally takes about a year or two before a child can speak the words, "My Father, and my mother," depending on the child. Thus, the Lord is telling Israel that the Assyrian army's invasion of the nations to the North, Syria and the northern ten tribes of Israel, would start to take place within the next few years. In 734 BC, Tiglath-pileser marched through Israel and Philistia to the Egyptian border and cut off any potential aid from the Egyptians. The next year (733 BC) Israel lost the Galiee and the TransJordan Area (see 2 Kings 15:29). Damascus falls to Assyria the next year in 732 BC and Isaiah's prophecy will be fulfilled.

Israel Refuses Christ

In the first four verses of this chapter, the birth of Isaiah's son Maher-Shalal-Hash-Baz would begin the downfall of the northern tribes. In verses 5–8, Isaiah compares this to the forthcoming domination of Judah by Assyria.

8:5 The Lord spake also unto me again, saying,

8:6 Forasmuch as this people refuseth the waters of Shiloah that go softly, and rejoice in Rezin and Remaliah's son;

Both Ephraim and Judah refused the protection of the sure, living God that their forefathers had trusted, of whom they had records and testaments in their possession. The soft peaceful waters of Shiloah run from the Gihon spring into Jerusalem. They were symbolic of the Davidic Monarchy (see I Kings 1:33–34, 45) and of the peace and protection of the Lord. This symbol of peace, protection, and the Davidic Monarchy had been rejected by the northern tribes. The king of the northern tribes, Ahaz had put his trust in Rezin, the king of Syria and Pekah, Remaliah's son. Without Jehovah protection, neither they would, nor will we, flourish and succeed. Since the people rejected the peaceful waters of the Lord, they would be given instead the Assyrian army which is compared to a torrid flood.

Lord Brings Assyria

8:7 Now therefore, behold, the Lord bringeth up upon them the waters of the river, strong and many, even the king of Assyria, and all his glory: and he shall come up over all his channels, and go over all his banks:

8:8 And he shall pass through Judah; he shall overflow and go over, he shall reach even to the neck; and the stretching out of his wings shall fill the breadth of thy land, O Immanuel.

Isaiah foretells how fast and powerful the Assyrians will come using two fascinating metaphors. He compares the calm waters of Shiloah and its spiritual elements to a mighty flood of "the river strong and many." This river is the Euphrates and Isaiah compares its power to the power of the world and the raging power of the oncoming Assyrian army to devastate the land. This powerful river is contrasted to the quiet faith required for waters of Shiloah and its symbolic power of God to save and protect. There would be no stopping this flood of Assyrian armies until they reached Jerusalem—or "even to the neck." Yet there was hope in that the head of the country (Jerusalem), would not be submerged by this army.

If Judah Aligns with Apostate Nations It Will Be Broken in Pieces

8:9 Associate yourselves, O ye people, and ye shall be broken in pieces; and give ear, all ye of far countries: gird yourselves, and ye shall be broken in pieces; gird yourselves, and ye shall be broken in pieces.

8:10 Take counsel together, and it shall come to nought; speak the word, and it shall not stand: for God is with us.

In verse 9, the prophet Isaiah tells both Judah and Assyria that if they proceed to follow this contract in seeking support or giving support to each other, they will both be broken in pieces. Isaiah speaks plainly and boldly, so he will not be misunderstood. He wishes Ahaz to understand fully what the result of his actions will be if he does not follow the Lord's council. The king of Assyria will bring great devastation upon each of their nations in the region.

In verse 10, the Lord invites Ahaz to take counsel with His prophet and these things shall "come to nought." If Ahaz wishes to repent and follow the prophet, all he has to do is "speak the word, and it shall not stand; for God is with us." This phrase also directly references Jesus Christ. The name "Immanuel" means "God is with us." So, this phrase could be restated as "speak the word, and it shall not stand; because of Immanuel." As we choose to accept Jesus Christ and covenant to obey His gospel, we are promised that God will be with us, as well through the Holy Ghost.

Walk Not in the Way of This People

8:11 For the Lord spake thus to me with a strong hand, and instructed me that I should not walk in the way of this people, saying,

Hand—symbolizes personal agency and power.

The way—mainly the lifestyle of the people including their thoughts, ideas, fears, or characteristics of his contemporaries (Moyer, 94)

The Lord in this verse is strongly encouraging Isaiah to use his agency to distance himself from the people.

8:12 Say ye not, A confederacy, to all them to whom this people shall say, A confederacy; neither fear ye their fear, nor be afraid.

The fear mentioned in this verse refers to the fears of the people. Isaiah understood what they feared but did not subscribe to these fears. Some translators emphasize this when they end this verse with the phrase ". . . nor make others to be afraid." Today we too are asked to understand the fears of our fear-ridden society, but not to fear them ourselves. We have no place in our hearts for fear of the world, but rather we should worry about what the Lord thinks. Let Him be our "fear," or in other words, deeply reverenced.

8:13 Sanctify the Lord of hosts himself; and let him be your fear, and let him be your dread.

"Sanctify the Lord of hosts"—the literal translation reads, "make him a temple, the Lord of Hosts" (Parry, *Understanding Isaiah,* 86).

The Lord was very precise with His instructions to His prophet in what he should tell king Ahaz about making a confederacy with Assyria. In this there was no room for negotiation on the issue. The people might attempt to pressure Isaiah to change the decree of the Lord, but God said under no circumstances was Isaiah to agree with the wishes of the people of Judah to make a confederacy with Assyria. They should sanctify themselves unto the Lord and overcome their sins and trust in His power and praise His name. They should repent and, with all their energy and faith, send their prayers heavenward, then He will fight their battles for them. They should fear the power of God and not go against His prophet's direction, which will help them keep on the path of eternal life. The only thing they and we should fear is displeasing God. Our attitude should be like that of Joseph of Egypt; when he was tempted, he said, "how can I do this great wickedness against my God?" (Genesis 39:9)

Christ Will Be for a Gin and for a Snare

8:14 And he shall be for a sanctuary; but for a stone of stumbling and for a rock of offence to both the houses of Israel, for a gin and for a snare to the inhabitants of Jerusalem.

Sanctuary (Heb. *miqdâsh*)—a consecrated thing or place not necessarily an asylum. A place where God dwells. The "he" in this verse should be capitalized since it is referring to the Lord. He is consecrated to be a spiritual refuge for the faithful, and He will be a "stone of stumbling" and a "rock of offence" to the rest.

A "gin" denotes the use of a noose or snare. A "snare" is designed for the victim to ensnare himself. Israel will ensnare themselves in their disobedience of the Lord Jesus Christ. By seeking support from Assyria, against the prophet's direction to the contrary, they were caught in the snare of their own making.

8:15 And many among them shall stumble, and fall, and be broken, and be snared, and be taken.

Using five verbs in this verse, there develops a "downward" pattern. Isaiah describes the downward results befalling those who reject the Lord. They stumble (they falter in their faith); they fall (they commit sins); they are broken (they suffer consequences for their transgressions); they are snared (they are enticed by Satan's temptations); they are taken (they are captured). This is a promise to both of the divided tribes of Israel, Ephraim and Judah. They stumbled on the teachings of the Lord and His prophets and were offended by the calls to repent. It is the same principle for Israel today: those who choose to ensnare themselves with wickedness will stumble, fall, and be broken.

Bind up Your Testimony and Wait upon the Lord

The Lord's Saints are under the direction of prophets of God. They are to help all who want come unto Christ to:

8:16 Bind up the testimony, seal the law among my disciples.

Bind (Heb. *tsârar*)—to wrap up, to safeguard from tampering
Seal (Heb. *châtham*)—to attest as final, to close up

We are to wrap up, or safeguard testimonies and prevent them from being tampered with. Those who are on the Lord's errand look for opportunities to build faith in Jesus Christ and deepen the conversion of one of His disciples or followers to His gospel. These servants "attest to" or become a witness to the Law of the Gospel as they are teaching. Testimonies and the gospel lead them to a sanctuary where they can be sealed together as family—the House of the Lord or His temple.

It would do each of us well to take the following prophetic pledge as we build other's faith in Christ:

8:17 And I will wait upon the Lord, that hideth his face from the house of Jacob, and I will look for him.

"I will look for him"—the literal translation is "I will hope for Him."

Isaiah just states that he is waiting upon the Lord to come, the same Lord that has hid "his face from the house of Jacob." The scriptures say, "he that feareth me shall be looking forth for the great day of the Lord to come." The Lord adds, "even for the signs of the coming of the Son of Man. . . . And, behold, I will come; . . . and he that watches not for me shall be cut off" (D&C 45:39, 44). To His Saints, the command is: "Prepare for the revelation which is to come, . . . when all flesh shall see me together. . . . And seek the face of the Lord always" (D&C 101:23, 38).

Isaiah and His Children's Testimony

8:18 Behold, I and the children whom the Lord hath given me are for signs and for wonders in Israel from the Lord of hosts, which dwelleth in mount Zion.

Sign—(Heb. *ôwth*)—a signal (literally or figuratively), as a flag, beacon, monument, etc.—mark, miracle.
Wonder (Heb. *môwphêth*)—Conspicuous, a miracle, a token or omen.

Isaiah bears testimony that he and his children have come as witnesses against the wickedness of Israel. He and his children are for signs and wonders in Israel given him from the Lord. They are visual witnesses with names to be seen and to bear testimony of the truth of Isaiah's prophetic words to King Ahaz, for and in behalf of both of the tribes of Judah and Ephraim. He took with him additional witnesses as the Lord instructed him to write in a notebook the prophecies that he made regarding the meaning of the names of his two son's names. Do you remember the name of his son Shear-Jashub? He took his son with him to meet King Ahaz to testify that after the lost remnant or ten tribes of Israel had been taken by the Assyrians, they should one day return to Zion.

His second visit dealt with the severity of the forthcoming attack of the army of Assyria. He took with him his son Maher-Shalal-Hash-Baz as a testimony of the speed of which the Assyrian army would come upon them to rob and plunder their nation. King Ahaz ignored the prophet's counsel and asked Assyria to assist Judah even though the conflict was reported by God to be basically over.

Isaiah himself was also a sign and a wonder. His name (*Yesha'yahu*) means "Yahweh is salvation" or "Yahweh saves." He is a living testimony that salvation comes in and through Jehovah. His actions will serve as a sign and a portent in Isaiah 20:1–6. It is interesting to note that the preposition "from" in "from the presence of the Lord" is literally translated "from with" and is "frequently used to stress 'from the very presence of'" the Lord (Moyer, 96). Isaiah had dealt with God personally and serves as a visible reminder that God wants to deal with each of us personally. A person's righteousness improves their relationship with God, and their closeness to Him.

Seek Christ

In verses 19–22, the Lord prepares Isaiah on how to deal with the leaders of Judah. They will approach him and encourage him to take part in practices that served as popular religion in his day and provides a warning that they will end up cursing their leaders and will reside in darkness.

8:19 And when they shall say unto you, Seek unto them that have familiar spirits, and unto wizards that peep, and that mutter: should not a people seek unto their God? for the living to the dead?

> Familiar spirits (Heb. *'ôwb*)—properly, a mumble, a necromancer (speaking like a ventriloquist, as from a jar).

It was the mode of operation for seekers of familiar spirits to try to contact the spirit of a departed person to learn things not known to man on this side of the veil. The Hebrew word for familiar spirit means "ventriloquist." The ventriloquist would throw his voice with the deception as if it were coming from a departed spirit. They would have their voice come from objects, such as a leather bottle, a bag, or even sometimes a pit. The house of Judah was more willing to hear the direction and predictions of familiar spirits than to hear the words of a living prophet of God. Judah desired that Isaiah should confirm his prophetic feeling that Judah should not join up with Assyria with the ventriloquist medium that had given them false reassurance in making a military pact with Assyria. By asking this they hope that Isaiah may see things as they, the leaders of Judah see them, and perhaps then he would stop being so harsh with them and join them. Isaiah responds to their desire by asking them a question: "Wouldn't it be better to seek direction from the God of heaven and earth than from wizards that peep and mutter?"

8:20 To the law and to the testimony: if they speak not according to this word, it is because there is no light in them.

Once Satan had gotten both Ephraim and Judah to leave the true and living God of Israel, it was natural for them to consult familiar spirits, such as wizards, for answers to life's problems and concerns of the day. However, if the familiar spirits do not speak according to the laws of God and the testimony of the Lord's prophets, it is because no light of revelation comes to them. The law (scriptures) and testimony bring hope, peace, and assurance. To reject these is to embrace hopelessness and despair.

Results of Not Following God's Law

If the people of the earth reject the testimony of Christ and choose to not follow God's law, what will be their consequence?

8:21 And they shall pass through it, hardly bestead and hungry: and it shall come to pass, that when they shall be hungry, they shall fret themselves, and curse their king and their God, and look upward.

8:22 And they shall look unto the earth; and behold trouble and darkness, dimness of anguish; and they shall be driven to darkness.

Bestead (Heb. *qâshâh*)—to be dense, i.e. tough or severe.

Fret (Heb. qâtsaph)—to burst out in rage: (be) anger(-ry)

"driven to darkness"—rather, "thick darkness" (Jer. 23:12). Driven onward, as by a sweeping storm.

In rejecting God's law, the people with pass through several trials. They will experience hunger (physical and spiritual). They will burst out in rage with themselves. They will curse their political and spiritual leaders and their decisions which result in their separation from God. There will be no hope anywhere for them. Not in the heaven nor in the earth. Israel has mocked God for so long that now they must pass through the mist of darkness they have created for themselves. What will the result of their divorce from God be? They "shall be driven to darkness," a place of misery, a place of fear and a place where the wicked fully realize that "wickedness never was happiness" (Alma 41:10).

ISAIAH CHAPTER 9

Christ's Indictment of Israel

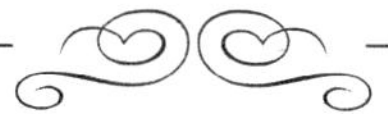

In chapter 8, Judah was warned against making an alliance with another nation. Judah was counselled to align with God and He would provide protection and peace. If they chose God, their path would be like a clear, cool stream refreshing them and purifying them. If they choose an alliance with the world, then they would be cursed with difficulty, trouble, and darkness. It is unfortunate that this prophetic council was not listened to.

With the rebellion of the Northern tribes against Assyria, Israel's power was smashed by 732 BC. Judah still remained independent although they had to pay tribute to Assyria or risk being destroyed. Samaria retained a little independence and boasted that she would rebuild and come to power again (Isaiah 9:10). At the death of Tiglath Pileser III in 727 BC, Hosea stopped paying annual tribute, conspired with Egypt, and rebelled against Assyria. Shalmaneser V, the next Assyrian king, attacked what remained of Israel and besieged Samaria. However, he soon died, and his successor, Sargon II, finished the campaign.

The fall of Samaria came in 722–721 BC and was the beginning of exile for the lost ten tribes of Israel. The Assyrians deported the conquered nation's inhabitants to break their national spirit and assimilate them into Assyrian culture. Shortly thereafter, Samaria was inhabited by pagan people from other nations. These people mixed with the remaining Israelites, for not all of them had been taken into captivity. Through the mixing of these groups, the Samaritans came about. As a result of this mixing, the Jews later felt that the Samaritans were no longer pure descendants of Abraham and therefore were not entitled to be remembered with the chosen people.

Verse 1 of chapter 9 bridges chapters 8 and 9, and its position might help clarify its meaning. In fact, it is included as the last verse of chapter 8 in the Hebrew versions of Isaiah but is made the beginning verse of chapter 9 in most English translations. Chapter 8 ends with a gloomy note of trouble and darkness, while, beginning in verse 2, chapter 9 speaks of light and joy. Chapter 9 picks up this theme and then compares their current condition of groping in the darkness to the great light of the Messiah that leads us all out of darkness.

Invasion of Israel by Assyria

9:1 Nevertheless the dimness shall not be such as was in her vexation, when at the first he lightly afflicted the land of Zebulun and the land of Naphtali, and afterward did more grievously afflict her by the way of the sea, beyond Jordan, in Galilee of the nations.

Galilee (Heb. *Galyil*)—a "circle," "circuit," and from it came the name Galilee.

Notwithstanding the calmness of the Ephraim and the northern part of Judah, the gloom of their indecision to follow a prophet was nothing to the affliction they would experience as a nation when the Assyrian army got there. The siege of Samaria by the Assyrians was begun by lightly afflicting Zebulun and Naphtali by Shalmaneser. The land of Zebulun was midway between the Sea of Galilee and the Mediterranean, and the land of Naphtali is along the western shore of the Sea of Galilee and extended northward. This invasion was concluded "by the way of the Red Sea, beyond Jordan, in Galilee of the nations" by Sargon (722–705 BC) (2 Kgs. 17:3). These two areas were the first to fall to Assyria. These people were deported, and their lands became three Assyrian provinces.

Jews Will See Jesus Christ

9:2 The people that walked in darkness have seen a great light: they that dwell in the land of the shadow of death, upon them hath the light shined.

The inclusion of Zebulun and Naphtali was prophetic in verse 1 because these lands were the site of the Savior's Galilean ministry. They who will see the great light, even the Savior of the World, never comprehended Jesus was the son of God the Father, not just the son of Joseph. At the time of Christ's birth, the Jewish nation will be walking in the spiritual darkness that they entered into by themselves. Isaiah foretold that Israel's Messiah would come as "a light to the Gentiles" (Isa. 49:6) and that His light would pierce the darkness of error and unbelief (Isa. 60:1–3).

The Righteous Receive Eternal Joy When Christ Comes to Earth

9:3 Thou hast multiplied the nation, and not increased the joy: they joy before thee according to the joy in harvest, and as men rejoice when they divide the spoil.

Note: The Joseph Smith Translation indicates that the word "not" should be deleted from the King James text.

The Jews did not have the spiritual ability to recognize Christ when He came, but His coming has multiplied and increased the joy of all mankind in all nations. His teachings give us knowledge, hope, comfort, peace, and joy. "Harvest" and "spoil" express the idea of two different types of joy, and joy in its completeness. Joy in the harvest is a divine gift given by God through nature. Joy in the spoil is a divine gift allowed by winning a contest of some sort. Divine gifts are given fully when the Messiah comes and delivers all from adversity (including sin and death) and gives a fullness of joy. At judgment day, "according to the joy in harvest," God's children will receive the degree of joy that they have qualified themselves for. Verse 4 further emphasizes how these gifts that bring us joy are given to us.

Christ Rescues Mankind from Sins and Physical Death

Isaiah speaking of what Jesus Christ has done for all mankind said,

9:4 For thou hast broken the yoke of his burden, and the staff of his shoulder, the rod of his oppressor, as in the day of Midian.

There are two sets of historical events that are alluded to in this verse. First, vocabulary is used which recalls Egypt, e.g. yoke (Lv. 26:13), burdens (Ex. 1:11; 2:11; 5:4–5; 6:6–7), and oppressor (Ex. 3:7; 5:6, 10–14). It also recalls the breaking of this yoke, burdens, and oppression though divine assistance during the exodus. Secondly, the defeat of Midian recorded in Judges 6–8 is remembered. This is an especially meaningful reminder of God's divine assistance in fighting a battle for Israel where Gideon and his very small force were the deliverer of Asher, Zebulun, and Naphtali (Jdg. 6:35).

A yoke is a bar or frame that is attached to the heads or necks of two work animals (such as oxen) so that they can pull a plow or heavy load. A staff is a stick and would bring back memories of suffering inflicted on Israel as the stick was struck across their shoulders. "Rod of his oppressor" represents suffering arising from personal hostility by one in authority. Three types of oppression and three types of suffering caused by too heavy of loads, inflicted suffering both physical and tyrannical. All three will be broken when the events of Isaiah 22:22 come to pass and the government will be upon the shoulder of Christ.

The end of this verse in the Bible includes the phrase "as in the day of Midian," but it is left out of the Book of Mormon Isaiah account. Maybe through the coming forth of the Book of Mormon and the restoration of Christ's Church on the earth, the last part of this verse in Isaiah's account is not needed to remind us of the days of Midian, for today is the day of redemption through Jesus Christ. We take on us Christ's yoke and He has taken care of the effects of endless suffering for sin and death.

One of the Last Great Battles against Wickedness

9:5 For every battle of the warrior is with confused noise, and garments rolled in blood; but this shall be with burning and fuel of fire.

Battle (Heb. *seh-own*)—boot. This is the only time in the Old Testament where this word is used and is often associated with warriors from the Egyptian or Assyrian armies (See Motyer, 101).

Confused noise (Heb. *ra'ash*)—vibration, bounding, uproar—commotion, confused noise.

The use of the warrior's boot used in battle symbolizes the breaking of the foreign power(s) that has afflicted the Lord's people. After a battle, boots, garments, weapons, chariots, and other items used during a holy war were not to become part of the booty or spoil of the victors. Damaged property like this had to be burned with fire (Joshua 7:23–26; 11:6; Psalms 46:9; Ezekiel 39:9–10).

In this verse, the confusion and blood associated with battles are over and they have become fuel for a fire. This verse continues the theme in verse four which spoke of God's power in overcoming the suffering of His Saints. Now the confusion of the world ends. The discarded bloody garments are rolled up, or gathered, in preparation for a burning. These garments may be spoken of in the Doctrine and Covenants where "the Lord shall be red in his apparel, and his garments like him that treadeth in the wine-vat" (D&C 133:48). Christ himself will personally take charge, for "his voice shall be heard: I have trodden the wine-press alone, and have brought judgment upon all people; and none were with me; And I have trampled them in my fury, and I did tread upon them in mine anger, and their blood have I sprinkled upon my garments, and stained all my raiment; for this is the day of vengeance which was in my heart" (D&C 133:50–51). It will be "Through the wrath of the Lord of hosts is the land darkened, and the people shall be as the fuel of the fire" (Isaiah 9:19).

Emmanuel Prophecy

Isaiah defines who Christ is. He says:

9:6 For unto us a child is born, unto us a son is given: and the government shall be upon his shoulder: and his name shall be called Wonderful, Counsellor, The mighty God, The everlasting Father, The Prince of Peace.

Wonderful (Heb. *pele'*)—a wonder, a miracle, a marvelous thing. Something out of the ordinary.

Wonderful Counsellor—Because there is no comma in the Hebrew text, some translations of this verse have "Wonderful Counsellor"

> in the text. This implies that Christ will be one who gives miraculous or supernatural advice or counsel.

This verse starts out stating that "unto us," or to the Jews, a son will be born. He will go to the Jews first, and then to the Gentiles. The Gospel of Matthew begins with the Son of David (king), the son of Abraham (prophet) being born. Matthew emphasizes in his first chapter that Jesus Christ is the legal successor to David's throne and even goes so far as to group the generations from Abraham to Christ in three groups of 14 to emphasize that even as three 14's in Hebrew is symbolic of David, so the legal government of Christ should be on His shoulders. Here the government on Messiah's shoulder is in marked antithesis to the "yoke and staff" of the oppressor on Israel's "shoulder." Their oppressions and burdens are lifted when His shoulders pick up the burden of rule. When we realize the role of God in our lives, and that He can lift our burdens partially and make them light (see Mosiah 23:21) or lift them completely off our shoulders, then we better understand the love He has for us.

Mighty is a military term and references in verses 3–5. He is the mighty (warrior) God born to, and for us. Everlasting Father describes our covenant relationship to Christ. Prince of Peace describes the condition that Christ as King will bring first spiritually in our lives today and in time literally to the world.

Taken together, this verse is often called the Emmanuel Prophecy. Christ is Emmanuel the King, signifying literally "God is with us" (D&C 128:22). God is with us (see D&C 68:6) in our days and He is Wonderful!

Christ's Millennial Government

> 9:7 Of the increase of his government and peace there shall be no end, upon the throne of David, and upon his kingdom, to order it, and to establish it with judgment and with justice from henceforth even for ever. The zeal of the Lord of hosts will perform this.

In this verse, Isaiah starts to use the future tense. He prophecies of the time when Christ will be "with us." During the Millennium, as His governing increases, peace will increase perpetually in the earth, and in our lives. It will not be a kingdom of mere might and triumph of force over enemies, but of righteousness where He will provide justice and mercy. In the Millennium, it is His right to reign, and the Jews understood about the government of the Lord, for Matthew said, out of Bethlehem "shall come a Governor, that shall rule my people Israel" (Matt. 2:6).

Isaiah also uses the throne of David to refer to Christ's eventual rule. He reminds Ahaz that the very promises of righteous rule that he has refused will one day be Christ's. He once again references that this future ruler will rightfully rule as a descendant of David. This will occur through "the zeal of the Lord." Zeal is a component of pure love that has no rivals and moves the Lord "to make his people's causes his own (Is. 42:13, 59:17, 63:15) and the passionate commitment of his nature to fulfil his purposes for them (37:12)" (Motyer, 103).

The remainder of chapter 9 and the first part of chapter 10 key off of the next verse. Isaiah has been prophesying about the future King Christ; he now switches his attention to the current leaders of Jacob and Israel. Isaiah will distinguish how the Lord's word has come to Jacob and how it came to Israel. Isaiah will then give four reasons why His message was not received by the northern kingdom Israel, and this will serve as a warning to the leaders and people of Jerusalem. With each of these four reasons, Isaiah will remind the people and their leaders that He is still there waiting for them to return to Him.

Christ's Message upon the Earth

9:8 The Lord sent his word unto Jacob, and it hath lighted upon Israel.

Lighted (Heb. *nâphal*)—fall

What is meant by "the Lord sent his word unto Jacob"? Isaiah is reminding all that God teaches truth through His word. Alma taught this when he said: "God gave unto them commandments, after having made known unto them the plan of redemption" (Alma 12:32). God has sent prophets (including Isaiah) to teach Jacob truths that lead all of us to greater peace and happiness. In time, Isaiah predicts that God will send Christ, or The Word, to teach the descendants of Jacob.

What is meant that the word of the Lord has "lighted [or fallen] upon Israel"? If we read the Hebrew word *nâphal* as "lighted," then we interpret this to mean that God's word lightly distilled on Israel. If we read the same word to mean "fall," we see the word of God as being like a sword—a two-edged sword (see D&C 6:2, 11:2, 12:2, 14:2, 33:1). The word falls on the righteous and cuts sin out of their lives. It builds them up. The word of God can fall on those who reject God's prophets and Christ. The Word brings those who repent closer to Christ and it also separates the righteous from the wicked.

Using the imagery that the word of God fell upon Israel, Isaiah will next give four reasons why the wicked of the house of Israel were scattered. We can see the same problems on the earth today that will cause the wicked to be destroyed. Isaiah reviews these four reasons with us so we will not make the same mistakes that ancient Israel had made. At the end of each reason, Isaiah provides a promise that God is there waiting with outstretched hands for the wicked to repent and turn back to Him.

First Reason for the Destruction and Scattering of Israel: Pride

9:9 And all the people shall know, even Ephraim and the inhabitant of Samaria, that say in the pride and stoutness of heart,

9:10 The bricks are fallen down, but we will build with hewn stones: the sycomores are cut down, but we will change them into cedars.

The pride of the nation has flowed from the king to all of the people of Ephraim. Their hearts are so prideful that they felt that if their dwellings were destroyed, they would just build them up again with better types of building materials. At this time in the East, bricks were generally sun-dried, and therefore soon dissolved by rain. The prideful now boast that they will replace these bricks with long-lasting and beautiful hewn stones.

Sycamore trees grew abundantly on the lowlands of Judea, and though useful for building on account of their antiseptic property (which induced the Egyptians to use them for the cases of their mummies), they were not very valuable. The cedar, on the other hand, was odorous, free from knots, durable, and precious (see 1 Kings 10:27). In essence these people are saying that "We will replace our cottages with palaces."

Syrians Before, and the Philistines Behind—My Hand Is Still Stretched Out

Now Isaiah speaks of the result of Ephraim's proud attitude; he said,

9:11 Therefore the Lord shall set up the adversaries of Rezin against him, and join his enemies together;

9:12 The Syrians before, and the Philistines behind; and they shall devour Israel with open mouth. For all this his anger is not turned away, but his hand is stretched out still.

Adversaries of Rezin—the Assyrians, who shall first attack Damascus, shall next advance "against him" (Ephraim).

Join —rather, "arm"; or cover with armor.

Syrians—Though now allies of Ephraim, after Rezin's death they shall join the Assyrians against Ephraim.

Behind—from the west.

Rezin is the king of Syria and the Lord will permit the newly hired Assyrian army to capture the land of Syria and of the Philistines. This is just a prelude to the humbling of the prideful and stout hearts of Israel. After their conquest of Syria, the Assyrians will come against Judah by using the very same Syrian army that had made a confederacy with Israel to go against Judah, their brethren in the north. This Assyrian army will be augmented with their newly captured Philistine recruits from the country supported by Hezekiah of Judah. The Assyrian army traditionally took those men who were captured and chose to live, then compelled them to fight in their ranks against their new opponent. This time it was Ephraim. The Syrians were forced to take the forefront position of the army, with the Philistines behind them and the Assyrian army in the rear (701 BC). Thus, the phrase "the Syrians before, and the Philistines behind" was coined. Even with all this, the Lord said He would come to their aid if they would only repent, for "his hand is stretched out still." He repeats this phrase five times to get their attention, but they will not repent and turn to Jehovah.

Second Reason for the Destruction and Scattering of Israel: The Wickedness of Its Leaders

9:13 For the people turneth not unto him that smiteth them, neither do they seek the Lord of hosts.

9:14 Therefore the Lord will cut off from Israel head and tail, branch and rush, in one day.

9:15 The ancient and honourable, he is the head; and the prophet that teacheth lies, he is the tail.

9:16 For the leaders of this people cause them to err; and they that are led of them are destroyed.

Branch (Heb. *kippah*)—a leaf of a palm tree.

Rush (Heb. *agmôwn*)—a rush growing in a marsh or collectively a rope of rushes.

Head . . . tail, branch . . . rush—These pair of opposites denote totality. The leader or the follower; the individual, or the collective whole—the entire nation will suffer a defeat as if in one day because of the wickedness of its leaders and their influence on the people.

Ephraim's evil began with the wicked political and religious leaders who taught the people how to err. These leaders are held responsible for their nation's destruction. Remember the lack of faith of Ahaz and how King Jeroboam promptly established calf idols for his people to worship to keep his subjects from worshiping the true God in Jerusalem. Jeroboam also instituted new worship ceremonies and set apart unrighteous priests when the Levite priests would not perform his false ceremonies. He also commanded his people not to go any more to Jerusalem to worship. Isaiah's reference to false prophets who lie and comparing them to the tail may be indicative of their desire to tell the people what they want to hear. Their words come as a result of what the rest of Israel wants them to say. Isaiah may be using a little humor to describe the actions of these false preachers. They are really tails wagging at the public's demand.

As a consequence of this action, the Lord said:

9:17 Therefore the Lord shall have no joy in their young men, neither shall have mercy on their fatherless and widows: for every one is an hypocrite and an evildoer, and every mouth speaketh folly. For all this his anger is not turned away, but his hand is stretched out still.

The King James phrase, "every one is a hypocrite," is changed in the Joseph Smith Translation to "every one of them is a hypocrite."

When these false prophets and leaders teach the people lies and condone their wickedness, the Lord has no joy in their wicked young men, and no mercy on the wicked fatherless and widows. Even these who are normally (due to circumstances) humble have become hypocrites and evildoers, and their mouths speak only words of folly. Yet we must remember that God's anger is not totally turned away as he was with Noah's people, for He tells them that, "his hand is stretched out still." God as a loving parent is still trying to get his people to repent.

The leaders of America today are just as wicked, maybe even more so. President Gordon B. Hinckley taught:

> Some to whom we have looked as leaders have betrayed us. We are disappointed and disillusioned. And their activity is only the tip of the iceberg. In successive layers beneath that tip is a great mass of sleaze and filth, of dissolute and dishonest behavior. (Hinckley, "Walking in the Light of the Lord")

The betrayal of their leaders causes the people of Israel to have no love for their brothers (vs. 19), no desire for a spiritual feast (vs. 20) which will lead to a general breakdown of society (vs. 21). They become a people who have no desire to change, nor listen to the Lord.

Third Reason for the Destruction and Scattering of Israel: Wickedness of the People Who Will Not Repent

9:18 For wickedness burneth as the fire: it shall devour the briers and thorns, and shall kindle in the thickets of the forest, and they shall mount up like the lifting up of smoke.

9:19 Through the wrath of the Lord of hosts is the land darkened, and the people shall be as the fuel of the fire: no man shall spare his brother.

9:20 And he shall snatch on the right hand, and be hungry; and he shall eat on the left hand, and they shall not be satisfied: they shall eat every man the flesh of his own arm:

9:21 Manasseh, Ephraim; and Ephraim, Manasseh: and they together shall be against Judah. For all this his anger is not turned away, but his hand is stretched out still.

briers. . . thorns—emblem of the wicked; especially those of low rank (Isa 27:4 2 Samuel 23:6).

Hungry—not literally. This is an image of unappeasable hunger, a hunger that wickedness will never satisfy.

Eat—not literally, but destroy (see Psa 27:2; Job 19:22).

flesh of. . . arm—those nearest akin: their former support (helper) (see Isa 32:2).

Verse 18 begins with the word for but could easily have been translated as the word surely. As verses 13–17 described the effects of leadership, verses 18–21 describe the effects of wickedness on the people. Wickedness is like a fire and if you play long enough with you, it will burn you. It is self-destructive and will then take a life of its own. The destruction of the briers and thorns seems to refer to the destruction of the wicked. Fire destroys the briers as well as the forest thickets and this symbolizes the totality of destruction that awaits the wicked. At the time the wicked will be burned, verses 19–20 indicate that great civil unrest and strife will be taking place in the land. People will not be satisfied with what they have, they "shall snatch on the right hand, and be hungry;" and "they shall eat on the left hand, and they shall not be satisfied." Their mind is so darkened that they realize not that the very thing that they are looking for is the gospel of Jesus Christ. There is no joy without it. They will not even be having joy in their own flesh. Fathers and mothers will be killing their own flesh and their children will be killing their parents. As it says in verse 19, their wickedness brings the wrath of the Lord and He will use fire to destroy the wicked, "for people shall be as the fuel of the fire." The Doctrine and Covenants gives additional light upon these things, in the following:

> And prepare for the revelation which is to come, when the veil of the covering of my temple, in my tabernacle, which hideth the earth, shall be taken off, and all flesh shall see me together.
>
> And every corruptible thing, both of man, or of the beasts of the field, or of the fowls of the heavens, or of the fish of the sea, that dwells upon all the face of the earth, shall be consumed. (D&C 101:23–24)

Before the Lord burns the wicked, He will first take away the veil and all on the earth will see Him together. And then through His wisdom, He will identify the telestial men and women of the earth, the beasts of the sea, the fowls of the heavens and the fish of the sea and He will consume them with fire. On earth the wicked telestial people will do the following:

> Therefore shall all hands be faint, every man's heart shall melt;
>
> And they shall be afraid; pangs and sorrows shall take hold of them; they shall be amazed one at another; their faces shall be as flames.
>
> Behold, the day of the Lord cometh, cruel both with wrath and fierce anger, to lay the land desolate; and he shall destroy the sinners thereof out of it. (2 Nephi 23:7–9)

> O ye wicked ones, enter into the rock, and hide thee in the dust, for the fear of the Lord and the glory of his majesty shall smite thee.
>
> . . . And they shall go into the holes of the rocks, and into the caves of the earth, for the fear of the Lord shall come upon them and the glory of his majesty shall smite them, when he ariseth to shake terribly the earth.
>
> In that day a man shall cast his idols of silver, and his idols of gold, which he hath made for himself to worship, to the moles and to the bats;
>
> To go into the clefts of the rocks, and into the tops of the ragged rocks, for the fear of the Lord shall come upon them

> and the majesty of his glory shall smite them, when he ariseth to shake terribly the earth. (2 Nephi 12:10, 19-21)

> And [the wicked] said to the mountains and rocks, Fall on us, and hide us from the face of him that sitteth on the throne, and from the wrath of the Lamb. (Revelation 6:16)

Before the fire destroys the wicked the Lord will do the following:

> And the saints that are upon the earth, who are alive, shall be quickened and be caught up to meet him.
>
> And they who have slept in their graves shall come forth, for their graves shall be opened; and they also shall be caught up to meet him in the midst of the pillar of heaven—
>
> They are Christ's, the first fruits, they who shall descend with him first, and they who are on the earth and in their graves, who are first caught up to meet him; and all this by the voice of the sounding of the trump of the angel of God. (D&C 88:96–98)

Wouldn't this sight be hard for the telestial people to watch? The heavens open up and the Lord reveals Himself to all and the wicked watch the righteous, living and dead, rise up to meet the Lord in the clouds. The telestial, meanwhile, will try to hide themselves and their worldly possessions which they know have made them unworthy to enter into God's presence. Each of us must ask ourselves, where do we want to be in the future? With the Lord sharing in His joy, or feeling the shame of our sins.

The fourth reason for the destruction of the wicked in Isaiah's day, and at the time of the Second Coming is found in Isaiah 10:1–4. In chapter 9, Isaiah discussed the general wickedness of the leaders and its effects on the people. In chapter 10 Isaiah returns to the topic of leadership, but addresses their interest in creating class divisions in creating advantages for themselves.

ISAIAH CHAPTER 10

Destruction of the Wicked at the Second Coming

In chapter 9, Isaiah discussed three reasons for Israel's destruction: pride, the wickedness of the leaders, and the wickedness of the people. In chapter 10 Isaiah gives a fourth reason for Israel's destruction as he returns to the topic of selfish leadership and its interest in creating class divisions that benefits themselves. The fourth reason for the destruction of the wicked in Isaiah's day, and at the time of the Second Coming is found in Isaiah 10:1–4.

Fourth Reason for Israel's Destruction: The Neglect of the Poor and the Needy

10:1 Woe unto them that decree unrighteous decrees, and that write grievousness which they have prescribed;

Grievousness (Heb. *'âmâl*)—toil, trouble, labour

This is a verse that lawmakers should pay close attention to, so they will not be party to making unrighteous decrees. It doesn't matter what position a person has, Isaiah condemns unrighteous dominion. Bad laws and regulations, whether spoken or written, include those that prescribe self-rewarding benefits for the powerful few. If a statute or law is framed in wickedness, it will prove to be trouble for the people. The Lord has often spoken of His concern for the poor and needy, and He condemns Israel, as He would any other nation, for their new unrighteous decrees by saying:

10:2 To turn aside the needy from judgment, and to take away the right from the poor of my people, that widows may be their prey, and that they may rob the fatherless!

"from judgment"—i.e. "from obtaining justice."

The purpose of the legislation in verse 1 is now explained: to deny justice and to manipulate justice for gain. Isaiah exclaims that the needy will not be able to find judgment in such laws and their rights will also be taken away. These new laws will prey on both the widows and the fatherless. The ones who need the help the most will not be able to get it. When towns, cities, and nations participate in such action, the Lord asks the following questions, in Isaiah's case these questions are directed toward Israel. He asks:

10:3 And what will ye do in the day of visitation, and in the desolation which shall come from far? to whom will ye flee for help? and where will ye leave your glory?

From far—i.e. Assyria
Leave your glory—i.e. deposit (for safekeeping) your wealth (see Psalms 49:17)

To whom will we turn when we are justly visited with the vengeance of a just God, which was the case when Israel was visited by the Assyrians? In the days of our troubles, He wants us to know that He turns a deaf ear to the prayers of those who have failed not to take care of the poor, needy, widows and fatherless and preyed upon their impoverished conditions. The Lord clearly states,

> Woe unto you, scribes and Pharisees, hypocrites! for ye devour widows' houses, and for a pretence make long prayer: therefore ye shall receive the greater damnation. (Matthew 23:14)

We are living in a day when every scheme and trick of the evil one is used to rob and cheat their fellow men, to gain power, prestige, and wealth. The Lord told the prophet Joseph Smith,

> For the earth is full, and there is enough and to spare; yea, I prepared all things, and have given unto the children of men to be agents unto themselves.
>
> Therefore, if any man shall take of the abundance which I have made, and impart not his portion, according to the law of my gospel, unto the poor and the needy, he shall, with the wicked, lift up his eyes in hell, being in torment. (D&C 104:17–18)

King Benjamin taught that each of us, either rich or poor, needs to be succored by the Lord:

> For behold, are we not all beggars? Do we not all depend upon the same Being, even God, for all the substance which we have, for both food and raiment, and for gold, and for silver, and for all the riches which we have of every kind? (Mosiah 4:19)

10:4 Without me they shall bow down under the prisoners, and they shall fall under the slain. For all this his anger is not turned away, but his hand is stretched out still.

> Under . . . under—rather, "among" (literally, "in the place of"). The "under" may be, however, explained, "trodden under the (feet of the) prisoners going into captivity," and "overwhelmed under the heaps of slain on the battlefield."

Without Christ's help, when the Assyrian army comes, the result for the citizens of Israel will be nothing less than to "bow down under the prisoners and they shall fall under the slain." If they would only put away their sin and take care of the poor and needy, the Lord would quickly turn His anger away, for His "hand is stretched out still." The Lord has the power to stop any advancing army if we are worthy of it.

The Assyrian army's coming is Israel's consequence of choosing sin over following the God of Israel. Thus, the Lord is justified in permitting the Assyrian army to come upon them. Israel was expected, as we are, to take care of those who cannot take care of themselves.

If the house of Israel will remember the Lord and deny their sins and come unto Christ, the Lord will give them power to do three things mentioned in the following scripture:

> I came unto mine own, and mine own received me not; but unto as many as received me gave I power to do many miracles, and to become the sons of God; and even unto them that believed on my name gave I power to obtain eternal life. (D&C 45:8)

The Wicked Will Be Used to Destroy the Wicked

Because of Israel's pride, the general wickedness of the people, and its leaders who create class divisions to benefits themselves at the expense of the poor, it is ripe and ready to be destroyed. Thus, the Lord will permit the Assyrian army to make their move on Israel. He said,

10:5 O Assyrian, the rod of mine anger, and the staff in their hand is mine indignation.

10:6 I will send him against an hypocritical nation, and against the people of my wrath will I give him a charge, to take the spoil, and to take the prey, and to tread them down like the mire of the streets.

> "O" or "Ah"—This word can be an expression of exclamation or it can be translated "Woe," as a warning as it is in 20 of the 22 times Isaiah uses the word.

Wicked Assyria becomes the rod of (or expression of) God's anger against Israel. Israel could have prevented this war and devastation if they had only followed the words of the prophet Isaiah. However, God's hand is still stretched out to receive a repentant Israel unto Himself, but they would not hear it, nor could they comprehend what awaits them as a result of their sins and arrogant attitude. It was by the power of the wicked Assyrian army that the Lord spoiled the hypocritical nations of Syria, Ephraim, and many towns leading up to Jerusalem, the neck of Judah. Years later, the Lord told the prophet Mormon that, ". . . it is by the wicked that the wicked are punished" (Mormon 4:5). The Assyrian army, even though more wicked than

Israel, was permitted by the Lord to come upon them, and into their choice lands and homes and "tread them down like the mire of the streets." The possessions and personal belongings of the hypocritical Israelite became the Assyrian's spoils of war. This great army preyed upon their people with all the ugliness of war and took their beautiful sons and daughters prisoner and carried them off to Assyria.

These verses also refer to a future event, Bruce R. McConkie explained,

> In a future day "he shall smite the earth with the rod of his mouth; and with the breath of his lips shall he slay the wicked." So shall it be in the day of burning. "For the time speedily cometh that the Lord God shall cause a great division among the people, and the wicked will he destroy; and he will spare his people, yea, even if it so be that he must destroy the wicked by fire." The polarization that will gather the righteous into one camp and the wicked into another has already commenced, and these processes shall continue until the Lord comes. In that day, "Righteousness shall be the girdle of his loins, and faithfulness the girdle of his reins." (2 Ne. 30:8-11.) His judgments in that day shall be just. Nephi's language, quoted and paraphrased from Isaiah, then goes on to describe millennial conditions. (McConkie, *Millennial Messiah*, 521–522)

The Real Plot of the King of Assyria

10:7 Howbeit he meaneth not so, neither doth his heart think so; but it is in his heart to destroy and cut off nations not a few.

"Howbeit" is an archaic word meaning "be that it may or nevertheless." It matters not what the king of Assyria said or signed in an arrangement when he was hired by Ahaz, he will never keep his word, nor was he ever intending to. In his heart, Sennacherib (Assyria's king) has his ambitions on conquering Egypt as well as Ethiopia (see. Isa 20:1–6; Zec 1:15). In saying this, Isaiah wants Ahaz to know that the king of Assyria is evil and a liar. Ahaz had already been advised of the inability of Syria and Ephraim to make any more of an advancement into his land, he did not need the help of Assyria. They had even given back the prisoners they had captured. The Lord knew the Assyrian king's heart was not upright and was set on making a sweep of all these nations as he made his way homeward, conquering them all in the region. The evil Assyrian king was just another prideful king seeking by any means to increase his kingdom and empire. The king's prideful claims in verses 8–11 were:

10:8 For he saith, Are not my princes altogether kings?

10:9 Is not Calno as Carchemish? is not Hamath as Arpad? is not Samaria as Damascus?

Is not. . . as—Six cities are named in pairs. In each pair, the first is farther south. The king is asking, "Were there any one of these cities able to withstand me?" Neither could the next city. Each of these cities was at one time a city of past glory.

Calno—Calneh, built by Nimrod (Gen 10:10), once his capital, on the Tigris and 50 miles south of Carchemish.

Carchemish—Circesium, on the Euphrates. Taken afterwards by Necho, king of Egypt; and retaken by Nebuchadnezzar: by the Euphrates (Jer. 46:2).

Hamath—in Syria, 100 miles north of Damascus. Taken by Assyria about 753 BC. From it, colonists were planted by Assyria in Samaria.

Arpad—50 miles away from Hamath.

Samaria—now overthrown.

The Assyrian king is here gloating over the nations that he has thus far conquered during his regime. He feels that as it was with these other kingdoms so it will be again. He asks, is not the capital city of Israel, Samaria the same as the nation of Damascus? He had conquered them both, and now he comes upon Judah, and is just saying that it is just a matter of time that like these two nations, Judah will fall. He will then place his princes over the newly conquered areas as kings and have them all pay tribute to him.

Kingdom of the Idols

The Lord knew very well the prideful heart of the Assyrian king, and for this reason He tried to get the king of Judah to follow His prophet Isaiah, and save himself and his nation a lot of turmoil. Again we must not forget who had control over Assyria, for it was the Lord that brought them up, or could have kept them far away. The Lord speaks of the wickedness of the Assyrian nation, He saying,

> 10:10 As my hand hath found the kingdoms of the idols, and whose graven images did excel them of Jerusalem and of Samaria;

In the past when Israel had worshiped Jehovah, they were blessed to defeat the oppressing armies, but now that they had turned to idol worship and from the true and living God of Israel, they have no promise. In their apostate condition, the Lord permitted an idol worshiping nation that excelled even themselves in their false worship, to succeed in coming against Israel and some of the cities of Judah because of their worship of false idols. The Assyrian conquest will bring many foreigners to the region with their own false Gods and idols, which will only add to future problems. This will further increase the problems of idolatry in the land where the Savior of the World will be born.

God Will Punish the Fruit of the Wicked

The Assyrian king seems to have believed in his false idols and their superiority to other nation's idols. Because of this belief he states:

> 10:11 Shall I not, as I have done unto Samaria and her idols, so do to Jerusalem and her idols?

The Assyrian king has no respect for Jehovah and is so prideful with self-acclamation that he concludes that he is the source of credit for his army's accomplishment in defeating Syria and Ephraim. And so why would Jerusalem be any different? Verses 12–15 shows signs of his evil heart and lack of respect for the very God that permitted him to humble these two apostate nations who had rejected Jehovah for idols. The Lord says,

> 10:12 Wherefore it shall come to pass, that when the Lord hath performed his whole work upon mount Zion and on Jerusalem, I will punish the fruit of the stout heart of the king of Assyria, and the glory of his high looks.

Stout (Heb. *gôdel*)—greatness of, i.e. the pride of.

It was the Lord that permitted the Assyrian king to come all the way to Jerusalem to do His bidding, and after He has permitted the Assyrians to humble Israel totally and to humble Judah to a degree, then He will "punish the fruit of the stout heart of the king of Assyria, and the glory of his high looks." The Lord will do this by the destruction of 185,000 of his soldiers outside Jerusalem in one night. God will allow the king to live and return home only to be killed by two of his sons as he worshipped in the temple of his false gods.

This prophecy not only refers to Assyria, but also refers to future wicked nations of the earth which one day will wage war against God's people. Though it appears that they will have success against Israel in the last times (see Rev 11:2), the wicked will again be destroyed quickly (see Rev. 11:13–18). You can almost hear the words of this proud arrogant Assyrian king echo through history:

10:13 For he saith, By the strength of my hand I have done it, and by my wisdom; for I am prudent: and I have removed the bounds of the people, and have robbed their treasures, and I have put down the inhabitants like a valiant man:

removed the bounds—set aside old and substituted new boundaries of kingdoms at will.

put down. . . inhabitants—i.e. "as a valiant man, I have brought down (from their seats) those seated" (namely, "on thrones"; as in Psa. 2:4, 29:10, 55:19), or "I have brought down (as captives into Assyria, which lay lower than Judea) the inhabitants."

King Sennacherib, the king of Assyria ascribes all of his success to himself. He claims that he is the one that determines the borders of kingdoms and is the rightful owner of all the treasure that lies therein. He is proud of his plundering and conquests. King Sennacherib continues his boasting:

10:14 And my hand hath found as a nest the riches of the people: and as one gathereth eggs that are left, have I gathered all the earth; and there was none that moved the wing, or opened the mouth, or peeped.

The riches of Ephraim and some of the cities of Judah were easily found by the Assyrians. One must remember that Hezekiah in his own prideful heart,

> And Hezekiah was glad of them, and shewed them the house of his precious things, the silver, and the gold, and the spices, and the precious ointment, and all the house of his armour, and all that was found in his treasures: there was nothing in his house, nor in all his dominion, that Hezekiah shewed them not. (Isaiah 39:2.)

With this blunder it was not hard for Assyria to lust after their riches. And when they have a city on the run and no one watching after it or really caring for anything more than their lives, it would be easy then for him to reach into the nest for the riches of the people and gather them as you would eggs after the birds have fled the nest. The boast is not a very powerful one on the Assyrian king's part. Neither the nation of Ephraim nor the cities of Judah that were captured had the force to "move a wing," which denotes the power to act against the opposing army or "open the mouth" to cry for help, for the Assyrian army was upon them. Only God could help them, but once the Assyrian army was there, and they had not repented, their lives were then in their own hands. Not even the wizards that peep (Isa. 8:9) could help them in their state of apostasy, nor their false god turn back the Assyrian's mighty army.

Can Men Prosper against God?

10:15 Shall the axe boast itself against him that heweth therewith? or shall the saw magnify itself against him that shaketh it? as if the rod should shake itself against them that lift it up, or as if the staff should lift up itself, as if it were no wood.

Shall the instrument boast against Him who uses it? Though free in a sense, and carrying out his own plans, the Assyrian was unconsciously carrying out God's purposes. In the King James Bible footnote of this verse, it says that the ax, saw, and rod are all "metaphors asking the same question: Can men (e.g., the Assyrian king) prosper against God?" The Assyrian king's bragging of his own power is very shortsighted. It was Jehovah that gave him the opportunity and the power to conquer and rule. His successes are due to the Lord, and the wickedness of the people of Ephraim and Judah.

The Judgment of the Assyrian King and the Final Judgment

The next three verses apply to the king of Assyria, and in time will apply to the wicked at the Second Coming of Christ:

10:16 Therefore shall the Lord, the Lord of hosts, send among his fat ones leanness; and under his glory he shall kindle a burning like the burning of a fire.

10:17 And the light of Israel shall be for a fire, and his Holy One for a flame: and it shall burn and devour his thorns and his briers in one day;

10:18 And shall consume the glory of his forest, and of his fruitful field, both soul and body: and they shall be as when a standardbearer fainteth.

> "As when a standard bearer fainteth"—rather, "they shall be as when a sick man" (from a Syriac root) wastes away."

The Lord will send among His fat ones, leanness; in other words, He will take from the rich and prideful of the earth, and permit during the Millennium His obedient children to have that which the rich and prideful had, but that they were not worthy to keep (2 Nephi 15:17). In His glory at the Second Coming, the Savior will consume all the wicked (D&C 101:23–24). He who has been the light to Israel, now will come as a flame to burn and devour His thorns and briers in one day. The Lord said He will use this people "as the fuel of the fire" (Isaiah 9:10). Thorns and briers symbolize all things that men have worshiped as their false gods, things that have led them off the path of righteousness. All those who have invested their time in the praise of the world and forgotten to love their neighbor as themselves, not lived His commandments; and have not stored up treasures unto their God will be cleansed from off the earth, as the earth is baptized by fire. He will take away from the wicked their meaningless accumulations and leave them without root or branch and consume them, "both body and soul." It would be good for us to remember what the Savior said unto the righteous,

> And fear not them which kill the body, but are not able to kill the soul; but rather fear him who is able to destroy both soul and body in hell. (Matt. 10:28)

When these events take place, it will surely be a time as when a "standard-bearer fainteth," or when spiritually the people are spiritually sick and waste away or dissipate any righteousness that they once possessed. It will be a time of confusion and disarray, when the unworthy "shall go into the holes of the rocks, and into the caves of the earth, for fear of the Lord, and for the glory of his majesty, when he ariseth to shake terribly the earth" (Isaiah 2:19). Daniel foretells of all the governments of the earth collapsing and the only government that will be upon the earth that will stand will be the government of the Lord, run by Him and His priesthood (See Dan. 7:9).

The great prophet Alma said of this day:

> For our words will condemn us, yea, all our works will condemn us; we shall not be found spotless; and our thoughts will also condemn us; and in this awful state we shall not dare to look up to our God; and we would fain be glad if we could command the rocks and the mountains to fall upon us to hide us from his presence. (Alma 12:14)

10:19 And the rest of the trees of his forest shall be few, that a child may write them.

> Rest—those who shall survive the destruction of the host.
> "his forest"—same image as in Isa. 10:18, for the once dense army.
> "Child . . . write"—so few that a child might count them.

The destruction of the king's army and the wicked at the Second Coming of Christ will be so complete that in comparison with the earth's entire population only a few who have been righteous will remain. Isaiah points out that the number of survivors will be so small that a "child may write" or count them.

Now the Promise Comes

10:20 And it shall come to pass in that day, that the remnant of Israel, and such as are escaped of the house of Jacob, shall no more again stay upon him that smote them; but shall stay upon the Lord, the Holy One of Israel, in truth.

10:21 The remnant shall return, even the remnant of Jacob, unto the mighty God.

This will fulfill the promise made through Isaiah and witnessed by his son, that the remnant will return to God (see Isaiah 7:3). Even though in our day some have now returned to God, this promise as a whole has not yet been fulfilled but will be fulfilled when the Lord comes. When the remnant returns, the house of Jacob will rejoice. Latter-day Israel, or today's steward of the house of Jacob, are those who have made baptismal covenants with the Lord with those who hold proper priesthood authority.

At this glorious future day when all Israel has accepted their true King and returned to their true Messiah, it will be a time when the full blessings of peace will bless the earth's inhabitants. "And the earth shall be given unto them for an inheritance; and they shall multiply and wax strong, and their children shall grow up without sin unto salvation" (D&C 45:58). This will only come when the remnant of Israel accepts Christ as their King and worships the Father in His holy name.

The Consumption Decreed

10:22 For though thy people Israel be as the sand of the sea, yet a remnant of them shall return: the consumption decreed shall overflow with righteousness.

10:23 For the Lord God of hosts shall make a consumption, even determined, in the midst of all the land.

Though Israel will now be as numerous as the sand, only a remnant or portion of them will come back. The great majority shall perish. The reason is added: because "the consumption [fully completed destruction] is decreed [literally: decided on, brought to an issue], shall overflow with righteousness [justice]." In other words, the destruction has been decided as the infliction of just punishment. The statement "shall make a consumption, even determined" in verse 23 could have been translated from the Hebrew "shall make a full end, as ordained."

The Doctrine and Covenants speaks of the "consumption decreed" in these words:

> And thus, with the sword and by bloodshed the inhabitants of the earth shall mourn; and with famine, and plague, and earthquake, and the thunder of heaven, and the fierce and vivid lightning also, shall the inhabitants of the earth be made to feel the wrath, and indignation, and chastening hand of an Almighty God, until the consumption decreed hath made a full end of all nations. (D&C 87:6)

In that day, when the "consumption decreed hath made a full end of all nations," kingdoms, organizations, and societies, then all tongues and people must yield to the kingdom of God set up by the Lord to reign supreme over all other powers. Daniel said,

> And there was given him dominion, and glory, and a kingdom, that all people, nations, and languages, should serve him: his dominion is an everlasting dominion, which shall not pass away, and his kingdom that which shall not be destroyed. (Daniel 7:14)

Joseph Smith said, "The saints have not too much time to save and redeem their dead, and gather together their living relatives that they may be saved also, before the earth will be smitten, and the consumption decreed falls upon the world" (*Teachings of Presidents: Joseph Smith*, 472).

Joseph Fielding Smith, commenting on what Joseph Smith had said added, "When that day comes, those who have professed to believe in the latter-day work, and who have rejected the doctrine of temple building and the ceremonial endowments therein, will find themselves shut out of the kingdom of God" (Smith, *Doctrines of Salvation*, 133).

Saints Shall Not Fear Gentiles or Their Trials

10:24 Therefore thus saith the Lord God of hosts, O my people that dwellest in Zion, be not afraid of the Assyrian: he shall smite thee with a rod, and shall lift up his staff against thee, after the manner of Egypt.

Those who dwell in Zion should be those people who are pure in heart. They should also have been spiritually born of God and be a people who have matured to the point that the Lord can come and dwell with them. The Lord told the Saints of Zion not to be "afraid of the Assyrian," referring to the Assyrians as well as the gentiles of the latter days. For the Lord will lift up His staff in Zion's defense and smite the Gentiles with His rod. He will do with those modern-day Assyrians, the gentiles of the world, as He did unto the Egyptians when Israel was in bondage. The Lord is keeping a watchful eye over His people. An example of this protection in our day comes from the life of Israel Barlow, a trusted bodyguard of the Prophet Joseph Smith. His grandson tells of one occasion when Joseph requested that he go on horseback and deliver a message to a certain brother who lived in one of the more hostile areas, and to observe conditions during his journey. The instructions the prophet gave to Israel were very specific and told him they were to be followed precisely. Joseph told him which day to leave, what time, what route to follow. He was also told it was okay to accept the hospitality shown him when he arrived at the destination, but under no circumstances was he to spend the night, no matter how much they encouraged him. He was to leave the same evening and return home. He was to "listen to the direction of the Spirit." Otherwise, his life would be in jeopardy.

Israel arrived safely at his destination and delivered the message. His grandson recorded what transpired next as he started on his return trip he said,

> He left promptly at sundown and rode along the country road until it became dark. Just before he came to the river bridge, a voice said to grandfather, "Ride faster." He sped up his horse and the voice repeated again, with more emphasis, "Ride faster." Again he increased the speed of the animal when the voice said to him: "Ride for your life." He then sped for all the

animals' strength. As the horse's feet clattered across the bridge he could hear the mob, which had gathered in the brush to intercept him, cursing at the top of their voices.

He had crossed the bridge but a short distance when the voice said to him: "Turn to the right," and he turned his horse off the road into the brush toward the river. There he stood in silence as the mob, who had mounted their horses, came racing over the bridge at break-neck speed, and down the road they went, supposedly after him. After they had gone by, he wound his way from the river's edge to the bed of the stream, and on through the willows. In the darkness he made his way along the river in the opposite direction from which the mob had expected him to go. Finally when he thought it was safe, several miles away, he emerged from the river and made his way over the country back into Nauvoo, just as the day was breaking. Returning to Nauvoo, Israel found Joseph Smith pacing the street in front of his home. He started to share his adventure with the Prophet, but Joseph stopped him and said he already knew everything that had transpired.

The Prophet told him that he had been up all night, waiting for his return, and stated "I saw it all, you have no need to tell me." Thereupon the Prophet laid his hand upon grandfather's shoulder and gave him a blessing and said: "Thee and thine shall never want." (See *Our Pioneer Heritage*, 19:324; *Faith Like the Ancients*, 1:196–7).

A Future Day of Redemption for the Lord's Saints

10:25 For yet a very little while, and the indignation shall cease, and mine anger in their destruction.

Just as the Assyrian army was destroyed, the Lord's Second Coming will be a day of vengeance, burning, and destruction for the wicked who have rebelled against His teachings. But for the righteous, it will be a day of redemption, blessing, and salvation, a glorious day of peace and righteousness. At that day, "Every corruptible thing . . . shall be consumed" (D&C

101:24). Only those who are worthy will be there to abide the day when the Lord comes in His glory.

> His voice shall be heard: I have trodden the wine-press alone, and have brought judgment upon all people; and none were with me;
>
> And I have trampled them in my fury, and I did tread upon them in mine anger, and their blood have I sprinkled upon my garments, and stained all my raiment; for this was the day of vengeance which was in my heart.
>
> And now the year of my redeemed is come; and they shall mention the loving kindness of their Lord, and all that he has bestowed upon them according to his goodness, and according to his loving kindness, forever and ever. (D&C 133:50–52)

Take Courage in the Lord

10:26 And the Lord of hosts shall stir up a scourge for him according to the slaughter of Midian at the rock of Oreb: and as his rod was upon the sea, so shall he lift it up after the manner of Egypt.

The Lord helps us take courage in these latter days by using some past examples of His courageous followers. Remember the victory of Gideon over the Midianites (Judges 6–7) and the powerful Egyptian army drowning in the red sea (Exodus 14). These victories recall the destruction of foes (and their leaders) clearly by God. The rock of Oreb (Judges 7:25) was named after a Midianite prince Oreb who had escaped death in the battle but was killed after he fled. The same will be true for the Assyrian king who will not perish with his army but will be assassinated by one of his sons when he returns home.

Millennial Day—The Burdens Shall Be Removed

10:27 And it shall come to pass in that day, that his burden shall be taken away from off thy shoulder, and his yoke from off thy neck, and the yoke shall be destroyed because of the anointing.

Just as the burden of the Assyrian oppression was taken from Judah, in a future day our burdens and trials will be taken from us when the Savior comes, and He alone will lift the yokes from those who have lived His commandments and trusted Him. In our lives today, we are encouraged to take off the yoke of sin and take the yoke of Christ for His "yoke is easy, and my burden is light" (Matthew 11:30). And this is done because He has the power as the Anointed One, the Savior of the World.

The Progress of the Assyrian Army through the Towns of Judah

Verses 28–31 describe the advancement of the Assyrian Armies as they conquered the various cities on their way to Jerusalem.

10:28 He is come to Aiath, he is passed to Migron; at Michmash he hath laid up his carriages:

10:29 They are gone over the passage: they have taken up their lodging at Geba; Ramah is afraid; Gibeah of Saul is fled.

10:30 Lift up thy voice, O daughter of Gallim: cause it to be heard unto Laish, O poor Anathoth.

10:31 Madmenah is removed; the inhabitants of Gebim gather themselves to flee.

Aiath lay about three miles south of Bethel, which had become Assyrian with the conquest of Samaria. If an Assyrian army mustered at Bethel, it would naturally enter Judean territory at Aiath. The army is traveling from the north toward Jerusalem. Michmash was nine miles north of Jerusalem and there he laid up his carriages, or he left his heavier baggage, so as to be more lightly equipped for the siege of Jerusalem.

As the army ventured further south, it traveled through Gibeah, the hometown of Saul. "Galah" means captive or captivity and "gallim" captives or captivities. Thus "Daughter of Gallim" means "Daughter of Captivities." Anathoth is still further south and was the hometown of Jeremiah. Finally, in verse 32, the Assyrian army will be at Nob which is one mile North of Jerusalem.

Which King Shall Rule

10:32 As yet shall he remain at Nob that day: he shall shake his hand against the mount of the daughter of Zion, the hill of Jerusalem.

10:33 Behold, the Lord, the Lord of hosts, shall lop the bough with terror: and the high ones of stature shall be hewn down, and the haughty shall be humbled.

10:34 And he shall cut down the thickets of the forest with iron, and Lebanon shall fall by a mighty one.

The king of Assyria stood on Mount Nob overlooking Jerusalem and shook his hand and, in essence, was telling Jerusalem that tomorrow would be their turn to be overthrown. The king remained on Nob that day, assuming that in the morning he would bring the same fate upon Jerusalem, the capital city of Judah. Yet the Lord of Hosts will destroy the Assyrian army and their king, so will he one day destroy the wickedness off the earth by fire as promised.

Isaiah's prophecy about the Assyrian king and his army was vindicated in 2 Chronicles 32, which gives the historical account of their overnight defeat at Nob. This event is also described in 2 Kings 18:13–19:37. Even as Isaiah's prophecy was proven to be correct, we can learn that prophets of God are always vindicated. We might not see how the Lord will accomplish something. It may be impossible to us. But if Lord inspires His prophet, He will always prove that prophet correct in the end.

ISAIAH CHAPTER 11

Millennial Reign of Christ

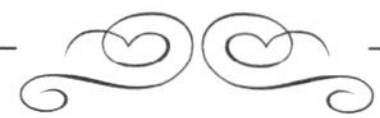

Coming Forth of the Church of Jesus Christ in the Latter Days

At the end of chapter 10, the lofty trees of Lebanon were cut down leaving only a stump. The cutting down of the tree referred to the destruction of Assyria and provides an introduction to this chapter. It should be noted that this chapter of Isaiah was quoted by the angel Moroni when he first appeared to the Prophet Joseph Smith on September 21, 1823. Moroni stated that the chapter "was about to be fulfilled" (JS-H 1:40). In this chapter, Isaiah foretells some of the great future events that will occur in reestablishing Christ's church. The Lord inspires Isaiah to prophesy:

11:1 And there shall come forth a rod out of the stem of Jesse, and a Branch shall grow out of his roots:

Rod (Heb. *chôṭêr*)—young growth, or twig
Stem—literally, "the stump" of a tree cut close by the roots
Branch (Heb. *nêtser*)—to grow green, a sapling

Roots:

The roots represent the stability, support, and the origin of all life that comes from Christ. Even though a branch or the trunk of the tree may be cut down, there is still life and hope arising from the roots. The Lord told Joseph Smith that the root of Jesse, "is a descendant of Jesse, as well as of Joseph, unto whom rightly belongs the priesthood, and the keys of the kingdom, for an ensign, and for the gathering of my people in the last days" (D&C 113:6).

Stem:

The scriptures identify Jesus as the stem of Jesse, the Root and offspring of David, and the lion of the tribe of Judah (Rev. 5:5; 22:16). The Lord identifies Christ as the Stem of Jessie in D&C 113:1–2. Bruce R. McConkie explained that the "Lord came as a descendant of that noble Israelite who sired David the King (Ruth 4:17)" (*Mormon Doctrine*, 766).

In further explaining the significance of Christ as a descendant of Judah, Elder McConkie wrote:

> When Father Jacob gave Judah his patriarchal blessing, Judah was likened both to a lion's whelp and to an old lion and was promised that the scepter should not depart from his descendants until the coming of Christ. (Gen. 49:8–12.) Accordingly, to denominate our Lord as the Lion of the Tribe of Judah is to point to his position as a descendant of Judah, to his membership in that tribe from which kings were chosen to reign, and also to show his status as the most pre-eminent of all that house, as the one who bore the banner of the tribe so to speak. *(Mormon Doctrine*, 449)

Rod:

The Lord Himself told Joseph Smith that the individual that Isaiah spoke of as the "rod" in verse one "is a servant in the hands of Christ, who is partly a descendant of Jesse as well as of Ephraim, or of the house of Joseph, on whom there is laid much power" (D&C 113:4). Bruce R. McConkie said, "Are we amiss in saying that the prophet here mentioned is Joseph Smith, to whom the priesthood came, who received the keys of the kingdom, and who raised the ensign for the gathering of the Lord's people in our dispensation?" (*Millennial Messiah*, 339–340).

Branch:

The branch is a green growth (or sapling) that grows out of the roots. The branch is tied directly to the unseen roots (Christ). A manifestation of a branch in our day is The Church of Jesus Christ of Latter-day Saints. Its strength comes from the stability, support, and priesthood keys rightfully originating from Christ.

In summary, the angel Moroni stated that this verse was "soon to be fulfilled" when he spoke in 1823. In the next ten years, the rod grew as Joseph Smith was called as a prophet and was given from the stem (Christ) the priesthood, and the keys of the kingdom so that he would be an instrument in the hands of the God to restore the ensign of the nations, and to gather the Lord's people in the last days. The Church can be seen as the branch that grew out of the roots (Christ). Even though a branch may be cut off (martyrdom of Joseph Smith), the Church would remain strong and rooted in Christ. There is nothing between the roots and the branch. There is nothing that stands between Christ, and His Church; Between Him and His prophet.

Strengths of Joseph Smith the Prophet

With the explanation of verse 1, it appears that Isaiah in verses 2–3 seems to be referring to seven personal strengths that the Lord gave to His servant Joseph Smith through the Holy Spirit. Not only can these strengths be gifts to a prophet, they are promised to anyone who has the gift of the Holy Ghost given to them.

11:2 And the spirit of the Lord shall rest upon him, the spirit of wisdom and understanding, the spirit of counsel and might, the spirit of knowledge and of the fear of the Lord;

11:3 And shall make him of quick understanding in the fear of the Lord: and he shall not judge after the sight of his eyes, neither reprove after the hearing of his ears:

Wisdom (1 Cor. 1:30, Eph. 1:17)—the application of knowledge.

Understanding—discernment and discrimination; the power to see at the heart of issues.

Counsel—the faculty of forming counsels.
Might—in this verse it is a power associated with counsels. It is the power that comes from counsel.
Knowledge—of the things of God. In other words, the truths given from God give us true knowledge (see Eph. 1:17).
fear of the Lord—reverential, obedient fear. The first step towards true "knowledge" (Job 28:28, Psalm 111:10).
quick understanding—literally "quick-scented in the fear of Jehovah." Those with the Spirit of God can quickly sense (or "smell") what leads or entices them towards God (Mor. 7:16; 10:5).

In these two verses, seven gifts of the Holy Spirit are specified as if to imply that the fullness or perfection of these gifts were to be in Christ's prophet. This promise is made to all who allow the Spirit of God to be in their hearts. The Spirit will help any who will listen and act on those promptings to have an increase of wisdom, understanding, power that comes with counsels, knowledge of the important truths of God, reverence of and obedience toward God, and increase our ability to be "quick to observe" (Mor. 1:2) and understand the things of God.

11:4 But with righteousness shall he judge the poor, and reprove with equity for the meek of the earth: and he shall smite the earth with the rod of his mouth, and with the breath of his lips shall he slay the wicked.

This verse is quoted by Nephi in 2 Nephi 21:4 and then again in 2 Nephi 30:9. Previous to Nephi's quoting this verse a second time in chapter 30, he wanted to "prophesy somewhat more concerning the Jews and the Gentiles" (2 Ne. 30:3). Nephi prophecies that after the Book of Mormon is published, there will be "many which shall believe the words which are written" (2 Ne. 30:3) and these words will be taken to his descendants and they will be "restored unto the knowledge of their fathers and also to the knowledge of Jesus Christ" (2 Ne. 30:5). Nephi also prophecies that after the Book of Mormon is published, that the Jews will begin to believe in Christ and begin to be gathered (see 2 Ne. 30:7). At this same time, the Lord will start His work among all nations and people and "bring about the restoration of his people" (2 Ne. 30:8).

Nephi then quotes verse 4 and adds one additional verse to Isaiah's teaching and afterwards will quote verse 5. Nephi states:

> For the time speedily cometh that the Lord God shall cause a great division among the people, and the wicked will he destroy; and he will spare his people, yea, even if it so be that he must destroy the wicked by fire. (2 Nephi 30:10)

What is the great division? Isaiah 11:4 gives one division—the division of the wicked from the righteous at the Second Coming. That is also true with what Nephi is saying, but there is definitely a second intended meaning. Before Nephi quotes Isaiah, the topic is the restoration of his people and hence the division would be among the Lord's people in the last days. Jacob added to this topic when he said the Lord will for the second time "recover his people, is the day, yea, even the last time, that the servants of the Lord shall go forth in his power, to nourish and prune his vineyard; and after that the end soon cometh" (Jacob 6:2). When will the Lord's vineyard be pruned and all of the non-producing trees cut out? At the Second Coming. Until then "there will be foolish virgins among the wise; and at that hour cometh an entire separation of the righteous and the wicked; and in that day will I send mine angels to pluck out the wicked and cast them into unquenchable fire" (D&C 63:54).

The Millennial Reign of Christ

The remainder of the chapter keys off of the events that will take place at the Second Coming and lead to Isaiah's next topic: The millennial reign of Christ on the earth.

11:5 And righteousness shall be the girdle of his loins, and faithfulness the girdle of his reins.

girdle—(Heb. *êzôwr*)—Waist-cloth, belt.

The girdle is often associated with the Biblical High Priest (Ex. 28:4, Rev. 1:13; 19:11). The girdle secures firmly the rest of the garments (1 Pe. 1:13) and like today's belt, it is symbolic of "readiness for action." Hence, at Christ's coming, he is ready to act in righteousness and faithfulness.

11:6 The wolf also shall dwell with the lamb, and the leopard shall lie down with the kid; and the calf and the young lion and the fatling together; and a little child shall lead them.

Each animal in this verse and the next is coupled with the one that is its natural prey. The peace existing during the Millennium not only exists among women and men, but within the animal kingdom as well. An appropriate state of affairs under the "Prince of Peace" (Isa. 65:25, Ezk. 34:25, Hos. 2:18).

11:7 And the cow and the bear shall feed; their young ones shall lie down together: and the lion shall eat straw like the ox.

11:8 And the sucking child shall play on the hole of the asp, and the weaned child shall put his hand on the cockatrice' den.

cockatrice—a fabulous serpent supposed to be hatched from the egg of a cock. The Hebrew means a kind of adder, more venomous than the asp.

Before "the sucking child shall play on the hole of the asp," the disposition of men must change. On one occasion, while the Prophet Joseph Smith's tent was being pitched at camp, the men saw three rattlesnakes and were about to kill them, but Joseph forbade the act. He asked the elders how the serpent would ever lose its venom while the servants of God made war upon it with desire to kill. Joseph then said that before this can happen: "Men must become harmless before the brute creation, and when men lose their vicious dispositions and cease to destroy the animal race, the lion and the lamb can dwell together, and the sucking child can play with the serpent in safety" (*Teachings of Prophets: Joseph Smith*, 71.)

11:9 They shall not hurt nor destroy in all my holy mountain: for the earth shall be full of the knowledge of the Lord, as the waters cover the sea.

After verse 9, Nephi adds three additional verses in 2 Nephi 30 that provide us a better understanding and knowledge of the earth that the Lord's righteous children will be given. He adds:

> Wherefore, the things of all nations shall be made known; yea, all things shall be made known unto the children of men.
>
> There is nothing which is secret save it shall be revealed; there is no work of darkness save it shall be made manifest in the light; and there is nothing which is sealed upon the earth save it shall be loosed.
>
> Wherefore, all things which have been revealed unto the children of men shall at that day be revealed; and Satan shall have power over the hearts of the children of men no more, for a long time. And now, my beloved brethren, I make an end of my sayings. (2 Nephi 30:16–18)

Another great promise is all secret things will be revealed. All works of darkness will be made known. All things that are sealed shall be opened. And to make life a lot better, Satan will be bound with no power over the children of men, for a long time, thus the gospel will be taught with greater power. The Doctrine and Covenants adds additional truth to the great things that shall be revealed:

> Yea, verily I say unto you, in that day when the Lord shall come, he shall reveal all things—
>
> Things which have passed, and hidden things which no man knew, things of the earth, by which it was made, and the purpose and the end thereof—
>
> Things most precious, things that are above, and things that are beneath, things that are in the earth, and upon the earth, and in heaven. (D&C 101:32–34)

The Church of Jesus Christ Will Be the Ensign to the World

In the next three verses Isaiah brings us back to the principles Nephi taught in his insert between verses 4–5 as well as what he taught in verse 1 of this chapter.

11:10 And in that day there shall be a root of Jesse, which shall stand for an ensign of the people; to it shall the Gentiles seek: and his rest shall be glorious.

Root—rather, "shoot from the root."

Rest—resting place (Isa. 60:13, Psm. 132:8, 14 Ezk. 43:7). The sanctuary in the temple of Jerusalem was "the resting place of the ark and of Jehovah." So the restored Church which is to be is described as an ensign to which all nations shall resort, and which shall be filled with the visible glory of God.

11:11 And it shall come to pass in that day, that the Lord shall set his hand again the second time to recover the remnant of his people, which shall be left, from Assyria, and from Egypt, and from Pathros, and from Cush, and from Elam, and from Shinar, and from Hamath, and from the islands of the sea.

Pathros—one of the three divisions of Egypt, Upper Egypt.

Cush—either Ethiopia, south of Egypt, now Abyssinia, or the southern parts of Arabia, along the Red Sea.

Elam—Persia, especially the southern part of it now called Susiana.

Shinar—Babylonian Mesopotamia, the plain between the Euphrates and the Tigris.

11:12 And he shall set up an ensign for the nations, and shall assemble the outcasts of Israel, and gather together the dispersed of Judah from the four corners of the earth.

These three verses began their fulfillment when Jesus Christ restored His church once again upon the earth to the Prophet Joseph Smith, which church will carry on through the Millennium. On April 6, 1830, in the little town of Fayette, New York, the Lord set up an ensign to all nations. This was the fulfilment of the prediction made by the Prophet Isaiah. Joseph Fielding Smith Jr. said the ensign "was the Church of Jesus Christ of Latter-day Saints, which was established for the last time, never again to be destroyed or given to other people. It was the greatest event the world has seen since the day that the Redeemer was lifted upon the cross and worked out the infinite and eternal atonement. It meant more to mankind than anything else that has occurred since that day" (*Doctrines of Salvation,* 254–255).

Isaiah, looking upon the western frontier, prophesied that this ensign "will hiss unto them from the end of the earth: and, behold, they shall come with speed swiftly" (Isaiah 5:26). This ensign is the new and everlasting covenant, the gospel of salvation (D&C 49:9); it is the great latter-day Zion (D&C 64:41–43); it is The Church of Jesus Christ of Latter-day Saints. The Church was restored on the earth so that all nations would be blessed.

A Peaceful Family Reunion

Verse 13 prophecies of the peaceful family reunion that will occur during the Millennium. "Ephraim was notorious for its jealousy of any success gained by any other tribe (Judg. 8:1; 12:1; cf. 2 Sam. 19:41–43). It was Ephraim's jealousy of Judah that in great measure brought about the separation of the two kingdoms" (Bible Dictionary, 666). The separation of the two kingdoms was set in motion as Solomon taxed his people exceedingly to pay the debts associated with his sin of having many strange wives that were not of the faith. After Solomon's death, his son was not wise enough to keep things together and the taxation issue escalated and, as a result, the northern ten tribes broke off from Judah. They have been vexing each other since then. What a great prophetic promise that after the gospel of Christ has returned to the earth:

11:13 The envy also of Ephraim shall depart, and the adversaries of Judah shall be cut off: Ephraim shall not envy Judah, and Judah shall not vex Ephraim.

It is the restoration of the gospel of Jesus Christ that is to bring the family of Israel together. The gospel is designed to bring the eternal family together by loving one's neighbor as oneself. In other words, those who accept the gospel of Jesus Christ will naturally gravitate toward following the great two commandments, loving God first and one's neighbor second. That is just how simple the gospel is.

Isaiah, looking down the corridor of time saw the latter-day gathering of the scattered House of Israel and said,

11:14 But they shall fly upon the shoulders of the Philistines toward the west; they shall spoil them of the east together: they shall lay their hand upon Edom and Moab; and the children of Ammon shall obey them.

Edom—south of Judah, from the Dead Sea to the Red Sea.

Moab—east of Jordan and the Dead Sea.

Ammon—east of Judea, north of Moab, between the Arnon and Jabbok.

Elder Orson F. Whitney, speaking of the phrase "they shall fly upon the shoulders of the Philistines toward the West," said:

> We recognize the fulfillment of that prophecy in the founding of this Church by Joseph Smith, a lineal descendant of Abraham, Isaac and Jacob, who thus lifted the Ensign of the gathering of their descendants from their long dispersion among the nations. But a part of the fulfillment rests with the Gentiles. Their steamships, their railroads, their means of rapid transit and communication—these are "the shoulders of the Philistines," upon which the children of Ephraim have been and are being brought to the West, to the land of Zion, where the New Jerusalem is to rise, where the pure in heart will assemble, and the necessary preparation be made for the coming of the Lord in his glory. God works outside as well as inside his Church, and uses big things and little things for the accomplishment of his purposes. (Conference Report, April 1919, 70)

Destruction of the Tongue of the Egyptian Sea

11:15 And the Lord shall utterly destroy the tongue of the Egyptian sea; and with his mighty wind shall he shake his hand over the river, and shall smite it in the seven streams, and make men go over dryshod.

Can you imagine the mighty wind that God will use in shaking His hand over the modern Egyptian sea and smiting it into seven streams so men will go over dry-shod, or with dry shoes? Undoubtedly with the reputation of the east wind, He will use it as He did for Moses to part the Red Sea, to let His people cross through on a dry roadway (see Ex. 14:21). Yet, this time will be a little different in that the mighty wind will leave seven rivers where a highway can stand for the remnant of His people to cross. What a prophetic testimony of events that are to take place when the times of the Gentiles are fulfilled. Nephi points out, "in the days that the prophecies of Isaiah shall be fulfilled men shall know of a surety, at the times when they shall come to pass" (2 Nephi 25:7).

Another thought to consider is, "As the Lord provided a highway through the Red Sea for his people anciently, as they traveled to their promised land, so will he provide a way for them to travel in the latter days. . . . Would we go too far astray if we were to suggest that the highway is created by the joined landmasses, and that as ancient Israel found a dry path through the Red Sea, so latter-day Israel will find a dry path where the Atlantic Ocean once was? It is at least a thought to ponder, for surely we are expected to seek for interpretations relative to all that has been revealed concerning the Lord and his coming" (McConkie, *The Millennial Messiah*, 624–625).

THE COMING FORTH OF THE TEN TRIBES

11:16 And there shall be an highway for the remnant of his people, which shall be left, from Assyria; like as it was to Israel in the day that he came up out of the land of Egypt.

The remnant of the Lord's people which escaped from the Assyrian captivity are the ten tribes who were taken into the north and lost. In the Doctrine and Covenants it speaks of a special highway to be raised for their benefit as they return: "And an highway shall be cast up in the midst of the great deep" (D&C 133:27). "And an highway shall be there, and a way, and it shall be called The way of holiness; the unclean shall not pass over it; but it shall be for those: the wayfaring men, though fools, shall not err therein" (Isaiah 35:8).

The priesthood keys for the gathering of the lost ten tribes were given to Joseph Smith and Oliver Cowdery by Moses on 3 April 1836. This was recorded as follows:

> After this vision closed, the heavens were again opened unto us; and Moses appeared before us, and committed unto us the keys of the gathering of Israel from the four parts of the earth, and the leading of the ten tribes from the land of the north. (D&C 110:11)

They were given the keys of "the gathering of Israel from the four parts of the earth" as well as the keys of "the leading of the ten tribes from the land of the north." Bruce R. McConkie said, "The gathering of Israel is a reality. When the ten tribes return they will come at the direction of the President of The Church of Jesus Christ of Latter-day Saints, for he now holds and will then hold the keys of presidency and direction for this mighty work" ("This Final Glorious Gospel Dispensation," 22).

ISAIAH CHAPTER 12

With Joy Will We Sing

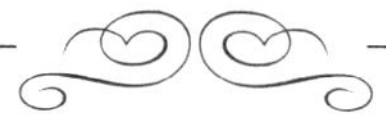

SONGS CAN BE USED TO COMMUNICATE MORE THAN JUST WORDS. THEY CAN convey greater emotion, emphasize overflowing gratitude, and increase love and reverence than just words alone. This chapter is a song that acts as a summary to chapters 6–11 and focuses its emotion, gratitude, love, and respect towards Christ and life with Him in the Millennium.

Chapter 6 started with the call of Isaiah as a prophet. He is tasked to preach of, and bring his people to, Christ. In chapter 7 Isaiah warned about the coming war but gave hope to Judah in the knowledge of Christ's birth. In chapter 8 Isaiah warned Judah's leaders not to align themselves with foreign powers, but to trust on the Lord of hosts. Chapter 9 and 10 reminded Israel that even though they may reject God, His arms are "stretched out still" waiting for them to return to God. At the end of chapter 10, God Himself will save Judah from Assyria, just as God Himself will save Israel in the last days from destruction. Chapter 11 brings us to Christ's triumphant return and His reign on the earth. The phrase "in that day" in chapter 12 (verses 1, 4) refer to the day when Christ will reign personally on the earth. This chapter is a book end to what Isaiah has been teaching in chapters 6–11 and its purpose is to provide hope to all that God does fulfill all of His promises. All of them.

Christ Is My Strength, Song, and Salvation

12:1 And in that day thou shalt say, O Lord, I will praise thee: though thou wast angry with me, thine anger is turned away, and thou comfortedst me.

12:2 Behold, God is my salvation; I will trust, and not be afraid: for the Lord Jehovah is my strength and my song; he also is become my salvation.

In the Millennial Day, the Lord's children will praise Him, for He will have turned away His anger and will give His children comfort. Verse 2 starts and ends with the similar statement—salvation is found in God. In between these statements are four characteristics of those who believe: 1) They trust God, 2) Their fears are conquered, 3) They have strength beyond their own, and 4) They express their great emotions, gratitude, love, and respect towards God in song. Through Christ we are all saved, and through our acceptance of Him as Lord and God, He also becomes our salvation as we choose to follow Him.

A literal translation of verse 2 also reveals the sacred names and name titles of Deity as they are used scripturally. "Behold El is my salvation, I shall trust and not be afraid; For my strength and my song is Yah, Yehovah, And he has become my salvation" (*Old Testament Student Manual*, 150).

Water out of the Wells of Salvation

Verse 3 is speaking of those who quench their spiritual thirsts from the water that Christ provides.

12:3 Therefore with joy shall ye draw water out of the wells of salvation.

Water is a common theme in the Old and New Testaments. For example, water comes from the rock (See Ex. 17), as well as wells. Christ taught a woman at the well that He will be the living water that will fully quench our spiritual thirsts (see John 4). That living water comes from the Holy Ghost (John 7:38–39) and leads to eternal life (Rev. 21:6). In that day of the Millennium, He will establish His earthly kingdom among His children and will direct His affairs as their king from that great city of New Jerusalem. Those who are sealed to be with the Savior upon His return will joyfully draw water out of Christ's living well. It is at this time that the floodgates of revelation will be opened and Christ will "reveal all things" including:

> Things which have passed, and hidden things which no man knew, things of the earth, by which it was made, and the purpose and the end thereof—
>
> Things most precious, things that are above, and things that are beneath, things that are in the earth, and upon the earth, and in heaven. (D&C 101:33–34)

With the outpouring of the Holy Ghost, what a joy it will be during the Millennium to have Christ teach His Saints. Until that time, we can taste of this living water as we draw closer to Christ through the well of the Holy Ghost.

A Song Is a Prayer unto the Lord

12:4 And in that day shall ye say, Praise the Lord, call upon his name, declare his doings among the people, make mention that his name is exalted.

"make mention" (Heb. *zâkar*)—to remember, to be brought to remembrance, be thought of, be brought to mind.

In that day of the Millennium, Isaiah prophesies that we as a people of the Lord will now praise Him, pray to Him, and share with others what He has done for us. We will do all things in His name and give credit to Him in all things. The phrase *qârâ shêm* (call upon His name) "has four meanings: to name a person for a function (Ex. 35:30); to call a person into fellowship (43:1); to invoke God by using his name (Gen. 12:8); and to proclaim the name (Ex. 34:5–6)" (Motyer, 130). While the third meaning is usually given for this verse, it is interesting to consider that as we call upon the Lord, we are also to call a person into fellowship. Our fellowship with Christ is sublime and epic. Our hope is that we can invite others into this fellowship of Christ so that their relationship with God is deepened and made closer.

We are not only to declare what God has done, but to declare who He really is. We are to "make mention" (remember) and bring Him forefront in our thoughts in such a way so that His name is exalted. A name in the Old Testament is a title that tells who you really are. Your name is an attribute of you. We are to not only remember God but declare His attributes to others. We encourage the fellowship of the faithful to remember themselves and to teach and testify to other about God and the hope that we have in Him.

In that day, we will also:

12:5 Sing unto the Lord; for he hath done excellent things: this is known in all the earth.

12:6 Cry out and shout, thou inhabitant of Zion: for great is the Holy One of Israel in the midst of thee.

The Lord has been, and will be, so loving and giving to those who believe on His name, especially to those who have eyes to see and ears to hear of the "excellent things" He has for the Saints of the earth. What a blessing to have the gospel of Jesus Christ on the earth and the understanding of the Atonement and the plan of happiness. What a blessing to have the companionship of the Holy Ghost to walk with us and help us keep a tight hold on the iron rod. Words cannot express the gratitude of coming before the sacrament table each week and renewing our covenants made with our Lord as we take time to remember Him and recommit ourselves to keep His commandments in love and thankfulness. The Lord is pleased when we sing our sacred hymns, written by people of faith. They have a powerful effect in our worship. They render strength for people to better live the principles of the gospel. They promote peace and spiritual growth in each of us. Such praises and singing are a prayer to the Lord, as He has said: "For my soul delighteth in the song of the heart; yea, the song of the righteous is a prayer unto me, and it shall be answered with a blessing upon their heads" (D&C 25:12).

ISAIAH CHAPTER 13

The Second Coming of Jesus Christ

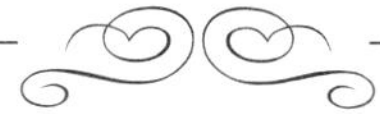

Chapters 6–12 taught and emphasized principles, blessings, and warnings to the people and leaders of Judah that would give them hope and lead them closer to God. The next few chapters (13–27) are mostly addressed to other nations but Isaiah applies the same principles, blessings, and warnings to these nations as he did in the previous few chapters. His purpose is to teach that truth applies to all of the world. Turning to God gives hope and peace—regardless of where you live. Isaiah will compare nations and their leaders to events that will happen in the last days. The first nation he will address is Babylon; a nation which is symbolic of worldliness and wickedness. The destruction of Babylon in this chapter serves as a type and shadow of the destruction of the wicked at the Second Coming. As we discuss the verses in chapter 13, the focus will be on how these verses apply to the destruction of modern-day Babylon, and the events leading up to Christ's coming.

13:1 The burden of Babylon, which Isaiah the son of Amoz did see.

Burden (Heb. *massâ'*)—weighty or mournful.

"of Babylon"—i.e. concerning Babylon.

The burden of Babylon refers to the weighty or mournful prophecies that Isaiah had seen. The rise and destruction of Babylon is identified as a type for the destruction of the wicked on the earth at the Second Coming of Jesus Christ. Babylon symbolically represents all governments and their citizenries which oppose or fight against the kingdom of God. The finery and glitter of Babylon are fundamental elements of Satan's great blueprint of his evil designs and practices.

The Fight against Satan Continues

13:2 Lift ye up a banner upon the high mountain, exalt the voice unto them, shake the hand, that they may go into the gates of the nobles.

High mountain (Heb. *shaphah har*)—bare, or "bald" hill. i.e. Ensign Peak

Exalt (Heb. *rûwm*)—to raise or rise.

Shake (Heb. *nûwph*)—to wave to and fro, shake.

"Gates of the nobles"—a symbolic reference to the entrances into Zion or to the temple's portals.

This verse prophesies that in the last days, a banner would be lifted up to the world and would serve as an invitation to the world for all to come into the gates of the nobles, or the gates of Zion. After the death of Joseph Smith, Brigham Young sought guidance from the Lord on what the Saints should do, and where they should go for safety:

> While they were fasting and praying daily on this subject, President Young had a vision of Joseph Smith, who showed him the mountain that we now call Ensign Peak, immediately north of Salt Lake City, and there was an ensign fell upon that peak, and Joseph said, "Build under the point where the colors fall and you will prosper and have peace." (George A. Smith, in *Journal of Discourses*, 13:85)

On July 24, 1847, Brigham Young arrived at an overlook where he saw the Salt Lake Valley. "While gazing upon the scene . . . he was enwrapped in vision for several minutes. He had seen the valley before in vision and upon this occasion he saw the future glory of Zion and of Israel, as they would be, planted in the valleys of these mountains. When the vision had passed, he said: 'It is enough. This is the right place. Drive on'" (Wilford Woodruff, qtd. In Faust, "Brigham Young: A Bold Prophet").

Soon after their arrival, Brigham Young led a small group to the top of Ensign Peak and suggested that the peak "was a proper place to raise an ensign to the nations" (Smith, in *Journal of Discourses*, 16:207). The banner Isaiah speaks of that shall be lifted up symbolically, high upon a mountain, is The Church of Jesus Christ in the latter days. The verbs "lift," "exalt" (raise or shout), and "shake" (beckon or wave to) create the impression that God has someone already in place to do this. God has His servants lift up the banner for all to see, raise their voices, and beckon all to gather to the banner.

The banner has been lifted high for all to see to gather the spiritual nobility out of Babylon. The banner, or The Church of Jesus Christ, was reestablished on April 6, 1830. The Lord moved His saints from the east to the western Rocky Mountains, where today stands the headquarters of God's kingdom upon the earth—in Salt Lake City, Utah. Since that time the voices of the Saints have been heard inviting all to accept the restored gospel. To shake the hand seems to denote the hand of fellowship that the Saints need to give to the world as they warn them of pending danger and to teach them the plan of happiness, which, if accepted, will prepare them to enter the "gates of the noble," which are the gates of Zion leading to the temple.

13:3 I have commanded my sanctified ones, I have also called my mighty ones for mine anger, even them that rejoice in my highness.

Sanctified (Heb. *qâdash*)—to consecrate, prepare, dedicate, be hallowed, be holy, be separate. Saints.

Mighty (Heb. *gibbôwr*)—powerful; by implication, warrior.

The footnotes to this verse teach that "Sanctified ones" and "Saints" are synonymously translated from either of two Hebrew words in the Old Testament. Both refer to individuals who are consecrated, prepared, and dedicated. Their desire is to be holy. God can rely on them to do as He commands with the timing that He intends. The JST adds the words "is not upon" after anger. The JST reads "I have commanded my sanctified ones, I have also called my mighty ones for mine anger is not upon that rejoice in my highness."

13:4 The noise of a multitude in the mountains, like as of a great people; a tumultuous noise of the kingdoms of nations gathered together: the Lord of hosts mustereth the host of the battle.

God's Saints (the sanctified ones, and mighty spiritual warriors) are the ones who have been enlisted into His army. The Savior is mustering (enlisting) His hosts to war against sin and wickedness, against Satan and the "servants of Satan that do uphold his work" (D&C 10:5).

What is the tumultuous noise of a great people in the mountains and among the nations of the earth? This is the power of the testimony of Christ, the word of God, and the standard that has been raised (the Church) for the world to see. The gospel of the Lord's kingdom is being preached and a warning is being given to all nations that permit the Lord's missionaries entrance. The Lord of Hosts is gathering all who will come to His supper, to battle Satan and his evil influences. The Lord loves His children and wishes them to come unto Him.

The Lord will make every effort to save every last person whom He can find who loves Him, before the end comes. John Taylor said,

> Before the Lord destroyed the old world, he directed Noah to prepare an ark; before the cities of Sodom and Gomorrah were destroyed, he told Lot to 'flee to the mountains,' before Jerusalem was destroyed, Jesus gave his disciples warning, and told them to 'flee out of it;' and before the destruction of the world, a message is sent; after this, the nations will be judged, for God is now preparing his own kingdom for his own reign, and will not be thwarted by any conflicting influence, or opposing power. (*The Government of God*, Ch.11)

After God's Saints have been enlisted into His army and they have gathered, then what will happen? Verse 5 explains:

13:5 They come from a far country, from the end of heaven, even the Lord, and the weapons of his indignation, to destroy the whole land.

Those who join the Lord's army will be gathered from all the nations of the earth. "Yea, verily I say unto you again, the time has come when the voice of the Lord is unto you: Go ye out of Babylon; gather ye out from among the nations, from the four winds, from one end of heaven to the other" (D&C 133:7). Their multinational force will originate from a country far away from where Isaiah lives. From this location far away from Israel, the Lord will direct His forces in preparation to His Second Coming through His prophets. This far country refers to America and Salt Lake City in particular. "The end of heaven may simply suggest the farthest reaches of the earth" (Parry, *Understanding Isaiah*, 132).

At Christ's coming, He will use His righteous living saints, along with resurrected saints, His holy ones, to be the "weapons of his indignation." Moses reports that the saints of the city of Enoch will also come back and rejoice together in the Lord's army (Moses 7:62). Then they come with the Lord to cleanse the earth, "cruel both with wrath and fierce anger." President Charles W. Penrose of the First Presidency once said of the Lord's coming:

> He comes! The earth shakes, and the tall mountains tremble; the mighty deep rolls back to the north as in fear, and the rent skies glow like molten brass. He comes! The dead saints burst forth from their tombs, and "those who are alive and remain" are "caught up" with them to meet him. The ungodly rush to hide themselves from his presence and call upon the quivering rocks to cover them. He comes with all the hosts of the righteous glorified. The breath of his lips strikes death to the wicked. His glory is a consuming fire. The proud and rebellious are as stubble; they are turned and "left neither root nor branch." He sweeps the earth "as with the besom of destruction." He deluges the earth with the fiery floods of his wrath, and the filthiness and abominations of the world are consumed. ("The Second Advent," 583)

Isaiah next says of modern-day Babylon:

13:6 Howl ye; for the day of the Lord is at hand; it shall come as a destruction from the Almighty.

> Destruction (Heb. *shod*)—Violence, desolation, literally "a devastating tempest."

All the wicked on the earth one day shall howl, for as Alma said, "wickedness was never happiness." In that great day of destruction, the wicked of the earth shall bewail the Lord's advent. They will know that the destruction originates from God Himself. Of this there will be no doubt.

Reactions of the Wicked at Christ's Second Coming

In the day Christ comes, He will come with power and His anger and wrath will be fierce. In verses seven through nine the Lord describes the physical expressions of fear that will fall upon the wicked. He said:

13:7 Therefore shall all hands be faint, and every man's heart shall melt:

Faint (Heb. *raphah*)—to sink, to be disheartened.

Melt (Heb. *mâçaç*)—to dissolve, or waste away. To fail.

Hands symbolize our visible actions or pursuits. The heart symbolizes our true inner self, our unseen intents and desires. The hand and the heart represent our seen and unseen self—the totality of an individual. Just as Babylon was taken by surprise on the night of Belshazzar's impious feast (Dan. 5:30), the Second Coming will come as a surprise to the wicked. Paralyzed by the devastating tempest that has come to them, the wicked will not be able to act, or even plan how to act on their wickedness. Hence their sudden fainting and powerlessness to act in evil, and their desires to act in wickedness, will waste away.

13:8 And they shall be afraid: pangs and sorrows shall take hold of them; they shall be in pain as a woman that travaileth: they shall be amazed one at another; their faces shall be as flames.

Amazed (Heb. *tâmahh*)—to be astounded, be stunned, be dumbfounded.

Faces as flames—bright red, full of shame and guilt, to be inflamed because of weeping.

At the Second Coming, terror will seize the wicked. Similar to a pregnant woman in the hour of delivering a child, the wicked will endure significant pain. There will be no epidural that will mask the pains that come from sin. The pain will be obvious, sudden, inevitable, and inescapable. They will look at each other in a bewildered gaze of consternation full of embarrassment, shame, and guilt.

13:9 Behold, the day of the Lord cometh, cruel both with wrath and fierce anger, to lay the land desolate: and he shall destroy the sinners thereof out of it.

"The land" should be translated "the earth," or "the world."

Isaiah restated this verse when he wrote: "Behold, the Lord maketh the earth empty, and maketh it waste, and turneth it upside down, and scattereth abroad the inhabitant thereof. And it shall be, as with the people, so with the priest; as with the servant, so with his master. . . . The land shall be utterly emptied, and utterly spoiled: for the Lord hath spoken his word. . . . The earth also is defiled under the inhabitants thereof, because they have transgressed the laws, changed the ordinance, broken the everlasting covenant" (Isaiah 24:1–5).

Signs Preceding Christ's Second Coming

Isaiah speaks of some special signs that will take place just before the coming of the Savior.

13:10 For the stars of heaven and the constellations thereof shall not give their light: the sun shall be darkened in his going forth, and the moon shall not cause her light to shine.

The promise of the great signs preceding the coming of the Lord indicates to the world that the sun shall be darkened and the moon shall not give of her light and the stars of heaven and the constellations shall also refuse to give their light.

There is no light in sin. The spiritual illumination of righteousness is withheld from the wicked. Light—symbolic of revelation, creation, and Christ will be denied to those who have chosen darkness. Divine judgment will encompass them with fear and will be a plague to them (see Ex. 10:21).

Message of Warning for Those Following Ways of the World

Isaiah reminds his readers why Christ will destroy the wicked at His Second Coming.

13:11 And I will punish the world for their evil, and the wicked for their iniquity; and I will cause the arrogancy of the proud to cease, and will lay low the haughtiness of the terrible.

Punish (Heb. *pâqad*)—to visit (with friendly or hostile intent).
Terrible (Heb. *'ârîyts*)—powerful or tyrannical.

In this verse the Lord uses three words to describe the wicked who are destroyed at the Second Coming: arrogant, proud, and haughty. Arrogance makes one believe that they are lord over another. Pride is in the comparison. The word "haughty" comes from a verb meaning to "boil or seethe." Their view of themselves has risen to the point where they overflow with contempt for others. They seethe (to be in a state of turmoil) within themselves and inflict their conflict with themselves onto others in a way to make their insecurities less noticeable to others. They desire to look better than others at the expense of how others view themselves.

The reasons why the Lord would punish the world and cause perilous times to come upon the wicked is because men are as Paul said, "lovers of their own selves . . .. Without natural affection . . . incontinent . . . " (2 Tim. 3:2–3). Paul also spoke of men in the last days as having ". . . vile affections: for even their women did change the natural use into that which is against nature: And likewise also the men, leaving the natural use of the woman, burned in their lust one toward another . . .. Being filled with all unrighteousness, fornication, wickedness, covetousness, maliciousness; full of envy, murder, debate, deceit, malignity; whisperers, backbiters, haters of God, despiteful, proud, boasters, inventors of evil things, disobedient to parents, without understanding, covenantbreakers, without natural affection, implacable, unmerciful: who knowing the judgment of God, that they which commit such things are worthy of death, not only do the same, but have pleasure in them that do them" (Rom. 1:26–27, 29–32). Many of the people in the last days will simply hate God. They will show this enmity towards God in their pride. Their "friendship of the world is enmity with God. Whosoever therefore will be a friend of the world is the enemy of God" (James 4:4).

Life to Be a More Precious Commodity than Gold

To those who love Him, the Lord makes the following promise:

13:12 I will make a man more precious than fine gold; even a man than the golden wedge of Ophir.

The phrases "man more precious than fine gold" and "golden wedge of Ophir" indicate two ideas. First, a great number of people will be slaughtered during the destructions identified in this section, so that those who remain on the earth will be scarcer than a precious metal like gold. Second, those who remain after the decreed desolations and survive the furnace of affliction will be purified like gold; they will no longer possess dross (sin). The location of Ophir is not known but was famous for its gold (1 Kings 9:28, Job 28:16).

The Lord told Isaiah, with reference to His Second Coming, that:

13:13 Therefore I will shake the heavens, and the earth shall remove out of her place, in the wrath of the Lord of hosts, and in the day of his fierce anger.

Because of the arrogance spoken of in verse 11, the Lord will "lay low the haughtiness of the terrible." Isaiah will also prophecy that: "Behold, the Lord cometh out of his place to punish the inhabitants of the earth for their iniquity" (Isa. 26:21). One of the ways this will be done is by the literal shaking of heavens and earth. John the revelator spoke of this event at the opening of the sixth seal when he wrote: "Lo, there was a great earthquake; and the sun became black as sackcloth of hair, and the moon became as blood; and the stars of heaven fell unto the earth, even as a fig tree casteth her untimely figs, when she is shaken of a mighty wind. And the heaven departed as a scroll when it is rolled together, and every mountain and island were moved out of their places" (Rev. 6:12–14).

Who will all this effect? John goes on to tell us, "The kings of the earth, and the great men, and the rich men, and the chief captains, and the mighty men, and every bondman, and every free man, hid themselves in the dens and in the rocks of the mountains" (Rev. 6:15).

Earth Moves as a Chased Roe

13:14 And it shall be as the chased roe, and as a sheep that no man taketh up: they shall every man turn to his own people, and flee every one into his own land.

Chased roe—i.e. a hunted deer.

The earth will move like a chased roe (hunted deer) darting back and forth. After the simile of the earth being like a chased roe, a comparative simile is given. The remaining people who have not a shepherd to call their own will be like a sheep that is alone and separated from the flock, wandering back and forth, trying to find its way. They will have chosen to not have the protection afforded by the shepherd and the flock and are terrestrial in nature. They will be worried about the welfare of their loved ones, so they will quickly attempt to make contact with their own families to see if they are okay. Both the earth shaking, and the fright of those without Christ as a shepherd will occur at the same time—preparatory to the Second Coming of Jesus Christ.

God Will Destroy the Wicked

The wicked in Babylon will be punished for their iniquity just like those of a telestial nature will be when the Lord comes. Speaking of this terrible destruction of the wicked in Babylon, and the wicked living right before the Second Coming, Isaiah wrote:

13:15 Every one that is found shall be thrust through; and every one that is joined unto them shall fall by the sword.

13:16 Their children also shall be dashed to pieces before their eyes; their houses shall be spoiled, and their wives ravished.

In verse 14 there was no protector for the wicked. In verse 15 there is no escape, and verse 16 tells us there is no mercy for the wicked both at the destruction of Babylon, as well as the Second Coming. Why is there no escape or mercy? Escape from death and hell comes from the Holy one of Israel (2 Nephi 9:19). Mercy comes from the Shepherd that was rejected in verse 14. If you, like a sheep, reject Christ, you choose to go alone into your lone wilderness. Your actions become less noble, and more self-centric.

13:17 Behold, I will stir up the Medes against them, which shall not regard silver; and as for gold, they shall not delight in it.

It is the Lord who will stir up the Medes. He is the one in control both in the destruction of Babylon, and in the destruction of the wicked at the Second Coming. Historically, the Medes, having formed an alliance with the Persians under Cyrus the Great's leadership, conquered the great Babylonian empire not by an expected assault, but by unexpectedly damming the Euphrates River. They simply marched through its riverbed and went under the great walls of Babylon almost without resistance.

> This event took place more than one hundred sixty years after Isaiah's prophecy. The phrase shall not regard silver and gold indicates that the Medes did not go into battle to obtain plunder (silver and gold) instead, their motivation was to kill, and gain power and control. Perhaps ancient Media points forward to all nations of the last days who have the same wicked designs. (Parry, *Understanding Isaiah*, 137–138)

13:18 Their bows also shall dash the young men to pieces; and they shall have no pity on the fruit of the womb; their eye shall not spare children.

The sequence of young men, infants (fruit of the womb), and children provides a picture of senseless slaughter. There is no thought of their enemy, nor of their future. It will be their pride that always leads the wicked to destroy the wicked. Destroying another human life is seen as a tool to gain power, prestige, and domination. The wicked care nothing of God, or about anything that reminds them of God, or would profess to desire to be more like God.

Babylon Destroyed and Never to Be Rebuilt

Babylon referred to here is the world polluted by wickedness that the Lord will destroy. He will be merciful unto the righteous, "but the wicked shall perish." Isaiah speaking of Babylon said:

13:19 And Babylon, the glory of kingdoms, the beauty of the Chaldees' excellency, shall be as when God overthrew Sodom and Gomorrah.

"When God overthrew Sodom and Gomorrah"—complete and total destruction.

13:20 It shall never be inhabited, neither shall it be dwelt in from generation to generation: neither shall the Arabian pitch tent there; neither shall the shepherds make their fold there.

"neither. . . Arabian pitch tent"—Not only shall it not be a permanent residence, but not even a temporary resting place. The Arabs, through dread of evil spirits, and believing the ghost of Nimrod to haunt it, will not pass the night there.

"neither. . . shepherds"—The region was once most fertile; but owing to the Euphrates being now no longer kept within its former channels, it has become a stagnant marsh, unfit for flocks; and on the wastes of its ruins (bricks and cement) no grass grows.

The greatest city in the world would not only be destroyed, but it would also never be rebuilt. It is tantamount to saying Rome will lie in dust and never be inhabited or New York or some other equally as important and well-situated city. It is one thing to predict the destruction of a city and another to foresee its complete disappearance and the location itself becoming desolate forever! So likewise will it be at the coming of the Lord.

13:21 But wild beasts of the desert shall lie there; and their houses shall be full of doleful creatures; and owls shall dwell there, and satyrs shall dance there.

Wild beasts (Heb. *tsiyim*)—animals dwelling in arid wastes. Wild cats.

Doleful creatures (Heb. *ôach*)—howling beasts.

Owls (Heb. bath *ya'ănâh*)—owl, ostrich, literally translated as "daughters of the owl."

Satyrs (Heb. *sâ'îyr*)—demon possessed goats or devil worshippers who dance on the ruins.

The location of Babylon will become a place not only where travelers nor shepherds will stay the night, but it will be a place that is seen as haunted. In this verse Isaiah picks up on various superstitions and uses them for effect. It is not meant to be evidence of their existence.

13:22 And the wild beasts of the islands shall cry in their desolate houses, and dragons in their pleasant palaces: and her time is near to come, and her days shall not be prolonged.

JST adds after the word prolonged: "for I will destroy her speedily yea, for I will be merciful unto my people, but the wicked shall perish."

Wild beasts of the islands (Heb. *'îy*)—jackals; called by the Arabs "sons of howling."

Cry (Heb. *'ânâh*)—answer, respond to each other, as wolves do at night, producing a most dismal effect.

Dragons (Heb. *tannîyn*)—serpents of various species, which hiss and utter dolorous sounds.

"her time. . . near"—though one hundred seventy-four years distant, yet "near" to Isaiah, who is supposed to be speaking to the Jews as if they are now captives in Babylon (Isa. 14:1, 2).

The days of Babylon were known and numbered. Babylon was destroyed by the Assyrians in 698 BC and then it was restored. Cyrus took the city in 539 BC and left as it was, but turbulent days followed. It was lastly attacked by Darius Hystapes in 518 BC and from that point on in history it would decline to desolation.

Joseph Fielding Smith said of the great kingdoms of the past, "History records the rise and the downfall of nations. We have before us the history of Babylon, of Assyria, of Egypt, of Rome, and other nations. Why were they destroyed? Because they refused to hearken to the spirit of truth, to the voice of righteousness, and to walk in that spirit before the Lord. In the days of their iniquity trouble came upon them, and the Lord's anger was kindled against them, and they fell from their high and exalted positions" (*Church News*, Feb. 6. 1932, 5).

ISAIAH CHAPTER 14

The Lord Will Again Choose Israel

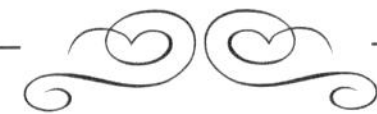

In chapter 13 Isaiah focuses on the destruction of Babylon and how that will be like the destruction of the wicked at the Second Coming of Christ. Chapter 14 continues with this topic and focuses on the leader of Babylon and compares his fall to the fall of Satan. At the second coming, both Babylon and its leaders will fall and their influence on mankind will cease. This chapter starts out explaining why Babylon will fall. It will fall so that Israel can flourish.

The Lord Will Have Mercy on Jacob, Yet Chooses Israel

14:1 For the Lord will have mercy on Jacob, and will yet choose Israel, and set them in their own land: and the strangers shall be joined with them, and they shall cleave to the house of Jacob.

Isaiah prophecies that God will, "yet" choose Israel and restore them to their land. Isaiah knew that Israel would be scattered and driven all over the earth. Yet one day when the time is right, the Lord promises Jacob that He will have mercy on His family. In speaking of this mercy, the Savior said:

> For a small moment have I forsaken thee, but with great mercies will I gather thee.
>
> In a little wrath I hid my face from thee for a moment, but with everlasting kindness will I have mercy on thee, saith the Lord thy Redeemer. (3 Nephi 22:7–8)

Jacob was his given family name, and Israel is his covenant name. Mercy comes to the individual and to the family through the Lord. Israel is chosen through the covenant. As Israel chooses to make the covenant with God to be His people, modern day prophets have authority from God to bless them. President Ezra Taft Benson, referring to his own calling as a prophet, seer and revelator said:

> By special assignment, [I have] been given authority in the house of Israel, I ask the God of Abraham, Isaac, and Jacob to bless my brethren of Judah and have mercy on them; that the land to which Judah has returned after a long night of dispersion shall be fruitful, prosperous, and become the envy of her neighbors; that the nation Israel shall be delivered from all her oppressors and enemies; that Judah will "draw water out of the wells of salvation" and fulfill all those prophecies that God declared through His prophets Isaiah, Ezekiel, Jeremiah; and that "the Lord shall inherit Judah his portion in the holy land, and shall choose Jerusalem again." (Zechariah 2:12). (*This Nation Shall Endure*, 141–42.)

14:2 And the people shall take them, and bring them to their place: and the house of Israel shall possess them in the land of the Lord for servants and handmaids: and they shall take them captives, whose captives they were; and they shall rule over their oppressors.

Note the blessings the Lord is giving to His people through having the gentiles assist them with the work of gathering of the Saints from the four corners of the earth. Elder McConkie gave a commentary of verse 2 in this way:

> And the people [Gentiles] shall take them, [Latter-day Saints] and bring them to their place; [valleys of the mountains] yea, from far unto the ends of the earth; and they [the Saints] shall return to their lands of promise [valley of the mountains] and

> the house of Israel shall possess them [Gentile*s*] in the land of the Lord for servants and handmaids; [gentiles will help Saints advance the work of God] and they [the saints] shall take them captives [Gentiles] unto, whose captives they were; [Satan's] and they [faithful members of the church] shall rule over their oppressors. [Israel shall rule; the Gentiles shall serve; the kingdom is the Lord's. His people are the governing ones.] (McConkie, *The Millennial Messiah*, 316)

In reviewing this verse a little closer we found that the "people" who are the gentiles will help the work of the Saints go easier. Their invention of the railroad helped the early pioneer Saints to migrate to the Rocky Mountains with much more ease and safety. The airplane helps with missionary work and the worldwide church as it grows bigger. The Lord will commission His anointed ones to find the true blood of scattered Israel and teach them of His ways. The Lord sends out missionaries "from far to the ends of the earth" and invites all who wish to come to know Christ to come and be taught His lifesaving principals and receive of His ordinances and covenants, and to come unto Zion, where the pure in heart dwell.

The gentiles, when converted, will be taken from Satan as his captive, and freed through the blood of the Lamb. Thus by accepting Christ, having faith, repenting, being baptized, and living the covenants they make with God, they will become rulers over their oppressors, for they will be given the Holy Ghost and will have, to the degree they live God's commandments, power to resist the temptations of the Devil. Through Christ's Atonement, Satan will no longer be able to hold them down in oppression through sin or death.

Millennial Promise to the Oppressed

14:3 And it shall come to pass in the day that the Lord shall give thee rest from thy sorrow, and from thy fear, and from the hard bondage wherein thou wast made to serve,

In the Joseph Smith Translation, verses 3–4 contain the phrase "in that day," indicating that these events pertain to the days of the gathering and then more fully during the Millennium. When the Lord gathers His people, He promises rest from their sorrow, fear, and hard bondage. The reward for His people is "peace in this world, and eternal life in the world to come" (D&C 59:23). During the Millennium, the righteous shall be given rest from their sorrows, fears, as well as the bondage of the task master that they endured during their earth life. This will all be taken away in Christ. Jesus has broken the bondage of sin and death for which we all should give thanks.

How Did Satan the Oppressor Cease to Rule over the Earth?

14:4 That thou shalt take up this proverb against the king of Babylon, and say, How hath the oppressor ceased! the golden city ceased!

As the Lord promised, a millennial day shall come when Satan is bound and all God's children will take up this proverb. The phrase "to take up a proverb" means to explain things as they truly are. This proverb causes the followers of Babylon to marvel, how it could be that their mighty king could no longer be relevant or feared. This proverb about the king of Babylon will parallel truths about Satan and bring them to light. How could he (Satan and/or the king of Babylon) have ceased to have any power or control over the wicked and their nations and cities of the earth? Isaiah answers this concern in the next two verses, he says,

14:5 The Lord hath broken the staff of the wicked, and the sceptre of the rulers.

14:6 He who smote the people in wrath with a continual stroke, he that ruled the nations in anger, is persecuted, and none hindereth.

The staff and the sceptre are symbols of rule. This king (and associated rulers under him) ruled in wickedness, with violence and anger, with a reign of terror (continual blows) and relentless aggression. The Lord will shatter their power through the use of His servants, His own voice, and the voice of natural destructive forces. The Lord explained how He does this when He said:

> How oft have I called upon you by the mouth of my servants, and by the ministering of angels, and by mine own voice, and

> by the voice of thunderings, and by the voice of lightnings, and by the voice of tempests, and by the voice of earthquakes, and great hailstorms, and by the voice of famines and pestilences of every kind, and by the great sound of a trump, and by the voice of judgment, and by the voice of mercy all the day long, and by the voice of glory and honor and the riches of eternal life, and would have saved you with an everlasting salvation, but ye would not! (D&C 43:25)

After Lucifer's reign is over, the Millennium rises and peace will warm the righteous.

14:7 The whole earth is at rest, and is quiet: they break forth into singing.

The Millennium is the time for singing praises unto the Lord. Wars will cease and peace will prevail. The awareness of this millennial peace and the magnificent things that the Savior of the world has done for His children, will bring His followers to great singing of praises unto Him, the Lamb of God. Maybe the words that will be sung at this time are recorded in Doctrine and Covenants 84:98–102. What a mighty message these words are, and it would be advisable for us to contemplate their great meaning. The Lord's covenant people will be the governing ones of this earth under Jesus Christ's direction in the Millennium.

Christ among His People in the Millennium

14:8 Yea, the fir trees rejoice at thee, and the cedars of Lebanon, saying, Since thou art laid down, no feller is come up against us.

The cedars of Lebanon are symbolic for what God has planted (see Psalms 104:16). These fir trees and the cedars of Lebanon in this verse seem to symbolize the most obedient children of the Lord that have lived on the earth, who rejoice in the right to live with their Redeemer during the Millennium. These trees were most desirous for their quality hard wood. They were used in building the temple by Solomon in Jerusalem and other royal government buildings. Like these woods, beautiful and enduring, the faithful Saints of this earth have remained firm in their convictions to their master Jesus Christ and the Lord has used them with their desiring qualities in the building of His Church in various dispensations. They stand tall and true in the qualities upon which the gospel principals are founded. They will rejoice in their God and in that day and will be found saying to their God, "Since Satan has been placed in spirit prison, no nations have come up to war against the Lord's people."

In Isaiah 37:24, the cutting down of these trees by the King of Assyria is symbolic of his pride. It is interesting to note that Satan will be seen as a pruned or discarded branch in verse 19. The Saints (trees) may think that the power of their destruction is in the feller (wood chopper) and that feller is Satan. But God knows that he has all power and only gives Satan as much power as He wants. In reality, Satan has no power of his own. He is like the diseased and broken branch that is pruned off and put on the pile of branches to be burnt.

Verses 9–15 contain a poem centering on Satan's visit to Hell (or Sheol). Several truths about the afterlife from the Old Testament can be seen in these verses. These truths are:

The dead are alive.
Sheol is the place where all of the dead live.
In Sheol there is personal continuity of personal recognition.
Sheol is a place of weakness with loss, not enhancement of earthly powers.
The dead wait in Sheol for a fullness, or future enhancement (see Motyer, 143–144).

At the start of the Millennium, Satan is bound and cast into spirit prison. Isaiah describes Satan's arrival in Shoel in the next few verses.

Satan Placed in Spirit Prison

14:9 Hell from beneath is moved for thee to meet thee at thy coming: it stirreth up the dead for thee, even all the chief ones of the earth; it hath raised up from their thrones all the kings of the nations.

Chief ones (Heb. *'attûwd*)—Literally he-goats i.e. the wicked leaders
Hell (Heb. *she'ôwl*)—hades, or the world of the dead.

When Satan is placed in the depths of the bottomless pit, those who have followed him will be stirred with excitement as they gather to meet him.

They will come unto him with hopes of being rescued from their imprisonment in spirit prison. Those who have been waiting to be delivered by Satan will find that he has been stripped of all the earthly power that he had been granted in his attempts to destroy the world. Isaiah prophesied of their conversation with Satan and their initial shock in that day as he said:

14:10 All they shall speak and say unto thee, Art thou also become weak as we? art thou become like unto us?

14:11 Thy pomp is brought down to the grave, and the noise of thy viols: the worm is spread under thee, and the worms cover thee.

> The grave (Heb. *sh*^{e}*'ôwl*)—hades. The same Hebrew word as in verse 9.
> Viols (Heb. *nebel*)—a skin-bag. The root word of *nebel* is *nabel* which means senseless or foolish.

These disillusioned followers of Satan upon seeing Satan placed as a common prisoner in spirit prison, will say, "Art thou also become weak as we? Art thou become like unto us?" Satan now finds himself in the same situation as they are, many of whom were kings, now without kingdom or servant. They will see Satan has not the lasting greatness and power that he proclaimed he had, for these have been taken from him. And as with the rest of Satan's followers, he has gone, as it were, to the grave and become as they who have died, and all there is left is the noise of the worms devouring their dead bodies. This is symbolic of the misery in which they will have been confined in spirit prison. At that time, it will be apparent to them that they have been "bamboozled" by the best of the soothsayers, the father of lies himself. And to their horror they will realize redemption comes only through Jesus Christ and His Atonement, that Satan has no power to deliver them as they had expected. It will be painful, yet a clear vision of reality to see the father of lies as he really is. The followers of Satan will be so amazed at seeing Satan imprisoned and stripped from all his powers, unable to fulfill his promises, that they will ask him the following questions:

14:12 How art thou fallen from heaven, O Lucifer, son of the morning! how art thou cut down to the ground, which didst weaken the nations!

Lucifer (Heb. *heylel*)—"light bearer"
Son of the morning (Heb. *ben shachar yalal*)—lit. son of the dawn to howl or a son who howls at the first light.

> Lucifer is apparently the title or name of the personage in the pre earthly existence who is now referred to as Satan or the devil. The fact that Isaiah refers to Lucifer and his role in the pre earthly existence seems to indicate that the Old Testament prophets were acquainted with the doctrine of a pre-earthly existence. (Ludlow, *A Companion to Your Study of the Old Testament*, 291–292)

Elder Critchlow used verses 12–20 to explain Satan's strategy to get as many spirits to side with him in the pre-existence, along with allies on earth. Satan deliriously reasons that if he can get a majority to follow him, then he will win the great war. Elder Critchlow explained:

> Approximately one third of the cast selected for the great drama defected and sided with Lucifer. For so doing, they were dropped from the cast and thus denied physical appearances on the stage. This infuriated them. They vowed to make the play flop, and to that end they have used freedom—the very agency they at first protested—to destroy "free agency."
>
> Lucifer's strategy is to induce the cast to use their individual agency in a way that will produce chaos on the stage. By exposing the cast to as much evil as possible, he hopes to gain numerical strength so that he might shout when the curtain rolls down at the end of the play, "I have the majority of the heavenly host on my side numerical strength is my power. Now I can claim `thine honor' now `I will ascend into heaven' now `I will exalt my throne above the stars of God'" (See Isa. 14:12–20). (Critchlow, 85)

14:13 For thou hast said in thine heart, I will ascend into heaven, I will exalt my throne above the stars of God: I will sit also upon the mount of the congregation, in the sides of the north:

14:14 I will ascend above the heights of the clouds; I will be like the most High.

Satan uses the word "I" five times in these verses as well as the word "me." Satan's only real interest is himself. He is saying he will yet go back and in a future day sit in the mount of the congregation, or in other words, the assembly of the Gods. He also boasts that he will be in the "sides of the north" which were the dwelling places for the Babylonian gods. Regardless who is God, Satan claims that he can be as great as, or greater than any god including God the Father Himself.

He rebelled against the Father and couldn't have his way, so he started a war in heaven. Because of this, he was thrust out of heaven, unto the earth, without a body. He is a natural-born liar, the father of all lies. He would say anything to deceive and obtain power. He did say a lot of things about his throne and being exalted above the stars of God and so on, but these are just aspirations and lies that he tells people in an effort to gain power. It is a game of deception he plays. He even tried to play it with Christ when he had been fasting for forty days, to cause him to falter and to worship Satan, yet Christ would not.

Satan and his third part of the hosts of heaven "kept not their first estate," and therefore rendered themselves ineligible for the glorious possibilities of an advanced condition or "second estate." He still wants the power and glory of the Father and the Son, and he will do any ungodly thing to obtain it. The scriptures say,

> And this we saw also, and bear record, that an angel of God who was in authority in the presence of God, who rebelled against the Only Begotten Son whom the Father loved and who was in the bosom of the Father, was thrust down from the presence of God and the Son,
>
> And was called Perdition, for the heavens wept over him—he was Lucifer, a son of the morning.
>
> And we beheld, and lo, he is fallen! is fallen, even a son of the morning! (D&C 76:25–27)

To better understand the numbers of spirits that were cast out with Satan to the earth to tempt the children of God who did receive bodies, a little math is in order. Some have estimated that 40 billion people have lived on the earth. The current population is more than seven billion today. If this estimate is even close to being correct it would mean when the Father lost one third of His spirit children, that at least 20 billion rebellious spirits were cast out with Satan. If these evil spirits were divided equally among the world's population, each of us would have three or four personalized devils following us around all the time.

Children of God who have no faith and have not been living God's commandments probably do not need many evil spirits to keep them in line. This, of course, would add many extra evil spirits to "hang around" the righteous to tempt them. It may well be that hundreds surround each faithful member of Christ's Church and chart every weakness in an effort to destroy their souls. Elder Harold B. Lee said of Satan's forces:

> There are carefully charted on the maps of the opposition the weak spots in every one of us. They are known to the forces of evil, and just the moment we lower the defense of any one of those ports, that becomes the D-Day of our invasion and our souls are in danger. (in Conference Report, 1949, 56)

With all the promises he made to his followers of what he would become, he will fail. He will find himself in spirit prison, not able to ascend anywhere. He may have been known as Lucifer, son of the morning, but that title was lost to him when he fell from heaven. Lucifer means "light bearer," which indicated the exalted position he once held. When he was cast out of the Father's presence, he was called "perdition," which means lost. In verse 15 Isaiah gives his resounding testimony of Satan's eventual destiny; he said:

14:15 Yet thou shalt be brought down to hell, to the sides of the pit.

> Sides (Heb. *yĕrekah*)—the rear or recess part, extreme part.
> "Sides of the pit"—figuratively the remotest part of hell (see Rev. 20:2–3)

The side of the pit indicates a place where you are not noticed. Satan will be cast into the fringes of hell. Unnoticed and unadorned. Who will put Satan in the pit? According to the scriptures Revelation 20:3; D&C 29:26; D&C 78:16; D&C 128:20, it will be an angel, who is Michael coming down from heaven with a key to the bottomless pit. He will be the one who will lay hold "on the dragon that old serpent, which is the Devil, and Satan, and bind him a thousand years." He will "cast him into the bottomless pit, and shut him up, and set a seal upon him, that he should deceive the nations no more, till the thousand years should be fulfilled: and after that he must be loosed a little season." Can you imagine how painful it must be to hit the sides of the pit, down to the bottom? Can you imagine the horror and disappointment on the faces of the wicked as:

14:16 They that see thee shall narrowly look upon thee, and consider thee, saying, Is this the man that made the earth to tremble, that did shake kingdoms;

Narrowly look (Heb. *shâgach*)—to glance sharply at; stare.
Consider (Heb. *bîyn*)—to discern or understand.

The contrast between the wicked's expectations and reality will be something that will make them stare in shame as they come to understand the nothing that their king has become. He now has no power. His threats are unenforceable. No kingdom is worried about him or his defeated army. All will see Satan as he really is—stripped of kingdom and power, and has been brought down with them to hell. They will marvel and realize their plight as they narrowly look upon him and say, "Is this the man that made the earth to tremble, that did shake the kingdoms." In other words, he will not be very impressive to look upon, disrobed of all his earthly preeminence, standing before them, not even with the power to quench his own thirsts.

The war in heaven has intensified here on the earth for the past six thousand years, as he has been enticing recruits to his dark and evil forces. He could not establish his earthly kingdom over that of the Father's and the Son's. He has tried to get something that he cannot have and has not earned: the birthright of Christ and the kingdom of his Father (see D&C 76:25). It must pain him very much to realize all the things that he cannot have, that any faithful follower of Christ and the Father will freely be given, because they lived the commandments and made covenants with the Son. And thus they can be joint-heirs with the Father and the Son (see D&C 84:33–38). Oh, how this knowledge must pain him.

Satan Wages War on Individuals and Christ's Church

14:17 That made the world as a wilderness, and destroyed the cities thereof; that opened not the house of his prisoners?

Opened not (Heb. *xtp pathach*)—freed not.

Satan, like the king of Babylon destroyed cities and their inhabitants. Both had prisoners. Satan's prisoners will never be freed by Satan. His desire is their eternal captivity. This hatred for individuals extends to Christ's Church as well. He makes war on Christ's Church and was effective enough to force it into the wilderness, or into a state of apostasy.

President Joseph Fielding Smith said:

> Satan in his wrath drove the [Church] into the wilderness, or from the earth; the power of the Priesthood was taken from among men, and after the Church with its authority and gifts disappeared from the earth, then in his anger the serpent continued his war upon all who had faith and sought the testimony of Jesus, desiring to worship God according to the dictates of conscience. So successful did he become that his dominion extended over all the known world. (Smith, *Progress of Man*, 166)

The church he fights so intensely against leads all who will listen towards Christ and His power to open the prison. He opened the way that each and every captive will be released through His Atonement, except the sons of perdition.

Earthly Kings Will Have a Glory, but Satan Will Be Cast Out

14:18 All the kings of the nations, even all of them, lie in glory, every one in his own house.

The kings of the earth have had the best the world has had to offer. They have ruled in great splendor and prestige. In their pride and wealthy influence, they have had statues and tombs erected out of magnificent marble and stone to preserve their memory. But Isaiah has informed us that once they have left the earth, they are no better off than any other spirit in the spirit world, unless they have obeyed the commandments of God. The Lord says of the self-proclaimed king of the earth:

14:19 But thou art cast out of thy grave like an abominable branch, and as the raiment of those that are slain, thrust through with a sword, that go down to the stones of the pit; as a carcase trodden under feet.

14:20 Thou shalt not be joined with them in burial, because thou hast destroyed thy land, and slain thy people: the seed of evildoers shall never be renowned.

"Like an abominable branch"—i.e. his body would remain unburied which anciently was considered to be a great curse. This can also represent that Satan won't even have a body!

"Trodden under feet"—unburied and unprotected.

Satan will never have a grave because he never had a body. He never will have a body. What does it mean Satan shall not be joined with the very kings of the earth that he has used to destroy the earth, to kill his own people and to be doers of evil? It means that in the end, the kings and their servants who have been wicked will eventually have a place of glory even if it is in the telestial kingdom. Yet Satan will be cast out of his grave like an abominable branch, because he never had a body and thus he could never die.

He is symbolically cast out of his grave never to be resurrected unto something he never had. The kings of the earth that were used and abused by Satan will be, at the end, greater than the evil one himself and will come unto some degree of glory. Satan has destroyed the land and lost his inheritance, so he will not even have any glory at all. He practiced the old motto: "Eat, drink, and be merry, for tomorrow we die; and it shall be well with us." But as you see from Isaiah, this is just another lie that Satan tells.

Satan is the king of all wickedness of this earth and has built himself a magnificent evil empire. Yet he will be placed in spirit prison for 1,000 years and then released for a short season to gather his forces, at which time he, and all the sons of perdition, will be cast out symbolically from their graves as an abominable branch of God's kingdom, out into outer darkness. The remnant spoken of in this verse is not a piece of clothing but a reminder to Satan that he will be cast out like a damnable branch of God's family. All those who follow him and who die in their sins, deprived of any possibility of celestial life, will symbolically be as stones that have fallen down into the bottom of the pit, which is spirit prison, from whence they cannot come, except upon the command of the Lord; but this will not happen until they have paid the price for their own sins, since they would not accept the atoning blood of the Savior and repent while in the flesh. For "they had their dominion taken away: yet their lives were prolonged for a season and time" (Daniel 7:12). They who are telestial "shall be delivered over to the buffetings of Satan until the day of redemption" (D&C 78:12). The time they spend being tormented by Satan will be for them "as a carcase trodden under feet" of the evil one.

The bottom line is that Satan will have no glory at the end of the earth. He will be cast into outer darkness, never to be reclaimed. The Lord speaking of those who were overcome by Satan said:

> And then shall it come to pass, that the spirits of the wicked, yea, who are evil—for behold, they have no part nor portion of the Spirit of the Lord; for behold, they chose evil works rather than good; therefore the spirit of the devil did enter into them, and take possession of their house—and these shall be cast out into outer darkness; there shall be weeping, and wailing, and gnashing of teeth, and this because of their own iniquity, being led captive by the will of the devil.
>
> Now this is the state of the souls of the wicked, yea, in darkness, and a state of awful, fearful looking for the fiery indignation of the wrath of God upon them; thus they remain in this state, as well as the righteous in paradise, until the time of their resurrection. (Alma 40:13–14)

Slaughter Prepared for Children of Satan

The Lord has declared a punishment for those who follow Satan. Satan's followers, or his children, will be destroyed.

14:21 Prepare slaughter for his children for the iniquity of their fathers; that they do not rise, nor possess the land, nor fill the face of the world with cities.

14:22 For I will rise up against them, saith the Lord of hosts, and cut off from Babylon the name, and remnant, and son, and nephew, saith the Lord.

A time will come when the Lord will rise up against the wicked and He will slaughter them and "throw down all their strongholds" (3 Ne. 21:14–21), in order to cleanse the earth of wickedness. This will be done to stop the continuation of evil filling the earth and to stop another wicked generation from arising and resuming their evil dynasty.

The Lord's Second Coming will destroy "every corruptible thing, both of man, or of the beasts of the field, or of the fowls of the heavens, or of the fish of the sea, that dwells upon all the face of the earth, shall be consumed" (D&C101: 23–24). "The names of the wicked shall not be mingled with the names of my people" (Alma 5:57). It doesn't matter who we are, how much money we have; or what relationship we have with anyone, these cannot save us from our sins. The promise of the Lord is clear, He will "cut off from Babylon the name, and remnant, and son, and nephew" leaving the earth a place where He can come to live during the Millennium. Only Christ can save mankind from their sins and make a difference, but only if they will repent.

The Lord Will Sweep the Earth

14:23 I will also make it a possession for the bittern, and pools of water: and I will sweep it with the besom of destruction, saith the Lord of hosts.

Bittern (Heb. *qippôwd*)—a hedgehog.

Pools (Heb. *'□gam*)—muddy pools of water, marshes; owing to Cyrus turning the waters of the Euphrates over the country.

Besom (Heb. *maṭ'□ṭê'*)—a broom that sweeps.

In verse 22 the Lord tells Satan and the Babylonian king that their land and their people would be destroyed. There will be no legacy for the wicked. No heirs. In this verse the Lord explains that the destruction will be so complete that their evil cities (like Babylon) will become heaps of desolate ruins surrounded by uninhabited marshes, only survivable by small wild animals.

The Lord has made His decree that He will cleanse the earth and establish His earthly kingdom, and that it shall never again be overthrown. His judgments shall lay waste the nations, remove the wickedness and evil and give a righteous kingdom room to grow, develop, and prosper. These judgments have already begun. Wilford Woodruff said the earth will be "swept as with the besom of destruction, until thrones are cast down and kingdoms overthrown, until each man draws his sword against his neighbor, and every nation and kingdom that exists will be at war with each other, *except the inhabitants of Zion*. The Lord has spoken it, and it will come to pass (see D&C 45:66–75)" (*Journal of Discourses*, 2:201).

A "besom" is a broom that the Lord will use first to sweep the earth of its wickedness by teaching righteousness and truth. He will also bring back to the Bible sacred truths that have over the years of translation been left out and discarded. President Ezra Taft Benson said, "The Book of Mormon is the instrument that God designed to 'sweep the earth as with a flood, to gather out [His] elect' (Moses 7:62)" (Benson, "Flooding the Earth with the Book of Mormon").

Elder Bruce R. McConkie said concerning the importance of the Book of Mormon,

> Few men on earth, either in or out of the Church, have caught the vision of what the Book of Mormon is all about. Few are they among men who know the part it has played and will yet play in preparing the way for the coming of Him of whom it is a new witness . . .. The Book of Mormon shall so affect men that the whole earth and all its peoples will have been influenced and governed by it. . . . There is no greater issue ever to confront mankind in modem times than this: Is the Book of Mormon the mind and will and voice of God to all men? We testify that it is. (McConkie, *The Millennial Messiah*, 159, 170, 179)

The Word of God to the Wicked

14:24 The Lord of hosts hath sworn, saying, Surely as I have thought, so shall it come to pass; and as I have purposed, so shall it stand:

The Lord prophesies and His word will stand. In the Doctrine and Covenants, the Lord further states, "What I the Lord have spoken, I have spoken, and I excuse not myself; and though the heavens and the earth pass away, my word shall not pass away, but shall all be fulfilled, whether by mine own voice or by the voice of my servants, it is the same" (D&C 1:38).

14:25 That I will break the Assyrian in my land, and upon my mountains tread him under foot: then shall his yoke depart from off them, and his burden depart from off their shoulders.

Just when Assyria is going to absolutely decimate everything, the Lord steps in.

The Lord wishes us to realize that it was He who had control over the Assyrian powers and their armies and He alone brought them upon Israel and into Judah. Even though Ahaz had invited them, the Lord has control over all armies. It was Israel's wickedness and their lack of willingness to follow the prophet Isaiah that the Lord permitted the Assyrian army to come into the land of David. His arm was always stretched out to stop the progress of the Assyrian army if Israel and Judah would repent. They would not, so the army was permitted to come. Isaiah warned King Ahaz not to make an alliance with Assyria in the first place and that nothing good would come of it. He told him if he did, they would come as a strong river overflowing its banks upon them and would move swiftly until they reached the very neck of Judah, which is Jerusalem (see Isaiah 8:7–8). The Assyrians in 701 BC under Sennacherib's leadership faced a revolt of Judah after Ahaz's death, when Hezekiah, supported by Egypt, refused to pay tribute to Assyria. He invaded Palestine and destroyed a number of cities, but at Jerusalem the Lord did "tred him under foot." He killed 185,000 in one night and the king ran home, only to be killed by his sons (see 2 Kings 19:32–37).

Another aspect to this verse lies in comparing the content of this scripture with what will take place in the land of Israel again before the Second Coming of Jesus Christ. It is prophesied that a great army will come upon the Jewish nation. The Assyrians symbolize evil gentiles of every nation who will make up this future army. The Lord will do to them as He had done to the Assyrians at the time of Ahaz's death. The evil yoke of the wicked will be broken and this event will prepare the way for the Lord not only to come to the Jews on the mount of Olives, but also to come in His full glory, in the sight of all the earth, to make a total cleansing of the wicked and to reign with glory and power upon the earth.

Bruce R. McConkie wrote of the Lord's future appearance to the Jews:

> At the very moment of the Second Coming of our Lord, "all nations" shall be gathered "against Jerusalem to battle" (Zech. 11; 12; 13; 14), and the battle of Armageddon (obviously covering the entire area from Jerusalem to Megiddo, and perhaps more) will be in progress. As John expressed it, "the kings of the earth and of the whole world" will be gathered "to the battle of that great day of God Almighty, into a place called in the Hebrew tongue Armageddon." Then Christ will "come as a thief," meaning unexpectedly and the dramatic upheavals promised to accompany his return will take place. (Rev. 16:14–21.) It is incident to this battle of Armageddon that the Supper of the Great God shall take place (Rev. 19:11–18), and it is the same battle described by Ezekiel as the war with Gog and Magog. (Ezek. 38; 39; *Doctrines of Salvation*, vol. 3, p. 45). (McConkie, *Mormon Doctrine*, 74)

> And seven months shall the house of Israel be burying of them, that they may cleanse the land. Has there ever been such an enterprise as this? Will there ever be such a graveyard as Palestine? There the embalmed bodies of the righteous rest in sacred tombs, awaiting the sound of the trump of God that shall call them forth in the resurrection of life; and there the mangled carcasses of the wicked shall lie in unmarked graves, awaiting the sound of a later trump that will call them forth in the resurrection of damnation. (McConkie, *The Millennial Messiah*, 487)

Who Can Disannul the Prophecies of the Lord?

14:26 This is the purpose that is purposed upon the whole earth: and this is the hand that is stretched out upon all the nations.

14:27 For the Lord of hosts hath purposed, and who shall disannul it? and his hand is stretched out, and who shall turn it back?

The purpose (Heb. *'êtsâh*)—the result of a counsel, i.e. plan

The Assyrians, Babylonians, and the Meads are all types of destruction of the wicked in the last days. The Lord has always used the wicked to destroy the wicked. However, a time will come when He will Himself come to destroy the wicked after much warning and great efforts have been made to save all who will turn from sin unto the Lord. The Lord has control upon the whole earth as He stretches His hand out over the nations of the earth. The nations cannot disannul or cancel the gospel promises the Lord has made to the wicked if they will not repent. The Lord reminded Israel and Judah several times through Isaiah that His "hand is stretched out still" to help them, if they would only repent.

The Lord has declared many things that shall transpire upon all nations before He comes to the earth at the beginning of the Millennium. They shall happen just as He has said they would. Our job is to abide in freedom and not get entangled in sin, but to keep our hands clean, and watch for the day when the Lord comes. He has set up signs for us to see and to know He will keep His promises and visit the earth. He makes mention of some of these signs when He says:

> [T]he earth shall tremble and reel to and fro as a drunken man; and the sun shall hide his face, and shall refuse to give light; and the moon shall be bathed in blood; and the stars shall become exceedingly angry, and shall cast themselves down as a fig that falleth from off a fig tree.
>
> . . . For after your testimony cometh the testimony of earthquakes, that shall cause groanings in the midst of her, and men shall fall upon the ground and shall not be able to stand.
>
> And also cometh the testimony of the voice of thunderings, and the voice of lightnings, and the voice of tempests, and the voice of the waves of the sea heaving themselves beyond their bounds.
>
> And all things shall be in commotion; and surely, men's hearts shall fail them; for fear shall come upon all people.

> And angels shall fly through the midst of heaven, crying with a loud voice, sounding the trump of God, saying: Prepare ye, prepare ye, O inhabitants of the earth; for the judgment of our God is come. Behold, and lo, the Bridegroom cometh; go ye out to meet him. (D&C 88:87, 89–92)

A Caution to the Wicked

14:28 In the year that king Ahaz died was this burden.

14:29 Rejoice not thou, whole Palestina, because the rod of him that smote thee is broken: for out of the serpent's root shall come forth a cockatrice, and his fruit shall be a fiery flying serpent.

Serpent's root (Heb. *nâchâsh sheresh*)—serpent's root. This probably refers to an ancestor whom Palestina despised (Uzziah) and this word for serpent is different than the one used below in "fiery flying serpent."

Fiery flying serpent (Heb. *saraph `uwph saraph*)—lit. Fiery serpent, flying, fiery serpent. Saraph is also translated as Seraphim, or a fiery angel with 6 wings (see Isaiah 6:2).

Before Ahaz's death, he had aligned himself with Assyria. He had tied Judah's fortunes with Assyria and Isaiah was opposed to this union. Isaiah had also tried to convince Ahaz to exercise his faith said, "If ye will not believe surely ye shall not be established" (Isaiah 7:9). This must be disheartening to a king to be told if he did not believe the word of the Lord's prophet, he would not keep his kingdom.

When Ahaz died, Palestina took the opportunity to approach the new king of Judah (Hezekiah) under the guise of offering condolences for Ahaz's death. Palestina, backed by Egypt, used this opportunity to offer an "anti-Assyrian alliance as the way for Judah to recover their national sovereignty" (Moyter, 147).

The country of Palestina consisted essentially of five city states, each governed by its own lord. Isaiah uses the term "whole Palestina" to indicate that this delegation was united in trying to get Judah to be a part of their anti-Assyrian alliance. This nation was home of the Philistines, detested enemies of Judah and the Israelites. This country was at the height of its power at the time of King Saul's death but declined during the reign of King David. It was King David who was consistently victorious over the Philistines and was referred to in the phrase "rod of him" which had struck at Palestina. Now the power of Judah under King David had been broken and Ahaz's policies had resulted in vassalage to Assyria.

David is broken but the Lord's power still resides in the fallen rod and Isaiah teaches this by referring to events in the early part of Exodus. In Exodus 4:2–3 and 7:10–12 Moses uses a rod and turns it into a deadly snake. Here the broken rod of David will be turned into the serpent's root, cockatrice (venomous viper), and fiery flying serpent. All three are "symbolic of evil to come upon her Philistia." Each one gets more intense, and more deadly.

The serpent's root also refers to a source that had defeated Palestina in the past. Following this imagery, the Rod of David is broken and Judah seems to be powerless after his death. Then from the Davidic line of descendants (the root of Jesse) comes ultimate power in Christ (See Isaiah 11:1). The power that will be exercised on the wicked is like the power that will be exercised on Palestina. It grows more intense and deadly to both Palestina and to wickedness and sin until God sends His messengers, or His Seraphim from His presence to do His work. Out of Christ's living roots arise a rod, which became Joseph Smith. Angels from God's presence descended and gave him power and authority to combat wickedness in our day. Satan had him killed, yet God's kingdom stills roll forward, for there came forth still another rod from the roots of Jesse and it was the prophet Brigham Young. Rods continue to spring forth as a prophet dies and the work of God rolls on faster and faster, and the strength always comes from the root of the stem of Jesse, Jesus Christ.

Instead of focusing on the renewal of, or changing of, political alliances at the death of a king, Isaiah will use Ahaz's death as an opportunity to reaffirm the promises that were made by God to Judah in the next few verses.

Christ Will Bless the Righteous in the Millennium

14:30 And the firstborn of the poor shall feed, and the needy shall lie down in safety: and I will kill thy root with famine, and he shall slay thy remnant.

The firstborn of the poor—i.e. the poorest of the poor

Verses 30–32 teach that those who are humble and who suffer (the poor and needy) will join Zion, which was founded by Jehovah. Starting in verse 30, Isaiah teaches that the poorest of the poor, the neediest, will become safe. These would be those Christ describes as the poor in spirit. They are taught Christ's gospel. In the Millennium, He will teach us, "Of things both in heaven and in the earth, and under the earth; things which have been, things which are, things which must shortly come to pass; things which are at home, things which are abroad; the wars and the perplexities of the nations, and the judgments which are on the land; and a knowledge also of countries and of kingdoms" (D&C 88:79). For he said, "Blessed are they which do hunger and thirst after righteousness: for they shall be filled." These are they that will be in His cities of New Jerusalem and Jerusalem, where He will teach them all things that pertain to the earth, as they lie down in safety within the fold of the true Shepherd.

President Joseph Fielding Smith explained that even though Christ will be here during the Millennium, there will still be nonbelievers on the earth. He wrote:

> There will be wicked men on the earth during the millennium' has been misunderstood by many, because the Lord declared that the wicked shall not stand, but shall be consumed. In using this term 'wicked' it should be interpreted in the language of the Lord as recorded in the Doctrine and Covenants, Section 84:49-53. Here the Lord speaks of those who have not received the gospel as being "wicked"as they are still under the bondage of sin, having not been baptized. 'The inhabitants of the terrestrial order will remain on the earth during the Millennium, and this class is without the gospel ordinances.' . . .
>
> The gospel will be taught far more intensely and with greater power during the millennium until all the inhabitants

> of the earth shall embrace it. Satan shall be bound so that he cannot tempt any man. Should any man refuse to repent and accept the gospel under those conditions then he would be accursed. Through the revelations gave to the prophets we learn that during the reign of Jesus Christ for a thousand years, eventually all people will embrace the truth. (Smith, *Answers to Gospel Questions*, 1:108–11)

Zechariah prophesied, that those of his children who will not embrace the gospel during the Millennium and come "unto Jerusalem to worship the King, the Lord of hosts, even upon them shall be no rain" (Zech. 14:16–19). Of these same people Joseph Smith taught, they "will be visited with the judgments of God, and must eventually be destroyed from the earth." (*Teachings of Presidents: Joseph Smith*, 269).

This verse also includes the phrase "thy root" in comparison with the spiritually strong root of David. If we tap into the roots of Christ, we will live through His living water. If we choose to use our own roots, our pride will result with spiritual famine. We will have no promise of spiritual increase now, or in the future.

14:31 Howl, O gate; cry, O city; thou, whole Palestina, art dissolved: for there shall come from the north a smoke, and none shall be alone in his appointed times.

All the wicked in every city will cry as a result their destruction. When the Lord comes to destroy the wicked it will come upon all Palestina, or the whole earth. The Lord will come as a smoke from the north. This smoke is a reference to the dust cloud that comes with an advancing army. There is an appointed time for the destruction of the wicked as they are burned and placed into spirit prison. The terrestrial people of the earth will be protected from the burning. Not a lot of information is provided for us on how this will be done in their behalf. And the celestial people, both dead and alive will be raised up to meet Christ in the clouds.

14:32 What shall one then answer the messengers of the nation? That the Lord hath founded Zion, and the poor of his people shall trust in it.

As the Lord comes in His glory, what will be the nation's answer to God's messengers? They will have either accepted the gospel message or rejected it. Those who are the "pure in heart" (D&C 97:21) will be a part of Zion. They will have trusted in the Lord. They will have accepted the messengers when they were sent to them.

ISAIAH CHAPTER 15

A Warning to the Nations of the World

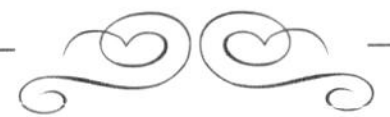

Beginning with chapter 15, Isaiah sends warnings to much of the world starting with Moab. These warning are found from chapters 15 to 23. In some cases, Isaiah warns the nation of their impending destruction especially those which surrounds Israel. Below is a summary list of these warnings:

The Warnings to the Nations—Isaiah 15–23

A message of warning is given to Moab (15:1–16:14; compare Genesis 19:30–38; Jeremiah 48; Ezekiel 25:8–11).

A message is given to Syria (17:1–14; compare Jeremiah 49:23–27).

A message is given to the land of America (18:1–7).

Messengers are sent out to the nations (18:1–6).

The people are gathered back to Zion (18:7).

A message of warning is given to Egypt (19:1–20:6; compare Jeremiah 46; Ezekiel 29–32).

It foretells the fall of Egypt as a mighty nation (19:1–15).

Judah will be a terror to Egypt (19:16–17).

The Hebrew language will be taught in Egypt (19:18).

An altar of the Lord will be in the midst of Egypt, and Egypt will be healed (19:1922).

Egypt will be blessed along with Assyria and Israel (19:23-–25).
Isaiah gives an object lesson of Egypt's captivity by Assyria (20:1–6).
A message of warning is given to the "desert of the sea" (Babylon?) (21:1–10; compare Jeremiah 50–51).
A message is given to Dumah (Edam) (21:11–12; compare Jeremiah 49:7–22; Ezekiel 25:12–14).
A message comes to Arabia (21:13–17; compare Jeremiah 49:28–33).
The Lord speaks to the "valley of vision" (Jerusalem) (22:1–25).
He foretells of a siege against Jerusalem (22:1–7).
He calls, but they continue in the Law of Moses (22:8–14).
A second siege will come against Jerusalem (22:15–19).
The throne of David will be established forever (22:20–25).
A message of warning comes to Tyre (23:1–18; compare Ezekiel 26–28).

Each of the prophecies in these chapters will be better understood, as Nephi said, by those who live in the day when they are fulfilled (see 2 Nephi 25:7). The prophecy in chapters 15 and 16 focuses on Moab. Moab was named after the firstborn son of Lot's eldest daughter (Gen. 19:37) and was the nation that bordered the Dead Sea on the east side of Israel. The prophet warns the Moabites that they will be destroyed, despite the fact that they are prosperous in trading and commerce. These two chapters create a wonderful chiasmas with the focus, or most important point, being in Chapter 16 verse 5 as seen below.

A1 Moab's certain ruin (15:1)
B1 Moab's grief expressed (15:2-4)
C1 The Lord's grief over Moab (15:5–9)
D1 Moab's plea for shelter (16:1–4)
E Security found in Zion (16:5)
D2 Moab's pride (16:6)
B2 Moab's grief explained (16:7–8)
C2 the Lord's grief over Moab (16:9–12)
A2 Moab's imminent ruin (16:13–14) (Motyer, 149)

The focus of this chiasmas is that security will be found in Zion and not in the pride of Moab. Pride brings destruction and Zion provides mercy, truth, judgment, and righteousness.

Moab's Certain Ruin

15:1 The burden of Moab. Because in the night Ar of Moab is laid waste, and brought to silence; because in the night Kir of Moab is laid waste, and brought to silence;

Ar (Heb. "the city")—the metropolis of Moab, on the south of the river Arnon.

Kir—literally "a citadel"; not far from Ar, towards the south.

This message of doom was addressed to Moab and was probably given in the first year of Hezekiah's reign. It will be fulfilled in the fourth of his reign (see Isaiah 15:5) when Sennacherib, king of Assyria, was on his way to invade Israel and seized on the strongholds of Moab. This destruction would come suddenly, as if in the night, on an unsuspecting and prosperous nation. In chapter 15, Isaiah will list sixteen cities and places which are located in both the northern and southern regions of Moab. This indicates that all of Moab will be affected by the devastation.

Moab's Grief

15:2 He is gone up to Bajith, and to Dibon, the high places, to weep: Moab shall howl over Nebo, and over Medeba: on all their heads shall be baldness, and every beard cut off.

Bajith (Heb. *Bayith*)—Literally "house," or rather, "to the temple."

Dibon (Heb. *Dîybôwn*)—Literally "wasting." Dibon was in a plain north of the Arnon, Same town as Dimon (Isa 15:9).

Nebo (Heb. *N^{e}bôw*)—Literally "prophet." The town Nebo was adjacent to the mountain, not far from the northern shore of the Dead Sea. There it was that Chemosh, the idol of Moab, was worshipped (compare Deut. 34:1).

Medeba (Heb. *Mêyd^{e}bâ'*)—Literally "water of rest." The town of Medeba is south of Heshbon, on a hill east of Jordan.

In this verse Isaiah indicates that when the time for Moab's destruction comes, the inhabitants of Moab go to their temples (Heb. *Byth*, "temple") and high places to mourn and lament because of the destruction. The high places were the usual places of sacrifice in the East. Moab will weep over this sudden calamity. They will have lost their access to the prophet, and to the peace (similar to the "waters of rest") that comes from hearkening to the prophet.

It was customary for males to demonstrate their sorrow by shaving their heads and beards (22:12; Micah 1:16). The once proud inhabitants of Moab are now reduced to humility and shame.

15:3 In their streets they shall gird themselves with sackcloth: on the tops of their houses, and in their streets, every one shall howl, weeping abundantly.

The tops of their houses were flat places where people resorted to be alone, but was a place where you could be seen. Whether they were on top of their houses, or in the streets, their extreme mourning was done in public places so that all could see.

15:4 And Heshbon shall cry, and Elealeh: their voice shall be heard even unto Jahaz: therefore the armed soldiers of Moab shall cry out; his life shall be grievous unto him.

Heshbon—an Amorite city, twenty miles east of Jordan; taken by Moab after the carrying away of Israel (compare Jer. 48:1–47).

Elealeh—near Heshbon, in Reuben.

Jahaz—east of Jordan, in Reuben. Near it, Moses defeated Sihon.

In the cities of Moab, the people will cry, and even the hardened men of war will feel sorrow and will cry out in despair instead of fighting in defense of their land. At this time of trauma, his [the soldiers] life, or better translated, his soul will be grieved.

The Lord's Grief

15:5 My heart shall cry out for Moab; his fugitives shall flee unto Zoar, an heifer of three years old: for by the mounting up of Luhith with weeping shall they go it up; for in the way of Horonaim they shall raise up a cry of destruction.

Zoar (Heb. *Tsô'ar*)—literally "insignificance." The fugitives fleeing from Moab, wander as far as to Zoar, on the extreme boundary south of the Dead Sea.

Luhith—a mountain in Moab.

Horonaim—a town of Moab not far from Zoar (Jer. 48:5). It means "the two poles," being near caves.

"My heart" in verse 5 refers to the same person as verse 9. This mourner is the Lord. "He grieves over the plight of the fugitives (in verse 5), the stricken environment (verse 6), the futile efforts to salvage something form the overthrow (verses 7–8) and over what is yet to come (in verse 9)" (Motyer, 150).

The mourning is over an event that will take place three years in the future. When a heifer is three years old, it is in its strength, or full of vigor. Zoar was considered to be a strong city but Isaiah prophesies that it soon would be destroyed when Sennacherib, king of Assyria, will invade in three years. Even though people will flee to what they perceive as their stronghold, in the end they will weep and cry.

15:6 For the waters of Nimrim shall be desolate: for the hay is withered away, the grass faileth, there is no green thing.

Nimrim (Heb. *Nimrîym*)—limpid or perfectly clear. A city in Gilead near Jordan.

As the fugitives flee southwards (see 2 Kings 3:19, 25), the northern regions and even the city Nimrim, its pure waters and vegetation seemingly vanish.

15:7 Therefore the abundance they have gotten, and that which they have laid up, shall they carry away to the brook of the willows.

As a result of the devastation of the land, anything that is over and above the necessities of life, or their abundance will be gone. The phrase the "brook of. . . willows" indicates that the fugitives will flee from Nimrim, where the waters have failed, to places better watered. Some scholars believe that they will flee to the "valley of Arabians"; that is, to the valley on the boundary between them and Arabia-Petraea; now Wady-el Arabah. "Arabia" means a "desert."

15:8 For the cry is gone round about the borders of Moab; the howling thereof unto Eglaim, and the howling thereof unto Beer-elim.

Eglaim (Heb. *'Eglayim*)—double reservoir. This town was on the very borders of Moab or perhaps beyond them.

Beer-elim—literally, "the well of God" and was beyond the east borders of Moab.

All of Moab will be in despair during this time. Its desperation will extend to its borders and beyond.

15:9 For the waters of Dimon shall be full of blood: for I will bring more upon Dimon, lions upon him that escapeth of Moab, and upon the remnant of the land.

The slain of Moab will be so many that the waters of Dimon (same as Dibon in verse 2) will be full of blood. And after this decimation, God will "bring more" destruction upon them by the lions. In essence, the lion will represent a fierce, strong, and deliberate attacker who will seek to destroy the refugees who remain in the land.

ISAIAH CHAPTER 16

Mercy, Truth, Judgment, and Rightesouness Are to Be Found in Zion

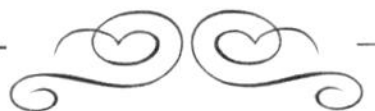

CHAPTER 16 CONTINUES THE PROPHESIES OF CHAPTER 15 AND IS A PART OF one chiasmas. The center of the chiasmas, or the most important principle taught in chapters 15 and 16 is found in verse 5. Mercy, truth, judgment, and righteousness are to be found in Zion.

MOAB'S PLEA FOR SHELTER

16:1 Send ye the lamb to the ruler of the land from Sela to the wilderness, unto the mount of the daughter of Zion.

Isaiah advises the Moabites who had fled southwards to Idumea, to send to the king of Judah the tribute of lambs. They had previously paid this tribute to Israel starting in the time of King David, but had stopped paying it (see 2 Kings 3:4–5). By restarting this practice, Moab would gain the favor and protection of Judah. Even more importantly, paying a tribute of lambs would teach Moab of the need of submitting to the Messiah (see Psalms 2:10–12, Rom. 12:1). The lambs would be sent to "the mount" or the temple in Jerusalem.

16:2 For it shall be, that, as a wandering bird cast out of the nest, so the daughters of Moab shall be at the fords of Arnon.

Arnon = "rushing stream"

"A wandering bird cast out of the nest" is bird that has just hatched and then is expelled from the nest. The children of Moab will be ill prepared for what is to come when they will be cast out of their home. The plight of a refugee is desperate, and the ones that suffer the cruelest fate are the young women. They will go to the "fords of Arnon," which is a boundary river of Moab, in order to escape out of the land.

16:3 Take counsel, execute judgment; make thy shadow as the night in the midst of the noonday; hide the outcasts; bewray not him that wandereth.

This is the message for the leaders of the refugees to do when they arrive in Zion. They are like someone in the brightness of noonday seeking the refuge of a cool mist at night. They will request asylum in Zion. The Jerusalem Bible renders their desire for others to "execute judgment" reads: "advise us what to do, decide for us." They want to be hid among the people and not extradited back to their enemy.

16:4 Let mine outcasts dwell with thee, Moab; be thou a covert to them from the face of the spoiler: for the extortioner is at an end, the spoiler ceaseth, the oppressors are consumed out of the land.

Even though this verse is awkwardly phrased, this second request is for a protective status for the refugees from Moab. They are to ask that Zion be a covert (a covering or disguise) for them. They seek protection against the extortioner, spoiler, and oppressor.

Security Found in Zion

16:5 And in mercy shall the throne be established: and he shall sit upon it in truth in the tabernacle of David, judging, and seeking judgment, and hasting righteousness.

Zion is not only a covert or protection, but is the destination for the spiritual refugee. Make no mistake about it, we are all spiritual refugees. We seek shelter from the heat of temptations. We want the promise of mercy, truth, judgment, and righteousness in our lives. In Zion, we find hope and peace. This verse is the center of the chiasmas in chapters 15 and 16 and is the focal point of these chapters. The most important point Isaiah wants us to understand in these chapters is that truth, judgment, and righteousness are found in Zion through Jesus Christ.

In the next few verses, the scene changes back to Moab and their wailing. Their wailing was not caused by a rejection from Zion but comes as a result of their pride. To enter Zion, Moab must submit to the King of Zion and they are unwilling to have Christ as their King. Their pride remains, and so does their fear and misery.

Moab's Pride

16:6 We have heard of the pride of Moab; he is very proud: even of his haughtiness, and his pride, and his wrath: but his lies shall not be so.

In verse 5 there are four words that describe what Moab could enjoy in Zion—mercy, truth, justice, and righteousness. In this verse there are five words that let us know what they choose instead—pride, very proud, haughtiness, pride, and wrath. Those with pride naturally paint themselves with flattering words but Moab's boasting, will not be allowed to stand.

Moab's Grief Explained

16:7 Therefore shall Moab howl for Moab, every one shall howl: for the foundations of Kirhareseth shall ye mourn; surely they are stricken.

Kirhareseth—literally, "a citadel of brick."

As a result of their pride, all hope of receiving sanctuary by the Jews will be in vain. Moab will be destroyed down to the "foundations." This means that when the houses will be pulled down, only the ruins of the foundations will remain.

16:8 For the fields of Heshbon languish, and the vine of Sibmah: the lords of the heathen have broken down the principal plants thereof, they are come even unto Jazer, they wandered through the wilderness: her branches are stretched out, they are gone over the sea.

Heshbon (Heb. *Cheshbôwn*)—Stronghold. A place east of the Jordan. Its exact location is not known.
Sibmah—"fragrance." Near Heshbon.
Jazer—"helped."

The cities mentioned in this verse are principal Moabite cities all connected with the wine industry and are mentioned here to indicate the industry's breadth. Isaiah also recounts that "her branches are stretched out, they are gone over the sea," which indicates that Moab's wine export business was regionally and perhaps even internationally known.

The lords of the heathen refer to those who have invaded Moab and destroyed the vines. As a result, the land languished, or in other words, was neglected and experienced a prolonged period of inactivity. Jazer was beyond the northern borders of Moab (see Numbers 12:32; Josh. 13:25) while the desert was to the east and the sea to the west. The languished land would cover all of the domain of Moab, from north to south, east to west.

The Lord's Grief

16:9 Therefore I will bewail with the weeping of Jazer the vine of Sibmah: I will water thee with my tears, O Heshbon, and Elealeh: for the shouting for thy summer fruits and for thy harvest is fallen.

The "I" in this verse refers to the Lord. In 15:5 God wept for Moab and He will weep with Moab. His tears will flow freely enough to be compared to the watering of the vineyards. Even though Moab has rejected God, He still loves them and is pained with their loss. God would love to be one who rejoices in a plentiful harvest of summer fruits, but such is not the case. That joy has past and only sorrow has been chosen.

16:10 And gladness is taken away, and joy out of the plentiful field; and in the vineyards there shall be no singing, neither shall there be shouting: the treaders shall tread out no wine in their presses; I have made their vintage shouting to cease.

All gladness, joy, singing, and shouts of victory are gone. This comes as a result of their pride in not accepting God's offering of assistance on His terms.

16:11 Wherefore my bowels shall sound like an harp for Moab, and mine inward parts for Kir-haresh.

Kir-haresh—"wall of potsherds." One of the two chief strongholds for Moab.

The bowels and the inward parts represent the emotional core of a person. In this verse, it is God who is in deep anguish for Moab and her people. When words can only fail you in expressing your emotions, you may turn to music to help explain how you feel. Even the harp is not enough to explain the sorrow God feels for these people.

16:12 And it shall come to pass, when it is seen that Moab is weary on the high place, that he shall come to his sanctuary to pray; but he shall not prevail.

This verse could be restated: "When Moab shall have appeared (before their false gods), when he is weary (with worthless rites and rituals to their false Gods), on the high place (usual places of sacrifice to false Gods), and shall come to his sanctuary (of the idol Chemosh on Mount Nebo) to pray, he shall not prevail." Moab's prayers to their false gods will have no effect.

Moab's Imminent Ruin

16:13 This is the word that the Lord hath spoken concerning Moab since that time.

This verse refers to other prophecies concerning Moab. Exodus 15:15 prophecies a time when the inhabitants of Moab will fear and have sorrow over their impending destruction. Numbers 21:29 provides a proverb concerning this future doom. But since "that time," a definite timeline for this destruction has been provided. This was given in Isaiah 15:5 and all this destruction will happen in three years from now.

16:14 But now the Lord hath spoken, saying, Within three years, as the years of an hireling, and the glory of Moab shall be contemned, with all that great multitude; and the remnant shall be very small and feeble.

Just as a hireling watches the clock waiting for their fixed term to expire, Moab can expect that in three years' time they will be destroyed. Everything that Moab has taken glory in will be dimmed. Only a small part of the people will remain and will have little power or influence. This will be fulfilled when the Assyrians led Israel into captivity.

Moab could never give up its pride. Pride prevented it from acquiring safety, security, and spirituality. Lasting peace is only found by the humble as they become closer to Christ. In our lives we too want the promise of mercy, truth, judgment, and righteousness. This is found in Christ. He has established Zion in our day where we can turn to for hope and peace.

ISAIAH CHAPTER 17

Be Mindful of the Rock of Thy Strength

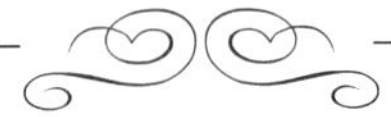

Chapter 17 is prophecy concerning Damascus (Syria) and its ally Samaria (Northern kingdom of Israel). In the fourth year of the reign of Ahaz, the Assyrian king Tiglath-pileser had carried away the people of Damascus to Kir (see 2 Kings 16:1–9). Ahaz will reign another 12 years. During his successor Hezekiah's rule, a further overthrow is foretold (Jeremiah 49:23, Zachariah 9:1). In the sixth year of Hezekiah's rule, Shalmaneser will carry away Israel from Samaria to Assyria (2 Kings 17:6, 18:10–11). Isaiah's prophecy in chapter 17 was given in the first years of Hezekiah's rule. The first three verses address Ephraim's alliance with Damascus. This alliance was made after they abandoned the security the Lord promises and chose to rely on the military power of another nation.

The Destruction of Damascus and Ephraim

17:1 The burden of Damascus. Behold, Damascus is taken away from being a city, and it shall be a ruinous heap.

The power and influence of Damascus will crumble.

17:2 The cities of Aroer are forsaken: they shall be for flocks, which shall lie down, and none shall make them afraid.

Aroer = "ruins"

There is no known city of Aroer in the area of Syria (Motyer, 156). Isaiah is building on verse 1 in stating that the cities of Aroer, that is, the cities round Aroer, will be cities of ruins, or a ruinous heap. "They" (ruined cities) will be uninhabited and will become a place where only flocks are kept.

17:3 The fortress also shall cease from Ephraim, and the kingdom from Damascus, and the remnant of Syria: they shall be as the glory of the children of Israel, saith the Lord of hosts.

The first part of this verse continues with the theme of the impending destruction. Their fortress (or strongholds) will be pulled down and destroyed. "Since Ephraim cannot be saved by seeking security in Damascus, neither can Damascus be helped by unbelieving Ephraim. The people of God cannot be made secure by worldly power nor, when they depart from sole reliance on the Lord, can they bring a blessing to the world" (Motyer, 156).

Verses 4–6 are the first of three "In that day" sections. The others begin in verses 7 and 9. Each section provides a description of the conditions in the day when Ephraim and Damascus will fall.

In That Day: A Lack of Food

17:4 And in that day it shall come to pass, that the glory of Jacob shall be made thin, and the fatness of his flesh shall wax lean.

In the day that Assyria will destroy Damascus (Syria) and Ephraim, the glory of Jacob, or the kingdom of Ephraim, and all that they rely on, will be "made thin." This glory is a false glory of quickly changing worldly power and prestige. They will become feeble, empty, and impoverished. Because of a lack of food, the people will become lean (famished or emaciated).

17:5 And it shall be as when the harvestman gathereth the corn, and reapeth the ears with his arm; and it shall be as he that gathereth ears in the valley of Rephaim.

Rephaim is a fertile plain at the southwest of Jerusalem toward Bethlehem. When it is time to harvest a crop, a harvestman will collect the standing grain "with his arm" so that he can cut it with the sickle in the other hand. Isaiah is comparing the inhabitants and wealth of Israel to ears of corn that will be swept away by an external force. Just like the timing of a harvest, it will be decided on when the time is right. After this event, there will only be a few ears of corn (inhabitants and wealth) left behind.

17:6 Yet gleaning grapes shall be left in it, as the shaking of an olive tree, two or three berries in the top of the uppermost bough, four or five in the outmost fruitful branches thereof, saith the Lord God of Israel.

In Old Testament times, what remains after the gleaners harvest a crop is left for the poor (see Deut. 24:19–20). Isaiah uses this imagery to again indicate that only a few poor people will be left "in it," or left in the land of Israel. Only "two or three" will be left "in the top," like the two or three olive berries left on the topmost boughs, indicates that this remainder is not worth taking the trouble to try to reach.

At That Day: Hope Remains in God

17:7 At that day shall a man look to his Maker, and his eyes shall have respect to the Holy One of Israel.

Man (Heb. *'âdam*)—Mankind.

This is the second "in that day" section and lets us know that there remains hope in God. Instead of trusting in their fortresses, they can put their trust in God after the harvest/gleaning in the previous verses. Isaiah uses the word "adam" and is translated "a man." This suggests that Isaiah is applying this hope more broadly than just to those who remain in Israel. There is always hope in God. As we trust in God, we look to our Maker. We are to "Look unto [Christ] in every thought; doubt not, fear not" (D&C 6:36). As we look to Christ, our doubts dissolve and our fears flee our hearts.

The eye is the window to the soul. The eye is symbolic of our reception of light, knowledge, insight, and revelation. The more we receive light, knowledge, insight, and revelation into our lives, the more respect we will have for the Holy One of Israel. The more you look towards Christ, the less you will look to false gods, and this is indicated in the next verse.

17:8 And he shall not look to the altars, the work of his hands, neither shall respect that which his fingers have made, either the groves, or the images.

The altars in this verse refers to incense alters used in the worship of the false god Baal. Any god that one creates by their own hands is a false god whether it be made of stone, wood, electronics, or metal. The groves referred to in this verse is a part of the worship of the gods Ashteroth (or Astarte the Assyrian queen of heaven) and Baal (or Bel the Assyrian king of heaven). In these groves, symbolical trees are often found in Assyrian inscriptions that represent the hosts of heaven ("Saba") that worship Ashteroth and Baal. Hence the expression images of the grove are these symbolic trees (see 2 Kings 21:7).

In That Day: Why Desolation Has Come

17:9 In that day shall his strong cities be as a forsaken bough, and an uppermost branch, which they left because of the children of Israel: and there shall be desolation.

Forsaken bough—what the axeman leaves behind after he cuts down the grove.

This is the third "In that day" reference that refers to the destruction caused by the Assyrians. When the Assyrians are done, the once strong cities will be broken and scattered like a forsaken bough. They will be small and weak like the uppermost branch on a tree. They (boughs and branches) will be left because of, or rather for the benefit of the children of Israel. God is leaving a remnant so Israel will remain in the land even though the people are weak and scattered.

17:10 Because thou hast forgotten the God of thy salvation, and hast not been mindful of the rock of thy strength, therefore shalt thou plant pleasant plants, and shalt set it with strange slips:

All this comes because the people have not remembered that one of the great attributes of God is salvation. Salvation only comes through God and in no other way. They have forgotten that God is the rock (stability, strength) on which we rely (see Deut. 32:15, 18). Instead of relying on the fortress rock, they plant beautiful plants that are sown from foreign seedlings. There is no defense in the perceived beauty of a false god. There is no spiritual strength coming from a false god that you may plant today in your heart but will quickly wilt, dry out, and become the dust of despair.

17:11 In the day shalt thou make thy plant to grow, and in the morning shalt thou make thy seed to flourish: but the harvest shall be a heap in the day of grief and of desperate sorrow.

In Alma 32, the word of God is compared to a seed. The seed comes from God. In this verse, the seed and plant is "thy plant." It is not God's. A person may spend considerable effort in the cultivation and encouragement in the worship of a false god. The phrase "in the morning" means "immediately after." So immediately after you plant the plant, it may grow and even flourish for a time. Tares will flourish for a time with the wheat, but there will come a time for the harvest.

The harvest of a god of electronics, ones-self (pride), or political correctness will always be worthless. It will be a heap of wasted time and effort. This day of expected gain and possession will become a day of grief and desperate sorrow.

After the imagery of the harvest, Isaiah turns in verses 12–14 to answer the question of who will actually rule the world and in the end, whose purposes will be accomplished. Isaiah will answer this question again in Isaiah 18:1–7.

17:12 Woe to the multitude of many people, which make a noise like the noise of the seas; and to the rushing of nations, that make a rushing like the rushing of mighty waters!

In Isaiah 17:12–18:7 the prophet will announce the sudden destruction of a great army in Judah (namely that of the Assyrian Sennacherib). The multitude of many people refers to the great army that Sennacherib will bring to destroy Israel. They will be so large that the noise of the army will be like the noise of the seas. Their motion will be steady and eroding like a powerful river swiftly moving towards the sea.

The Assyrian army destroyed cities all along their path to Jerusalem. In an effort to deprive the Assyrians of water, springs outside the city were blocked. Workers then dug a 533-meter tunnel to the Spring of Gihon, providing the city with fresh water. Additional siege preparations included fortification of the existing walls, construction of towers, and the erection of a new, reinforcing wall. The Assyrian army was camped next to Jerusalem and 2 Kings records that God destroyed 185,000 men in one night (see also Isaiah 10).

17:13 The nations shall rush like the rushing of many waters: but God shall rebuke them, and they shall flee far off, and shall be chased as the chaff of the mountains before the wind, and like a rolling thing before the whirlwind.

This is a prophecy that God will stand and fight for Jerusalem. The large Assyrian army will be compared to "chaff of the mountains." In the East, threshing floors would be in the open air on elevated places, so as to catch the wind in order to separate the chaff from the wheat. The winds would be stronger on the mountains. The Assyrian army will be blown away seemingly without difficulty away from Jerusalem. They will blow away like a "rolling thing" (tumbleweed) in a very strong windstorm.

17:14 And behold at eveningtide trouble; and before the morning he is not. This is the portion of them that spoil us, and the lot of them that rob us.

This prophecy will be fulfilled to the letter in the destruction of the Assyrian army. They will go to bed and "before morning" of the vast host that "at eveningtide" was such a terror ("trouble") to Judah will be destroyed.

Isaiah Chapter 18

The Gathering

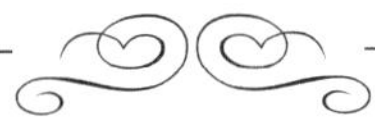

In this chapter, Isaiah answers the question of who will actually rule the world and in the end, whose purposes will be accomplished. His conclusion is similar to what he wrote at the end of chapter 17.

The Destruction of Damascus and Ephraim

18:1 Woe to the land shadowing with wings, which is beyond the rivers of Ethiopia:

This chapter starts off with the word "Woe." Most commentators suggest that "Lo," "Ho," "Alas," "Hark," or "Hail" would be more accurate, and they are almost unanimous in thinking that this is not a message of doom but of hope. It is a call for attention. Our attention should be on a land that is beyond the rivers of Ethiopia, or a land that is much further away from Jerusalem than is the African nation of Ethiopia. What land is Isaiah talking about? Joseph Fielding Smith explained that the land is America when he wrote:

> I will read from the 18th chapter of Isaiah because this has to do with this latter day work. I think I will present it all. The way it begins in the King James Version is: "Woe to the land shadowing with wings, which is beyond the rivers of Ethiopia." This is a mistranslation. In the Catholic Bible it reads: "Ah, land of the whirring of wings, beyond the rivers of Cush," and

> in Smith and Goodspeed's translation it reads: "Ah! Land of the buzzing of wings, which lies beyond the rivers of Ethiopia." The chapter shows clearly that no woe was intended, but rather a greeting, as indicated in these other translations. A correct translation would be, "Hail to the land in the shape of wings." Now, do you know of any land in the shape of wings? Think of your map. About twenty-five years ago one of the current magazines printed on the cover the American continents in the shape of wings, with the body of the bird between. I have always regretted that I did not preserve this magazine. Does not this hemisphere take the shape of wings; the spread out wings of a bird? (*Old Testament Student Manual*, 157)

The word "shadowing" means protecting or stretching out its wings to defend a feeble people, namely, the Hebrews. Wings are a symbol of the ability to move, or of protection and gathering. Isaiah is prophesying that Israel can look forward to that hope that America will bring as it protects and gathers Israel. Hyrum Smith said in April 1844, "The gathering will continue here [Nauvoo, Illinois] until the Temple is so far finished that the Elders can get their endowments; and after that the gathering will be from the nations to North and South America, which is the land of Zion. North and South America, are the symbols of the wings" (*History of the Church*, 6:322).

18:2 That sendeth ambassadors by the sea, even in vessels of bulrushes upon the waters, saying, Go, ye swift messengers, to a nation scattered and peeled, to a people terrible from their beginning hitherto; a nation meted out and trodden down, whose land the rivers have spoiled!

terrible (Heb. *ary yare'*)—feared
meted out (Heb. *qav qav*)—measured and secured
trodden down (Heb. *howbm mebuwcah*)—victorious
spoiled (Heb. *azb baza'*)—cut through

From America, the prophet sends forth his ambassadors. These ambassadors represent Jesus Christ. President Smith noted that the term "vessels of bulrushes" in this verse should read "vessels of speed," and that the "nation scattered and peeled" is Palestine. The land of Palestine was denuded or "peeled" of its forests under Turkish misrule. The ensign's being lifted up refers to the restoration of the gospel in America; ambassadors would then go from America to the nations of the earth to gather those people who are "scattered and peeled" (Smith, *Signs of the Times*, 46).

The abuse of the land of Palestine started in earnest in the 1920s. Between 1920 and 1924 there were nearly 3 million trees planted and since 1948, around 240 million trees have been planted in Israel (Revell, "Trees and Humans in the Holy Land").

President Joseph Fielding Smith summarized the beginnings of these reforestation efforts and applied them to the spoiled and trodden land of Palestine when he wrote:

> The work of afforestation began 40 years ago, when the first Jewish settlements were founded, but received a great impetus after the war, when, under the British mandate, greater opportunities for development were opened for Jews. The government department of agriculture has planted 1,285,062 trees during the past four years; the Palestine foundation fund, affiliated agencies of the World Zionist organization, 672,933 trees; the supreme Moslem council, 14,700; while the balance were planted by individuals, mostly settlers in the Jewish agricultural colonies.
>
> We read in the Scriptures of the great cedars of Lebanon, and the trees upon the mountains. These were swept off when the curse came upon the land, and the rains have washed down the soil into the valleys where the rivers have spoiled the land as Isaiah predicted. If you wish to read more about this curse which came upon Palestine, you will find it recorded in the 26th chapter of Leviticus, the 4th and 28th chapters of Deuteronomy, and many other places, where Moses and the prophets predicted that it would come. (Smith, *Signs of the Times*, 47–48)

President Smith summarized verses 1 and 2 in this way:

> America was discovered because the Lord willed it. The gospel was restored in America, rather than in some other land, because the Lord willed it. This is the land "shadowing with

> wings" spoken of by Isaiah that today is sending ambassadors by the sea to a nation scattered and peeled [Israel], which at one time was terrible in the beginning. Now that nation [Israel] is being gathered, and once again they shall be in favor with the Lord. (Smith, in Conference Report, April 1966, 14).

18:3 All ye inhabitants of the world, and dwellers on the earth, see ye, when he lifteth up an ensign on the mountains; and when he bloweth a trumpet, hear ye.

Elder Orson Pratt also identified the land of North and South America as the land spoken of in this verse, and he emphasized that the ensign mentioned in verse 3 was to go to all the world (see *Journal of Discourses*, 16:84–85). President Joseph Fielding Smith added that "The Lord calls upon all the world to take notice when this ensign is lifted upon the mountains, and He was to send ambassadors by vessels of great swiftness to this nation scattered and peeled, whose land the rivers had spoiled" (*Signs of the Times*, 48).

> This chapter is clearly a reference to the sending forth of the missionaries to the nations of the earth to gather again this people who are scattered and peeled. The ensign has been lifted upon the mountains, and the work of gathering has been going on for over one hundred years. No one understands this chapter, but the Latter-day Saints, and we can see how it is being fulfilled. (Smith, *Signs of the Times*, 48)

18:4 For so the Lord said unto me, I will take my rest, and I will consider in my dwelling place like a clear heat upon herbs, and like a cloud of dew in the heat of harvest.

In the first three verses, the Lord has sent His messengers from America into the world. Now the Lord watches from "my dwelling place" unobserved. He watches like the "clear heat" and like the "cloud of dew." Both are felt, observed, quiet, and often overlooked as common occurrences. It is a time of spiritual harvest. God is providing the needed heat and moisture to complete the ripening process before the harvest occurs.

In our lives we too can feel the warmth of the gospel. God's effects on us are like heat and moisture. It warms us and softens us. It sustains us and helps us, and also allows us to assist in the preparation of the Great Harvest which will occur at Christ's Second Coming.

18:5 For afore the harvest, when the bud is perfect, and the sour grape is ripening in the flower, he shall both cut off the sprigs with pruning hooks, and take away and cut down the branches.

It is the Lord who determines when it is time to harvest. We trust not only in God but in His timing. "Afore" or before the harvest comes, He will determine when the "sprigs" or undesired twigs and branches are cut off. He will prune the vineyard of the wicked and then the harvest is gathered. This pruning is comparable to the parable of the wheat and tares in Matthew 13.

Verse 6 should be taken together with verse 5. When the harvest comes, God reaps and leaves behind only what the birds and animals will get. Kings may think they will be the ones to get it all, but in the end, they will get nothing.

18:6 They shall be left together unto the fowls of the mountains, and to the beasts of the earth: and the fowls shall summer upon them, and all the beasts of the earth shall winter upon them.

After the Great Harvest of souls, the only thing remaining will be given to the beasts and fowls. The phrase that the fowls will "summer upon them" and the beasts will "winter upon them" indicates that this will not be a temporary harvest but will last all year long. This harvest will be complete.

This refers to one of the two great feasts yet to occur in the future. This feast is also mentioned in Ezekiel 39:4, 17 and in D&C 29:18–20. The other great feast will be held with the righteous saints and Christ in Adam-ondi-ahman (see D&C 116, Dan. 7:9–14, 21–27; 12:1–3).

18:7 In that time shall the present be brought unto the Lord of hosts of a people scattered and peeled, and from a people terrible from their beginning hitherto; a nation meted out and trodden under foot, whose land the rivers have spoiled, to the place of the name of the Lord of hosts, the mount Zion.

This verse reemphasizes what was taught in verse 2. "In that time," or the last days, the scattered people will be gathered by His messengers and brought again to the Lord as a present. President Joseph Smith indicated that the gift that Christ will be given is the gift of a righteous people who have been restored to the gospel truth (see *History of the Church,* 132). He will take them from nations of the earth and gather these "scattered and peeled" people to the temple, or the place that has the "name of the Lord of hosts" upon it. The mount in Zion.

ISAIAH CHAPTER 19

They Shall Know the Lord, and He Shall Heal Them

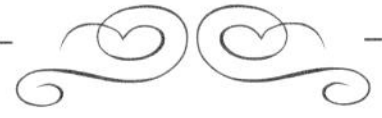

The 19th and 20th chapters of Isaiah are connected, but with an interval between. Egypt had been held by an Ethiopian dynasty—Sabacho, Sevechus, or Sabacho II, and Tirhakah—for forty or fifty years. Sevechus (called So, the ally of Hoshea, 2 Kings 17:4), retired from Lower Egypt on account of the rebellion of the priests along with the threat from the Assyrians on Lower Egypt. On his withdrawal, Sethos, one of the priestly caste, became their leader, having Tanis ("Zoan") or else Memphis as his capital, 718 BC; while the Ethiopians kept Upper Egypt, with Thebes as its capital, under Tirhakah. A third native dynasty was at Sais, in the west of Lower Egypt. This dynasty later belonged to Psammetichus, the first who admitted Greeks into Egypt and its armies. He was one of the dodecarchy, a number of petty kings between whom Egypt was divided, and by aid of foreign auxiliaries overcame the rest in 670 BC. Some have referred to this Psammetichus as being the "cruel Lord" referred to in Isaiah 19:4.

It is in this context that Isaiah 19 and 20 was given. Egypt was not a united nation, and Assyria was also having problems of its own. "Assyrian texts report a number of rebellions in the conquered territories and even in the newly conquered Samaria. Gaza and Damascus were reestablished as Assyrian provinces (See Pritchard, *Ancient Near Eastern Texts*, 285). The rebellious vassals of Assyria sought aid from Egypt. In the face of such action, the prophet Isaiah warned Judah against the unstable Egyptians. The prophet further warned of Assyria's defeat of weakened Egypt, now dominated by foreign (Ethiopian) rulers. The Babylonians were also rebelling, eventually causing Assyria to shift her attention and presence from the land of Israel" (See John Bright, *A History of Israel*, 263).

Elder Bruce R. McConkie indicated that this chapter deals with the local affairs of Judah, Assyria, and Egypt. It also prophesies salvation for Egypt in the day of restoration (see McConkie, "Ten Keys to Understanding Isaiah").

19:1 The burden of Egypt. Behold, the Lord rideth upon a swift cloud, and shall come into Egypt: and the idols of Egypt shall be moved at his presence, and the heart of Egypt shall melt in the midst of it.

There will come a time when the Lord will swiftly go into Egypt and will punish this nation. Even their idols of the bull, crocodile, Ra, etc., will be moved with fear at the presence of a mightier God.

19:2 And I will set the Egyptians against the Egyptians: and they shall fight every one against his brother, and every one against his neighbour; city against city, and kingdom against kingdom.

There will be a civil war—the upper against the lower parts of Egypt. The Septuagint replaces "kingdom against kingdom" with "nome against nome." Egypt was divided into forty-two nomes or districts. Historians refer to these civil wars as being between Apries and Amasis at the time of Nebuchadnezzar's invasion; as well as between Tachos, Nectanebus, and the Mendesians, just before Ochus subdued Egypt.

19:3 And the spirit of Egypt shall fail in the midst thereof; and I will destroy the counsel thereof: and they shall seek to the idols, and to the charmers, and to them that have familiar spirits, and to the wizards.

Charmers (Heb. *aṭ*)—softly, or literally "those making a faint sound."

Familiar spirits (Heb. *ôwb*)—a mumble, i.e. a water-skin (from its hollow sound); hence a necromancer who acts as a ventriloquist projecting their voice into a water-skin or a jar.

Wizard (Heb. *yidd*[e]*'ônîy*)—one who knows or utters words that delude people. A false prophet.

The famed spirit of Egypt was their wisdom. As a result of these civil wars, their wisdom will fail, and the counsel that wisdom brings will be destroyed. They will ask anyone but God for advice. They will seek answers from the dumb (idols) and the deceivers (charmers, familiar spirits, and wizards). Isaiah uses three different spiritual deceivers who deceive in slightly different ways. The charmer uses personal appeal and the victim's vanity to softly pull them into their deception. The familiar spirit seeks to imitate the faint sounds that are attributed to the spirits of the dead. Hence, the familiar spirit attempts to attach its deception to a trusted source like a close family member who has passed away. The wizard pretends to have authority to speak and deceives publicly.

Isaiah uses three types of deceivers to symbolically represent how they're fully turning toward a fullness of deception. Whether the source is knowing or unknowing, the intent is the same: to deceive all so that they no longer have God as their source. Each deception in some way imitates the Spirit of God but is designed to delude, or cause the people to believe something that is not true.

19:4 And the Egyptians will I give over into the hand of a cruel Lord; and a fierce king shall rule over them, saith the Lord, the Lord of hosts.

As a result of the civil war, Egypt will be given a dictator who will be a "cruel Lord." Historians make reference to three different people who could have been the cruel Lord referred to in this verse. First, it could refer to the Persian King Cambyses (reigned 530–522 BC), son of Cyrus the great and conquered Egypt in 525 BC. The second was Ochus (reigned 358–338 BC) and was noted for his "fierce cruelty" as he defeated Nectanebo II, the Pharaoh of Egypt, in 343 BC. The third is Psammetichus (reigned 664–610 BC) and brought into Egypt Greek and other foreign mercenaries to subdue the other eleven princes of Egypt into a united empire.

Primary Effect on Egypt of Little to No Water in the Nile River

19:5 And the waters shall fail from the sea, and the river shall be wasted and dried up.

The sea referred to in this verse is the Nile. The drying up of the Nile is a figurative expression of a coming economic collapse. The Nile does not need to dry up for this to happen. It just does not rise to a level where it will water the crops of Egypt. When it fails to rise high enough the result will be a famine in the land. Records at Cairo have been kept of the daily rise of the Nile's water. It overflows in August and waters the land so crops can grow. Ancient records indicate that if it rises to a height less than twelve cubits (18 feet), it will not overflow the land, and famine must be the result. So, also, when it rises higher than sixteen (24 feet) the waters are not able to drain off in time for seeds to be planted.

19:6 And they shall turn the rivers far away; and the brooks of defence shall be emptied and dried up: the reeds and flags shall wither.

As a result of the Nile not overflowing, "they shall turn the rivers," or it would be better written that "the streams shall become putrid." That means that the artificial streams made for irrigation will become stagnant and offensive when the waters fail. This will cause the brooks (canals) to dry up.

19:7 The paper reeds by the brooks, by the mouth of the brooks, and every thing sown by the brooks, shall wither, be driven away, and be no more.

Paper reeds (Heb. *ârâh*)—a naked (i.e. level) plot of land.

Normally the land closest to the canals will be the lushest and well watered. Without the water from the Nile, the land will be naked—there will be no plants growing. Everything that is planted will wither away. The water of the Nile is referred to three times in this verse and this stresses the enormity of the calamity.

Secondary Effects on the Economy of Egypt

19:8 The fishers also shall mourn, and all they that cast angle into the brooks shall lament, and they that spread nets upon the waters shall languish.

Without the overflow of the water of the Nile, there will be three secondary effects on Egypt's economy. First, the major industry of fishing will be ruined.

19:9 Moreover they that work in fine flax, and they that weave networks, shall be confounded.

The next consequence of little to no water in the Nile is that the great linen economy will be severely impacted. Egypt will lack the flax needed to create their luxurious product. Scholars note that the linen from Egypt has five hundred forty (or two hundred seventy double) threads in every inch. It was the finest and most dense cloth of its time. In comparison, today's fabric, like the Cambric weave that has been "preferred for ecclesiastical wear, fine shirts, underwear, shirt frills, cravats, collars and cuffs, handkerchiefs, and infant wear" (Steele, 217), has between 100 and a hundred and sixty threads per inch.

19:10 And they shall be broken in the purposes thereof, all that make sluices and ponds for fish.

Sluices are dams. Naturally those employed in making dams and ponds to capture the overflow of the Nile will not be able to earn a livelihood and is the third of these secondary effects of the Nile not overflowing its banks in August. Jerusalem Bible reads: "The weavers will be dismayed and all the workmen dejected."

Political Collapse of Egypt Foretold

In verses 11–13 there is a repetition of several words to emphasize the enormity of the effect on Egypt. Isaiah will use "wise" three times, "princes" three times, "counsel" (noun and verb) three times, "Egypt" four times, and "fool" occurs both as a noun and a verb (Motyer, 165). All this indicates that their wisdom will fail. Their princes will not be able to rule. No council or wisdom will be found. Egypt will be left with fools to mislead them.

19:11 Surely the princes of Zoan are fools, the counsel of the wise counsellors of Pharaoh is become brutish: how say ye unto Pharaoh, I am the son of the wise, the son of ancient kings?

The Greeks called Zoan the city of Tanis and was in Lower Egypt. It was one of the Egyptian towns nearest to Palestine (see Num. 13:22). The priests in Zoan boasted that they were descendants of wise and royal ancestors. These priests were the usual "counsellors" of the Egyptian king. They were generally chosen from the priestly caste, or, if from the warrior caste, they were admitted into the sacred order and were called a priest. These priests are, therefore, meant by the expression, "son of the wise, and of ancient kings." They have no council for Pharaoh. Not only the false gods mentioned in verse 3 are unable to give council, the wisest of Egypt's wise are also unable to do so. Wisdom and counsel come from the true God.

19:12 Where are they? where are thy wise men? and let them tell thee now, and let them know what the Lord of hosts hath purposed upon Egypt.

Even though they can boast of knowing things, they do not know what really matters. They do not know God, and His son Jesus Christ. Coming to know the only true God and Jesus Christ is to know of eternal truths and eternal life (see John 17:3).

19:13 The princes of Zoan are become fools, the princes of Noph are deceived; they have also seduced Egypt, even they that are the stay of the tribes thereof.

Noph was also called Moph, or in Greek, Memphis. It was on the western bank of the Nile and was capital of Lower Egypt. It was the residence of the kings and was ruled by the military caste. So in writing "they also are deceived," Isaiah indicates that they deceive themselves in believing that their country is secure from an Assyrian invasion. Their self-deception will cause them to behave like fools having lost their ability to lead the people.

19:14 The Lord hath mingled a perverse spirit in the midst thereof: and they have caused Egypt to err in every work thereof, as a drunken man staggereth in his vomit.

In everything that matters most, Egypt has not understood what God is doing. They are as helpless as a "drunken man."

19:15 Neither shall there be any work for Egypt, which the head or tail, branch or rush, may do.

There is nothing Egypt can do to escape this difficulty. The head (Egypt's leaders) and tail (the followers) will be unable to be productive in either the quality or the quantity of their work.

The Healing of Egypt in the Days of the Restoration

19:16 In that day shall Egypt be like unto women: and it shall be afraid and fear because of the shaking of the hand of the Lord of hosts, which he shaketh over it.

When their day of this judgment comes, they will be helpless and timid. The "Shanking of the hand of the Lord" refers to His judgments by means of the coming invaders.

19:17 And the land of Judah shall be a terror unto Egypt, every one that maketh mention thereof shall be afraid in himself, because of the counsel of the Lord of hosts, which he hath determined against it.

Isiah prophecies that the land of Judah (Israel) will be a terror to Egypt. Many historians have tried to put the fulfillment of this verse into the past, but the first time that Israel became a terror to Egypt during or after the time of Isaiah was in 1967. Between June 5–10, 1967 Israel fought the neighboring states of Egypt, Jordan, and Syria. During this short war, Israel destroyed the entire Egyptian air force and inflicted heavy losses on the Egyptian army. Israel captured the Gaza strip and the Sinai Peninsula from Egypt, the West Bank from Jordan, and the Golan Heights from Syria. This verse moves this prophecy to our days, the days of the restoration of the gospel of Jesus Christ. The gospel must be restored before the people of Egypt will.

19:18 In that day shall five cities in the land of Egypt speak the language of Canaan, and swear to the Lord of hosts; one shall be called, The city of destruction.

Some have labeled the language of Canaan as being Phoenician and Hebrew. Others emphasize that Canaan was the grandfather of the Palestinians who today speak Arabic. Most of the population of Egypt today speaks Egyptian Arabic which replaced Coptic as the language of daily life after the Muslim conquest. Coptic is still used by Coptic Christians in their liturgy.

Hebrew was the language of the prophets of the Old Testament, and of the apostles in the New Testament. Five is symbolic of God's grace, goodness, and favor toward mankind. In this verse, Isaiah is prophesying that the language of God will be spoken in the last days in a portion of Egypt. There will be cities in Egypt in the last days where faithful Saints will have gathered and will covenant with the Lord to do His will.

One of the Dead Sea Scrolls changes "City of Destruction" to "City of Sun." This change in the translation is favored by many modern scholars of Isaiah. The City of the Sun is the Egyptian city of Heliopolis, and it is likely that the original Hebrew was making a pun: The City of the Sun (*heres*) becomes the City of Destruction (*hheres*). Heliopolis is today a suburb of Cairo. In Egypt today there are over 10 million Christians.

Salvation for Egypt in the Days of the Restoration

Salvation for Egypt may begin with five cities, but it will spread from the center of the land to the border (vs. 19). Their conversion to the gospel of Jesus Christ will come through five acts that will bring them to God. First, they will be reconciled at the altar of the Lord and make a covenant to remember Him and become His people (vs. 19). Second, the Egyptians will have a personal relationship to God through prayer (vs. 20). Third, they will receive revelation from God and they will "know the Lord" (vs. 21). Fourth, they will act on this knowledge by making and keeping covenants (vows) as well as serving the Lord (vs. 21). Lastly, they will be chastened and healed as they "return even to the Lord" (vs. 22).

19:19 In that day shall there be an altar to the Lord in the midst of the land of Egypt, and a pillar at the border thereof to the Lord.

In the last days there will be a place of worship, a true altar, built to the Lord in Egypt. This is probably not an altar for sacrifice but will be a place for reconciliation with God. They will commit to serve the Lord and this commitment will be manifest as they chose to covenant to follow Christ. It will be a "pillar" for a memorial and for worship. This also recalls the purpose of the pillar set up in Joshua 22 that was to remind of God and serve as a testimony that they have become God's people.

19:20 And it shall be for a sign and for a witness unto the Lord of hosts in the land of Egypt: for they shall cry unto the Lord because of the oppressors, and he shall send them a saviour, and a great one, and he shall deliver them.

When the day comes that the faithful will cry to God because of their oppression, God will send them a Saviour, a great one who will deliver them from their oppressors. Prayer will open the way for them to have a personal relationship with God and will allow them to receive personal revelation in their lives.

19:21 And the Lord shall be known to Egypt, and the Egyptians shall know the Lord in that day, and shall do sacrifice and oblation; yea, they shall vow a vow unto the Lord, and perform it.

In the last days, Egyptians will come to know Christ. They will worship Him. They will make covenants with Him, and then "shall do" or keep the covenants. They will perform what they have promised to do and become.

19:22 And the Lord shall smite Egypt: he shall smite and heal it: and they shall return even to the Lord, and he shall be intreated of them, and shall heal them.

"For whom the Lord loveth he correcteth; even as a father the son in whom he delighteth" (Proverbs 3:12). The Lord's chastening of His people will assist them in the healing process. The Lord will heal Egypt through the truth of the gospel of Jesus Christ, their return to Him, and through the promises of His covenants.

Salvation Spreads beyond Egypt

19:23 In that day shall there be a highway out of Egypt to Assyria, and the Assyrian shall come into Egypt, and the Egyptian into Assyria, and the Egyptians shall serve with the Assyrians.

The spreading of the gospel and its covenant is the focus of verses 23–25. In Egypt, it started out with 5 cities (vs. 18) and then spread to the whole nation (vs. 19). The gospel taught in Egypt is the same that is taught throughout the region, and the world. The highway in this verse starts in Egypt and ends in Assyria and goes right through Israel. Israel is the family name associated with the covenant. Israel made a covenant with God. The highway of peace can only be established through a covenant with God. The only way to peace comes through the gospel.

19:24 In that day shall Israel be the third with Egypt and with Assyria, even a blessing in the midst of the land:

There will be an alliance between Israel, Egypt, and Assyria and that alliance will come through the Lord. The covenant of Israel will be in the middle of them and will be a blessing to both of these great nations.

19:25 Whom the Lord of hosts shall bless, saying, Blessed be Egypt my people, and Assyria the work of my hands, and Israel mine inheritance.

The faithful are rewarded. Whether they live in Egypt, Israel, or Assyria. In the last days that is one of the great messages to the entire world. In Christ you are "blessed" to be "[His] people," you are in "[His] hands," and you are "[His] inheritance." It does not matter where you live, or what the past has been, each individual, and each nation, is capable of being blessed by the Lord through the gospel of Jesus Christ. Peace will only come to individuals or nations when we act as true Christians.

ISAIAH CHAPTER 20

Where Can We Go for Help and How Will We Escape?

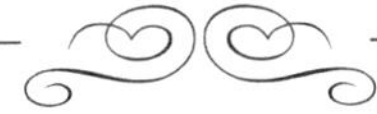

CHAPTER 20 ALSO DEALS WITH FUTURE EVENTS THAT WOULD SOON OCCUR in Egypt, Assyria, and Israel. Verse 1 starts with the Assyrian campaign against Ashdod which took place in 711 BC. "For the previous four years Egypt had been unsettling the western Palestinian states with promises of aid should they rise against Assyria, and by 713 BC, Ashdod was in rebellion. As a consequence, Assyria deposed its king and put another in his place, but Ashdod was not to be deterred. The new king was ousted and (with the evil genius of Egypt looming in the background) envoys were sent to call Judah, Edom, and Moab to join the rising. Since Hezekiah suffered no Assyrian reprisals at this time, he probably held aloof; it could even be that he was swayed by Isaiah's views as expressed in chapter 18. But Ashdod did not escape. Sargon II, now at the height of his power, sent his supreme commander to wage the campaign. Ashdod was defeated and became an Assyrian province. After this defeat Egypt reneged on its promises to Judah, Edom, and Moab (Motyer, 170).

This prophecy is set after Isaiah spoke of Egypt becoming God's people and being healed. Isaiah records this prophecy when Egypt and Assyria were in the height of their powers. He teaches that even though a nation may be a world power, they are subject to the Lord. What the Lord has spoken will occur. It always has, and it always will in the future.

20:1 In the year that Tartan came unto Ashdod, (when Sargon the king of Assyria sent him,) and fought against Ashdod, and took it;

Ashdod = "powerful." A major Philistine city on the Mediterranean Sea.

The year spoke of in this verse is 711 BC. The supreme commander of the Assyrian army is Tartan (i.e. second to the king, see 2 Kings 18:17). Sargon II reigned from 722–705 BC and was considered one of the greatest kings of Assyria.

20:2 At the same time spake the Lord by Isaiah the son of Amoz, saying, Go and loose the sackcloth from off thy loins, and put off thy shoe from thy foot. And he did so, walking naked and barefoot.

Sackcloth was a loose outer garment of coarse dark haircloth worn by mourners (2 Samuel 3:31) and by prophets, fastened at the waist by a girdle (Matt. 3:4; 2 Ki. 1:8; Zec. 13:4). Isaiah is asked to take off his clothes made of sackcloth and he does so. He is a living object lesson and walks around dressed like a slave for three years. The Lord explains why in the next two verses.

20:3 And the Lord said, Like as my servant Isaiah hath walked naked and barefoot three years for a sign and wonder upon Egypt and upon Ethiopia;

Isaiah had been acting out his message for three years. The phrase "naked and barefoot" mentioned three times in the section, emphasizes the Lord's command to Isaiah to remove his clothing. It is probable that Isaiah removed only his upper garment, which would have made only the upper portion of his body bare. The Assyrians forced their captives to march naked and barefoot to humiliate them, and the naked and barefoot Isaiah prophesied of the time when Egypt and Ethiopia, as Assyria's captives, would be forced to walk naked. In a spiritual sense, naked and barefoot represents the way we stand without the Atonement, "uncovered" before the Lord, for the Hebrew term for atonement (*kapar*) signifies a covering.

During this time there had been intense anti-Assyrian diplomacy by the Egyptians (Motyer, 171). The people were left to wonder what Isaiah's message meant, and what it portended. It was a three years' sign, that is, a sign that a three years' calamity would come on Egypt and Ethiopia. It would also serve as a "wonder" or rather an omen or threat of what would happen in the future. Egypt and Ethiopia would be stripped of their power and prestige. In three years' time, Assyria would overrun Egypt.

20:4 So shall the king of Assyria lead away the Egyptians prisoners, and the Ethiopians captives, young and old, naked and barefoot, even with their buttocks uncovered, to the shame of Egypt.

Isaiah predicts the sad sight of captives being humiliated and deported. This happened after the battle of Eltekeh in 701 BC. Belzoni, the prolific Italian explorer and pioneer archaeologist of Egyptian antiquities says that captives are found represented thus on Egyptian monuments (see also Isa. 47:2–3; Nah. 3:5, 8–9).

20:5 And they shall be afraid and ashamed of Ethiopia their expectation, and of Egypt their glory.

"They" are the Philistine allies of Egypt who trusted that they would get help against Assyria. This serves as a warning to Israel that Egypt will not help you. You cannot expect protection from a military power. Protection comes from God.

20:6 And the inhabitant of this isle shall say in that day, Behold, such is our expectation, whither we flee for help to be delivered from the king of Assyria: and how shall we escape?

This question could be restated and said in all ages: "Where can we go for help to be delivered from our enemy: and how will we escape?" The solution is simple. Christ. He alone can help. He alone can save. He alone can save us from the greatest of our enemies—death and sin.

ISAIAH CHAPTER 21

Lasting Safety and Security Are Not Found in Military Power, but in Christ

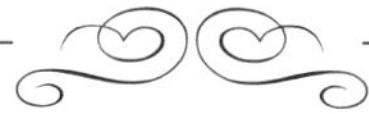

THIS CHAPTER FOCUSES ON THE FUTURE OF BABYLON. IT IS A MESSAGE OF prophecy and doom for the great kingdom of Babylon and is a vision that causes Isaiah great pain and distress (see verse 3).

> 21:1 The burden of the desert of the sea. As whirlwinds in the south pass through; so it cometh from the desert, from a terrible land.

The phrase the "desert of the sea" refers to Babylon. The capital was located in a dry and dusty plain and had the Euphrates River running through it. In the spring the waters of the Euphrates would overflow and flood the entire plain. As a result, Babylon sat both in a desert and at time on a sea. When the south wind blows on Babylon, they first go over the deserts of Arabia. These hot and dry winds were often fierce because their course flowed over an unbroken plain (see Job 1:19).

> 21:2 A grievous vision is declared unto me; the treacherous dealer dealeth treacherously, and the spoiler spoileth. Go up, O Elam: besiege, O Media; all the sighing thereof have I made to cease.

The severity of the events shown Isaiah in this vision is difficult for him to view. The treacherous dealer in this verse is Babylon. Dealing treacherously refers to the military stratagem employed by Cyrus in taking Babylon. In essence, Isaiah states that Babylon is going to be repaid for its treachery with treachery. The moral instability of the world is often repaid in kind. What comes around will go around for these morally bankrupt nations. This prophecy will be fulfilled in 588 BC, about 200 years after Isaiah lived.

Elam was a province of Persia and the original place of the Persian's settlement (see Gen. 10:22) and was east of the Euphrates. The name "Persia" was not in use until the Babylonian captivity and the name Persia means a "horseman." It was Cyrus who first trained the Persians in horsemanship that lead to that name.

21:3 Therefore are my loins filled with pain: pangs have taken hold upon me, as the pangs of a woman that travaileth: I was bowed down at the hearing of it; I was dismayed at the seeing of it.

> The pain caused by the vision given to Isaiah was so intense that its descriptive words in Hebrew portray his condition to be more than mere sorrow: "Chalchalah [Hebrew for pain] is the contortion produced by cramp, as in Nahum ii. 11; tzirim [Hebrew for pangs] is the word properly applied to the pains of childbirth; na avah [Hebrew for bowed down] means to bend, or bow one's self, and is also used to denote a convulsive utterance of pain; bahal [Hebrew for dismayed] indicates that Isaiah was disturbed, dismayed, terrified, anxious. (Keil, 7:1:379).

Similar to how ancient Babylon was destroyed, modern day Babylon, a symbol of wickedness, will be destroyed at the Second Coming of the Lord. While faithful Saints look forward to the Second Coming, Isaiah sees and describes the hopelessness of the wicked at that same day. He does not take any joy in the wicked's suffering. Suffering of any kind pains his soul.

21:4 My heart panted, fearfulness affrighted me: the night of my pleasure hath he turned into fear unto me.

"*Te ah*" (Hebrew for "panted") denotes a feverish and irregular beating of the pulse. The darkness of evening and night, in which the prophet found so much pleasure [Heb. *cheshek*—delight, desire or pleasure] and always longed for is symbolic of the judgment of the wicked at the Second Coming. What Isaiah had longed for, had hoped for, and had prayed for, now includes a horrible vision. That day is truly dreadful for the wicked.

21:5 Prepare the table, watch in the watchtower, eat, drink: arise, ye princes, and anoint the shield.

"Prepare the table" refers to getting ready for a feast in Babylon. In Babylon they are complacent and are choosing to be totally unaware of what awaits them. During this feast the guests were to be watched over in security as the city's watchtowers were manned. But Isaiah raises an alarm and calls on the princes to "arise." Their previous efforts to prepare to use their shields by adding oil to its leather so that it would not become hard and crack must now be used.

It was during such a feast that Cyrus opened the dykes made by Semiramis to confine the Euphrates to one channel and suffered them to overflow the country, so that he could enter Babylon by the channel of the river. Cyrus will enter Babylon through this channel and bypass the extensive defenses that surround the city.

21:6 For thus hath the Lord said unto me, Go, set a watchman, let him declare what he seeth.

God's direction to Isaiah to set a watchman to "declare" what he sees. Four verses later (verse 10), Isaiah himself is represented as the one who saw and then "declared." In verse 6 the prophet positions himself so that he can view what needs to be seen. In verse 7 the prophet foretells what he will see and he describes this faithfulness in doing his duty in verse 8. When the prophet sees what he had foretold (verse 9), he then reports that Babylon the great has fallen. So it is with prophets in our day. They are in position to see the enemy's forces and they tell us of the spiritual attacks that are being planned against us. They are faithful and what they prophecy will always come to pass.

President Harold B. Lee used these verses to show what a prophet sees and understands about the power of Satan and his unseen hosts. He stated:

> In a revelation to the Prophet Joseph Smith the Lord said that Satan drew after him a third part of the spirits whom God created, and that they with Satan became the force in the world to try to destroy the work of righteousness. That power was spoken of by Isaiah in a vision which he received which he called a grievous vision, in which it was said: "Set a watchman on the tower to tell what he seeth and report the coming of horsemen and chariots," but a voice spoke out of Mount Seir saying, "Watchman, what of the night," suggesting that, more to be feared than the enemies that could be perceived with the physical senses or could be seen by physical eyes were the powers of darkness that came unseen by physical eyes.
>
> That same thought was in the mind of the Master, no doubt, when he said: "And fear not them which kill the body, but are not able to kill the soul; but rather fear him which is able to destroy both soul and body in hell" (Matthew 10:28).
>
> The Apostle Paul seemed to understand very clearly this same power when he declared: "For we wrestle not against flesh and blood, but against principalities, against powers, against the rulers of the darkness of this world, against spiritual wickedness in high places" (Eph. 6:12). (Lee, in Conference Report, October 1949, 56)

21:7 And he saw a chariot with a couple of horsemen, a chariot of asses, and a chariot of camels; and he hearkened diligently with much heed:

"The verse is (lit.) 'When he sees a mounted troop, pairs of horses, a mounted troop on donkeys, a mounted troop on camels . . . '. M. S. Seale has pointed out that 'Arabian nomads, preparing to go into battle, rode one mount, whether camel or horse, and trailed another—usually their best mare—which they mounted just before flight'" (Motyer, 175). Isaiah is seeing an invading army approaching and is about to give a warning in verse 8.

Isaiah's reaction is impressive. He "hearkened diligently with much heed." To "hearken" means to listen; to give respectful attention; to give heed to. In Chinese there are several characters that make up the verb "to hearken." These characters are (1) ear, (2) you, (3) eyes, (4) undivided attention, and (5) heart. This suggests that with your eyes, you ears, and your heart you must give undivided attention. The Chinese character paints the aspects of active listening very well.

21:8 And he cried, A lion: My Lord, I stand continually upon the watchtower in the daytime, and I am set in my ward whole nights:

"And he cried, A Lion" is literally "And the lookout is A Lion." The point in comparing the prophet to "a lion" is the same as in Rev. 10:3. It refers to the loudness of the cry. Like a lion the prophet is also vigilant. The lion's eyelids are short, so that, even when asleep, he seems to be on the watch, awake; hence he was painted on doors of temples as the symbol of watchfulness, guarding the place. The prophet is diligent to do his duty to God and the people.

21:9 And, behold, here cometh a chariot of men, with a couple of horsemen. And he answered and said, Babylon is fallen, is fallen; and all the graven images of her gods he hath broken unto the ground.

The men in this verse are riding together in the chariot. They are returning home with a victory in hand. Babylon, its wickedness, morals, ideology, philosophies, and atrocities are shattered. Its gods are broken and lie scattered on the ground. This refers not only to the historical event, but to one of the greatest events of history—the Second Coming of the Lord.

21:10 O my threshing, and the corn of my floor: that which I have heard of the Lord of hosts, the God of Israel, have I declared unto you.

> Threshing (Heb *m^{e}dushshâh*)—a threshing, i.e. (concretely and figuratively) of a down-trodden people.
>
> Corn (Heb. *ben*)—son of.

Isaiah now concludes the first section of this chapter and his report of the dire message of the destruction of Babylon and all that it stands for. The message focus on "my threshing" and "my floor." Isaiah has reported this to Israel and to King Hezekiah. He knows that his people are downtrodden. Like corn that has gone through the threshing process, they are to be taken away from the field of Israel, crushed, and taken captive to Babylon. But the message is also clear that they are on "my," or the Lord's, floor. His is still in control even in our times of greatest despair.

Prophecy Concerning Edom (Dumah)

21:11 The burden of Dumah. He calleth to me out of Seir, Watchman, what of the night? Watchman, what of the night?

Dumah (Heb. *Dûwmâh*)—silence.

Dumah was a son of Ishmael (Gen. 25:14) and is the name of a town in Edom. Isaiah uses the city Dumah to represent not only a country (Edom), but also his silence on the prophecy of the future concerning this nation. This prophecy reflects a nation that is just trying to "hold on" to the night as time passes. They ask, "What of the night?" Or in other words, how much time is left? And they ask it multiple times as they try to "hold on." Today, these are a class of people that are not necessarily trying to do well, nor are they trying to change their lives. They are self-absorbed and ignorant of how much time remains until the Second Coming. They are simply trying to "hold on" to what time they have left.

21:12 The watchman said, The morning cometh, and also the night: if ye will enquire, inquire ye: return, come.

Isaiah indicates that the morning of deliverance is coming for Israel, but so is "the night of darkness wherein there can be no labor performed" (Alma 34:33). There is also an invitation here to all of Edom, or to all of the world. If you want to inquire about the light of the gospel, then first enquire and that will lead you to return back to God. The way is open for all to come home.

Prophecy That Arabia Would Be Overrun by a Foreign Foe within a Year

21:13 The burden upon Arabia. In the forest in Arabia shall ye lodge, O ye travelling companies of Dedanim.

Forest (Heb. *ya'ar*)—from an unused root probably meaning to thicken with verdure; a region of thick underwood, rugged and inaccessible.

Dedanim = "low country." A city in North Arabia.

There are no forests in Arabia but there are regions of thick underwood. It is mostly inaccessible. Isaiah is prophesying of a time when the inhabitants of Arabia would flee to the scanty shelter anywhere they could find it. They will be coming in a time of distress, fleeing for safety. This prophesy was likely fulfilled in 715 BC when Sargon II campaigned against the tribes between Tema (see vs. 14) and the Gulf of Aqabah. In 703 BC the Arabs joined in the campaign but were conquered by Sennacherib.

21:14 The inhabitants of the land of Tema brought water to him that was thirsty, they prevented with their bread him that fled.

Tema was an oasis city and a center for caravan routes a hundred miles south of Elath and two hundred miles east of the Red Sea in Arabia. The fugatives (those who flee) mentioned in the previous verse coming from Dedanim, were in need of food and water. Isaiah is encouraging the inhabitants of Tema to be compassionate to these refugees and provide for their needs. Even though their immediate needs are provided for, they will not find safety from the swords and bows mentioned in the next verse.

21:15 For they fled from the swords, from the drawn sword, and from the bent bow, and from the grievousness of war.

These fugitives fled "for" or as a result of the swords that were drawn either against them or because they were caught in the middle of the conflict.

21:16 For thus hath the Lord said unto me, Within a year, according to the years of an hireling, and all the glory of Kedar shall fail:

The prophecy is simple, within a year, all of the pomp and glory of Kedar (Arabia) will be gone. Kedar was a wandering tribe (see Psalms 120:5). Kedar is representative of the land where they wandered—Arabia in general.

21:17 And the residue of the number of archers, the mighty men of the children of Kedar, shall be diminished: for the Lord God of Israel hath spoken it.

The remaining archers will be diminished (or to be made small or few). There will be little power left in Kedar and only a few survivors who will remain.

This chapter notes that even though other gentiles will show mercy to the refugees, there is no safety for any of them in other gentile nations. There is only lasting safety and security in Jesus Christ.

ISAIAH CHAPTER 22

Security and Peace Come Only through God

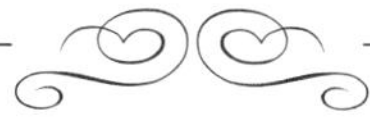

This chapter prophecies on the future of Jerusalem and on the future of two of its inhabitants—Shebna and Eliakim. Earlier chapters of Isaiah had focused on northern Israel and on their apostasy from the way of God. Now Isaiah focuses on Jerusalem's loss of faith in God, and their reliance in themselves (verses 1–14). He will condemn the individual (Shebna) who is only concerned with security in worldliness (verses 15–19), and will also condemn looking for the security in the world for others (Eliakim) through worldliness. You cannot find security in worldliness for a city (Jerusalem) and individual (Shebna) or for your family (Eliakim) without God. Security and peace only come through God (See Motyer, 179–180).

The Defense of Jerusalem—A Defense without God

In the first four verses of this chapter there is a stark contrast between the people and the prophet: they rejoice, but he weeps.

> This is because he sees what they do not see: death, defection and capture (2b-3), in fact nothing less than (lit.) "the destruction of the daughter of my people" (4). Verse 5 (beginning with "For") adds the further explanation that this is a special "day of the Lord." Are we to believe that such a day had come and

> gone without the populace noticing it? Is not Isaiah in principle saying, "If you could see coming what I see coming, there would be no rejoicing"? Such a forward view makes the reference to Elam intelligible. Isaiah has long known that Jerusalem will fall to some foe, though not to Assyria. It was revealed to him at the time of the Babylonian visit (chapter 39) that Babylon would be the destroyer. This truth is here veiled by referring to Babylon's remoter ally, Elam, and to the unidentifiable Kir in verse 6. (Motyer, 181)

22:1 The burden of the valley of vision. What aileth thee now, that thou art wholly gone up to the housetops?

"The valley of vision" spoken of here is the Kidron Valley. Kidron is the largest valley in Jerusalem and Gethsemane is a part of this valley. From the top of the valley, you can overlook a large part of Jerusalem. In Isaiah's day the people of Jerusalem would climb on their rooftop in the evening to cool down and relax. It also became a custom in ancient Israel to go to the rooftop to mourn and to celebrate (Jer. 48:38).

22:2 Thou that art full of stirs, a tumultuous city, a joyous city: thy slain men are not slain with the sword, nor dead in battle.

> Stirs (Heb. *teshu'ah*)—noise
> Tumultuous (Heb. *hâmâh*)—to make a loud sound, noise, or roar.

Jerusalem is full of noise. A lot of noise. It is not a sound associated with sorrow—but with joy. Why are they so happy? Why are they celebrating on the housetops? The people of Jerusalem are seeing their condition as something to celebrate over. They have full confidence in their security because they are well defended with swords. They don't see their situation the same as the prophet will see it. Isaiah sees what will happen to the men of the city when they are attacked by Nebuchadnezzar in Zedekiah's reign.

22:3 All thy rulers are fled together, they are bound by the archers: all that are found in thee are bound together, which have fled from far.

Isaiah sees the time that while the enemy was approaching Jerusalem, her leaders will flee the city in cowardice and fear. Nevertheless, they will be captured and bound by the archers and sent into captivity. After the captives were taken into exile, "none remained, save the poorest sort of the people of the land" (2 Kgs. 24:14).

22:4 Therefore said I, Look away from me; I will weep bitterly, labour not to comfort me, because of the spoiling of the daughter of my people.

The phrase "daughter of my people" lets us know that Isaiah is seeing what will happen in the future to his people. Israel, and Jerusalem in particular, will be spoiled. The people of his time may be rejoicing in their man-made defenses, but Isaiah knows what will happen and is crying over their demise.

22:5 For it is a day of trouble, and of treading down, and of perplexity by the Lord God of hosts in the valley of vision, breaking down the walls, and of crying to the mountains.

This verse explains again why he will weep bitterly when Jerusalem is destroyed. "For" or because, it will be a very difficult, confusing (perplexing), and violent day. Isaiah sees the crushing of the walls surrounding Jerusalem and the people "crying to the mountains." Some have translated this as "Crying towards the mountains." Either way, the mournful cry of the townsmen "reaches" to the mountains and is echoed back by them. Josephus describes in the very same language the scene at the assault of Jerusalem under Titus. Some see this prophecy as indicating that the people will "cry" as they escape towards the mountains as the Savior said they would do in Matthew 24:16.

22:6 And Elam bare the quiver with chariots of men and horsemen, and Kir uncovered the shield.

Elam = "eternity." Is east of Babylon as throughout Isaiah's lifetime was an ally of Babylon against Assyria.

Kir = "wall." A place in Mesopotamia.

"The quiver" and "the shield" in this verse are two classes of light and heavy armed troops. When the troops "uncovered" their shields,

> they would take off for the battle the leather covering of the shield which was intended to protect the embossed figures on the shield from dust or injury during the march.

The day of trouble is coming towards Jerusalem. The enemy will bring its attack on foot, with cavalry, and with chariots. Each have weapons of offense (bows) and defense (shields) and seem to be a very mobile attack force.

22:7 And it shall come to pass, that thy choicest valleys shall be full of chariots, and the horsemen shall set themselves in array at the gate.

Seeing their choicest valleys being full of their enemy's chariots would indicate the swiftness of the approaching army. They are unopposed as they come towards Jerusalem. Soon they will be ready to break down, and then enter the gates of the city.

22:8 And he discovered the covering of Judah, and thou didst look in that day to the armour of the house of the forest.

> Discovered (Heb. *gâlâh*)—to uncover or remove.

Judah's covering was its defenses. At this day all of the defenses that Judah had relied on will be stripped away. In that day of distress, they will look to the house of the forest for defensive armor. The house of armory was built of cedar from the forest of Lebanon by Solomon, on a slope of Zion called Ophel (1Ki. 7:2; 10:17; Ne. 3:19). It was used for the storing and display of valuable arms and utensils . . . and so called because it rested upon four rows of cedar columns that ran all round (it was in the centre of the fore-court of the royal palace) (See Keil, 7:1:394).

When their reliance on themselves is removed, it only exposes their shame as a captive to their own pride. They relied on their own ability to defend themselves and would not place any trust in God.

22:9 Ye have seen also the breaches of the city of David, that they are many: and ye gathered together the waters of the lower pool.

The source of Jerusalem's water supply was the Gihon Spring which lies east of the city. Previous to the reign of Hezekiah, the conduit from the Gihon Spring to Jerusalem was over ground. Hezekiah saw this as a vulnerability for

Jerusalem, and as a result engineered a new conduit underground (2 Kings 20:20; 2 Chron. 32:2–4). In so doing, the Gihon Spring was now concealed and Jerusalem made secure in its water supply. The lower pool spoken of in verse 9 was the reservoir at the end of Hezekiah's Tunnel in Jerusalem.

Isaiah sees their day of distress where the city's walls have been breached and the people are gathered together where they can get water. Their monumental efforts in securing the city with walls and tunnels by their own efforts have failed.

22:10 And ye have numbered the houses of Jerusalem, and the houses have ye broken down to fortify the wall.

Jerusalem's "do-it-yourself" strategy for salvation was through walled strength. This verse refers to the number of houses that they deemed expendable. These houses could be pulled down with the least loss to the city, and with most advantage for the repair of the walls and rearing of towers (2 Chron. 32:5). This becomes a parable to us in our day. One of the people's greatest achievements (the tunnel) and some of their most costly sacrifices (the lost buildings) were wasted. Without faith in Christ, there are no lasting achievements, and no personal sacrifice made for an earthly possession matters. Faith in Christ brings an achievement that is greater than you ever could have made by yourselves. It enables you to apply Christ's grace into your heart to become like Him. At His coming, you will know Him, because you are now like Him (1 John 3:2).

22:11 Ye made also a ditch between the two walls for the water of the old pool: but ye have not looked unto the maker thereof, neither had respect unto him that fashioned it long ago.

> Hezekiah was a wall-builder, adding considerably to the fortifications of Jerusalem. The reference in verse 11 to the two walls may be to an area between a new wall and an existing wall of the old City of David. The point, however, is to indicate that now for the first time the city had a protected water supply. (Motyer, 184)

Isaiah condemns their reliance on themselves for their security and their rejection of the security that comes from God. They "have not looked . . . neither had respect" for God. Instead, they, in verses 8 and 9, ". . . didst look to the armor, ye have seen ('had respect', or 'regard to') the breaches." It was God who had made Jerusalem in such a way that it would always require faith in order to be defended. The city itself was a constant reminder of their need for God.

22:12 And in that day did the Lord God of hosts call to weeping, and to mourning, and to baldness, and to girding with sackcloth:

When the calamity comes, God will call on Israel to repent. In Isaiah's day, baldness and sackcloth were an outward sign of a person's repentant heart (see Jeremiah 47:5 and Amos 8:10). In the day of our sins, God uses consequences of our actions, and the day of our difficulty to invite us to change our hearts and repent.

22:13 And behold joy and gladness, slaying oxen, and killing sheep, eating flesh, and drinking wine: let us eat and drink; for to morrow we shall die.

In the day of their distress, their attitude was to seek pleasure. They wanted to turn to hedonism, or to satisfy the desires of the flesh one last time before their demise. They reasoned that if their weapons (verse 8), defenses (verse 10), or their engineering (verse 11) could not save them, then nothing would. They simply wanted to eat and drink, and they reasoned that tomorrow we die (see also 2 Ne. 28:8; 1 Cor. 15:32). This is the attitude held by those who do not believe in God or in a post-mortal existence.

22:14 And it was revealed in mine ears by the Lord of hosts, Surely this iniquity shall not be purged from you till ye die, saith the Lord God of hosts.

The first 14 verses of this chapter are what caused Isaiah to weep bitterly as he described in verse 4. Now the Lord reveals to the prophet that his people will not repent. They will continue in this sin even when they are exposed to the ravages of this destruction and perish. When a person with this type of attitude dies and enters the post-moral realm, God will use the experience of death as one more invitation to repentance. Death itself will serve as a witness of God's plan and will be a warning for us to repent. God desires for us to turn our hearts to Him and return to His presence.

Personal Warning to Shebna

Verses 15–19 serve as a personal warning to the treasurer Shebna. Shebna is attempting to set up his own little kingdom. It appears that he has a position of trust and is the king's "right hand man" and is in charge of the palace (verse 15). He displays his wealth for all to see "the chariots of his glory" (verse 18) as well as for all to see in the future with his "sepulcher on high" (verse 16). He serves as an individual who has the sickness of the land—his desire is to satisfy his own desires. He only serves himself. In this way, Shebna symbolizes all wicked people of his day and ours. If they choose to forget God, God will withdraw temporary riches and rewards (verse 19). If they choose to remember God, God will always remember to bless. Both in this life with peace, hope, and assurance, and even more so in the world to come.

22:15 Thus saith the Lord God of hosts, Go, get thee unto this treasurer, even unto Shebna, which is over the house, and say,

22:16 What hast thou here? and whom hast thou here, that thou hast hewed thee out a sepulchre here, as he that heweth him out a sepulchre on high, and that graveth an habitation for himself in a rock?

Shebna, a leading official in the royal courts of Judah, had become proud and wicked. Isaiah asks Shebna, "Who do you think you are, that you make a great sepulchre for yourself? Are you trying to exalt yourself?" Shebna tries to imitate God and God's glory with the counterfeits of permanence (sepulchre), prominence (its height) and self-aggrandizement (a visible habitation in a rock). The location of Shebna's sepulchre is unknown, although some scholars place it with other tombs carved in rock in the valley of Kidron, east of Jerusalem.

22:17 Behold, the Lord will carry thee away with a mighty captivity, and will surely cover thee.

Carry thee (Heb. *lwj tuwl*)—certainly grab you
Captivity (Heb. *ṭalṭêlâh*)—a hurling, captivity
Cover thee (Heb. *hje atah*)—hurl you away

Verse 17 and the first part of verse 18 could be literally translated as "Look, the Lord is going to throw you far away, big man—taking you in His grip, rolling you up really tight—like a ball into a limitless land" (Motyer, 188). This likely occurs when Shebna is carried away as a captive to Assyria by Sennacherib's forces.

22:18 He will surely violently turn and toss thee like a ball into a large country: there shalt thou die, and there the chariots of thy glory shall be the shame of thy lord's house.

He will die as a stranger in a foreign land and all of his efforts to protect himself with the weapons of the world will have failed. We are not saved by the quantity or quality of our chariots, guns, or missiles, we are saved by our faith in God. In the end, all who put their trust in themselves and in what they can create will be "the shame of thy Lord's house." They will be remembered as a disgrace.

22:19 And I will drive thee from thy station, and from thy state shall he pull thee down.

As a symbol for all of us, if we put our trust in man, we will lose our heavenly position, and will lose our inheritance in the kingdom of God.

Eliakim Is Symbolic of Christ

22:20 And it shall come to pass in that day, that I will call my servant Eliakim the son of Hilkiah:

Eliakim = "God raises" or "God sets up"
Hilkiah = "my portion is Jehovah"

Eliakim serves as a type of Jesus in several ways: as Eliakim replaced an evil ruler of Judah (Shebna), so Christ will replace all of the temporal rulers of Judah and Israel when He takes His rightful place as King of kings;

Eliakim's name is prophetic and points to Christ's power to lift us from both sin and death as a priest, Eliakim points to Jesus's role as the priest (Heb. 7:17) and similar to Eliakim's ministry "over the house" of Hezekiah, king of Judah, Christ possesses eternal power over the house of Judah or Israel. The name Eliakim also testifies of the resurrection of the Lord; for the hope of salvation only comes through Him.

When the patriarch Israel gave his son Judah his blessings, he said, among other things: "The sceptre shall not depart from Judah, nor a law-giver from between his feet, until Shiloh come; and unto him shall the gathering of the people be" (Genesis 49:10). Right to rule is only enjoyed through the holy priesthood of God. This power was focused upon Jesus Christ (Isaiah 9:6; Revelation 3:7).

22:21 And I will clothe him with thy robe, and strengthen him with thy girdle, and I will commit thy government into his hand: and he shall be a father to the inhabitants of Jerusalem, and to the house of Judah.

Just as Eliakim is given clothes as symbols of authority, so will Christ be given the same. The girdle mentioned in this verse refers to the temple's sacred vestments. By priestly authority will he (Christ and Eliakim) rule the government and will be the father and protector of Jerusalem and all of Judah. Christ will also reign as the great High Priest and King over all of Israel and the world.

22:22 And the key of the house of David will I lay upon his shoulder; so he shall open, and none shall shut; and he shall shut, and none shall open.

As in Isaiah 9:6, the government will be laid on the shoulder of Christ. He will have the key of the house of David. The key of David is a symbol of power and authority both temporally and spiritually. In the book of Revelation this key is mentioned. John wrote: ". . . These things saith he that is holy, he that is true, he that hath the key of David, he that openeth, and no man shutteth; and shutteth, and no man openeth; I know thy works: behold, I have set before thee an open door, and no man can shut it: for thou hast a little strength, and hast kept my word, and hast not denied my name" (Rev. 3:7–8).

Elder McConkie explained:

> From the day of Adam the term key has been used by inspired writers as a symbol of power and authority. Keys are the right of presidency, and the one holding them holds the reins of government within the field and sphere of his appointment. In ancient Israel, David was a man of blood and battle whose word was law and whose very name was also a symbol of power and authority. Accordingly, when Isaiah sought to convey a realization of the supreme, directive control and power resident in our Lord, the Son of David, he spoke these words in the Lord's name: "And the key of the house of David will I lay upon his shoulder so he shall open, and none shall shut and he shall shut, and none shall open." (Isa. 22: 22.) Thus the key of David is the absolute power resident in Christ whereby his will is expressed in all things both temporal and spiritual. (*Mormon Doctrine*, 409)

22:23 And I will fasten him as a nail in a sure place; and he shall be for a glorious throne to his father's house.

Sure (Heb. *âman*)—to support, confirm, be faithful. It also means to stand firm, to trust, to be certain, to believe in.

Just as Eliakim wants to be faithful and stand firm in righteousness, Christ would do this perfectly. The imagery of a "nail in a sure place" leads us to remember the crucifixion of Christ when a second nail was hammered into His wrists. The reason why it is nailed there is a witness of the glorious throne that we can have through Christ. The nail that is fastened "in a sure place" may be a reference for the Jews in the last days to help them identify Christ when He appears upon the Mount of Olives at His Second Coming (see D&C 45:48–53; Zachariah 12:10; 13:6; 14:4, D&C 19:18; John 17:12).

22:24 And they shall hang upon him all the glory of his father's house, the offspring and the issue, all vessels of small quantity, from the vessels of cups, even to all the vessels of flagons.

"offspring and the issue"—i.e. "the offshoots of the family, high and low."
vessels of cups—of small capacity: answering to the low and humble offshoots.
vessels of flagons—larger vessels: answering to the high offshoots.

The entire family of Adam's future happiness hangs on Christ. Whether we have a small amount of talent, time, or money, or if we have a larger amount, our future hangs on what Christ did for us. In comparison to Him, we are "all vessels of small quantity."

22:25 In that day, saith the Lord of hosts, shall the nail that is fastened in the sure place be removed, and be cut down, and fall; and the burden that was upon it shall be cut off: for the Lord hath spoken it.

Removed (Heb. *mûwsh*)—to withdraw (both literally and figuratively), to depart, remove.

In this verse, the comparison of Christ and Eliakim ends. Christ will never fail, but Isaiah prophecies that the person named Eliakim one day will falter. He will withdraw (remove) himself, or depart from what God has set up for him. This will be his choice and as a result will be "cut down" (sheered off) from where God had fastened him. For any person, if we withdraw from Christ, we weaken our spiritual stability. We will remove ourselves from the Spirit of God and in the end we will fall. No more will we assist Christ with His kingdom and His "burden of government." We will be left alone, cut off from the lasting joy that comes through Christ.

ISAIAH CHAPTER 23

If We Lose Our Desire for Righteousness, We Lose Our Joy

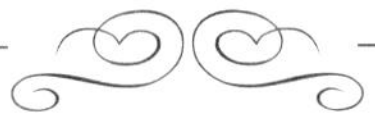

Tyre was a famous Phoenician city noted for her commercial enterprises, great wealth, and materialism. Tyre was so well known that she was called a "market place of nations" (23:3), and her traders and merchants were so celebrated that they were equated with the princes and the "honorable of the earth" (23:8). The Lord spoke against Tyre (and her inhabitants), decrying her pride by calling her a harlot. He also warned her inhabitants to repent, lest she become a desolate city. Tyre's inhabitants did not listen to the prophet and were thus destroyed.

23:1 The burden of Tyre. Howl, ye ships of Tarshish; for it is laid waste, so that there is no house, no entering in: from the land of Chittim it is revealed to them.

Tyre (Heb. *Tsur*)—"Rock."

During the reigns of David and Solomon, Israel had a good relationship with Tyre.

> Hiram of Tyre "always loved David" (1 Ki. 5:1) and renewed his covenant with Solomon (1 Ki. 5:12), co-operating commercially over the temple (1 Ki. 5:6). But there was

> another side. Solomon took Phoenician wives and imported the cult of the Sidonian Ashtoreth (1 Ki. 11:1, 5). These high places remained (2 Ki. 23:13) and Isaiah would have grown up with an awareness of Tyre's corruption of Israel's most favored king. Phoenician influence was an evil genius to the northern kingdom also, even to the extent of almost replacing Yahweh with the Baal of Sidon (1 Ki. 16, 18). (Motyer, 189)

The prophet predicts that Tyre, its ships, along with its false gods and economic influence, will be laid waste. No houses will remain, and the harbor (entering in) will be destroyed. Tarshish was probably Spain. Chittim is the early name for present-day Cyprus.

23:2 Be still, ye inhabitants of the isle; thou whom the merchants of Zidon, that pass over the sea, have replenished.

> Be still (Heb. *dâmam*)—to be in awe, astonished or struck dumb.
> Zidon = "Fishing station"

Zidon was the older city of the Phoenicians and started out as a fishing station. As the ships from Tarshish were on their way to Tyre, they learned about the destruction of Tyre. Zidon received her revenue from the grain (seed) of Sihor (the Nile waters of Egypt) mentioned in verse three.

23:3 And by great waters the seed of Sihor, the harvest of the river, is her revenue; and she is a mart of nations.

The harvest spoken of came from Egypt. At this time period, Egypt was known for its fertile fields that were watered by the Nile River. From Egypt came the grain to Tyre where it was marketed and traded.

23:4 Be thou ashamed, O Zidon: for the sea hath spoken, even the strength of the sea, saying, I travail not, nor bring forth children, neither do I nourish up young men, nor bring up virgins.

There is a sense of despair in this verse that matches the silence of the harbor mentioned in verse 2. Tyre's success relied on the sea, and now the sea speaks to a barren city. According to Israelite tradition, shame fell on the woman who was barren or violated, or who lost all her children through death.

Tyre and Sidon, portrayed as women, will be humbled and shamed. Tyre, referred to as the "strength of the sea," will be virtually depopulated, her people killed, enslaved, or made refugees, and therefore unable to raise up a new generation of young men and virgins to populate the island.

23:5 As at the report concerning Egypt, so shall they be sorely pained at the report of Tyre.

When (as) the report of Tyre's demise reaches Egypt, they will react the same way as Tyre did of its own demise. Isaiah states it this way to amplify the magnitude of this disaster and the far-reaching implications it will have for other nations (see Motyer, 191).

People of Tyre Will Go to Tarshish as Refugees

23:6 Pass ye over to Tarshish; howl, ye inhabitants of the isle.

23:7 Is this your joyous city, whose antiquity is of ancient days? her own feet shall carry her afar off to sojourn.

The phrase "carry her afar off to sojourn" indicates that after the destruction of their city, Tyre's refugees will migrate to distant places. All that will be left of a once joyous city will be a silent ruin.

23:8 Who hath taken this counsel against Tyre, the crowning city, whose merchants are princes, whose traffickers are the honourable of the earth?

The question of "who" in this verse is answered in the next verse. It is the Lord who allowed this to happen to this great and ancient city. The city's inhabitants are called the "honourable of the earth" in this verse. Tyre's merchants were so well respected and famous, it was as if they were considered princes, or sons of kings.

23:9 The Lord of hosts hath purposed it, to stain the pride of all glory, and to bring into contempt all the honourable of the earth.

Tyre represents the wealth and prestige that is valued by the world. It does not matter how you become prideful. It matters not how honourable you consider yourself and those around you to be. The Lord will humble the proud. Some commentators believe that "the pride of all glory" may refer to the Tyrian temple of Hercules. This temple was one of the most ancient in the world and was a source of pride to the city of Tyre.

23:10 Pass through thy land as a river, O daughter of Tarshish: there is no more strength.

The people of Tarshish can now travel freely throughout their land. Tarshish, as a colony of Tyre, has become independent.

23:11 He stretched out his hand over the sea, he shook the kingdoms: the lord hath given a commandment against the merchant city, to destroy the strong holds thereof.

23:12 And he said, Thou shalt no more rejoice, O thou oppressed virgin, daughter of Zidon: arise, pass over to Chittim; there also shalt thou have no rest.

Oppressed (Heb. *'âshaq*)—defraud, violate, or oppress.

Isaiah prophecies four results of Tyre's demise. First, their rejoicing will have been brought to an end. Fun, or good times are temporary, the joy that comes from Christ can last eternally. Second, just as a virgin is oppressed, defrauded, or violated, they will lose peace, innocence, and their sense of security. Both peace in the physical sense, but also the peace that results in the heart and mind and comes as a result of being righteous. Third, they will lose permanence or physical establishment as they are forced to relocate. Lastly, they will have no rest.

The inhabitants of Tyre can be compared to us today. Just like the inhabitants of Tyre, if we lose our desire for righteousness, we lose our joy, our peace, the hope of our permanent residence with God, and we will not have rest. Rest, peace, and joy come from our covenant with God and our hope of one day dwelling with Him.

23:13 Behold the land of the Chaldeans; this people was not, till the Assyrian founded it for them that dwell in the wilderness: they set up the towers thereof, they raised up the palaces thereof; and he brought it to ruin.

The Chaldees ("them that dwell in the wilderness") lived a nomadic life in the mountains of Armenia located in the north and east part of Assyria. They were described as a people who "were not," or had no existence as a recognized nation. "Founded it," means that the land was assigned to them who had "dwelt in the wilderness" as a permanent settlement. The ancient Greek historian Herodotus indicated that the towers that the Chaldes set up where the siege-towers of Babylon that were used against Tyre. These towers made possible an attack on high walls by hurling large objects and this is depicted in several Assyrian sculptures. As a result, they raised up (or rather, they "lay bare") the foundations of "her [Tyre's] palaces" and utterly destroyed them (see Psalms 137:7).

Tyre Represents the World

23:14 Howl, ye ships of Tarshish: for your strength is laid waste.

In verses 14–19, Tyre, like Babylon, "represented the world and so eventually would come under the judgments of God. Like Babylon, she was seen as a harlot committing fornication (joining in wickedness) with the kingdoms of the world (see Isaiah 23:15, 17–18; compare Revelation 17:1–2). The seventy years may refer to her coming judgments. Isaiah 23:18 shows that eventually the merchandise of Tyre (the world) shall be put to proper use in building the kingdom of Jehovah" (*Old Testament Student Manual*, 159).

23:15 And it shall come to pass in that day, that Tyre shall be forgotten seventy years, according to the days of one king: after the end of seventy years shall Tyre sing as an harlot.

The days of one king are said to be seventy years and during this timeframe, the prosperity and success of Tyre will simply be forgotten. They will be like a harlot that has been forgotten, but who attracts notice again by her song. Large marts of commerce are often compared to harlots seeking many lovers, that is, they court merchants of all nations, and admit any one for the sake of gain (compare with Nahum 3:4; Revelation 18:3).

23:16 Take an harp, go about the city, thou harlot that hast been forgotten; make sweet melody, sing many songs, that thou mayest be remembered.

23:17 And it shall come to pass after the end of seventy years, that the Lord will visit Tyre, and she shall turn to her hire, and shall commit fornication with all the kingdoms of the world upon the face of the earth.

The number 70 is symbolic of a period of judgment (see Jeremiah 25:11). Isaiah uses this symbolism in describing Tyre's future. When Tyre is again remembered after her time of judgment, she will again be like a harlot in her fornication. She will return to immoral practices, greed, or idolatry. Tyre, as a symbol of the world, will once again sell to the world's kingdoms and gain riches. Like the world, Tyre will one day suffer the wrath for her immorality.

Tyre had its Golden Age around the 10th century BC. By the 8th century it was still going strong and was a great trade center in the days of Isaiah. The prosperity of Tyre attracted the attention of King Nebuchadnezzar II of Babylon who lay siege to the city for thirteen years in the 6th century BC without breaking their defenses. During this siege, most of the inhabitants of the mainland city abandoned it. After the siege, Tyre slips from the main pages of history. To regain prominence in the world, their king began to set apart Tyre as being special in the eyes of God. The king even introduced a new, elaborate, and exclusive ceremony to celebrate the annual festival of their god Melqart. Its exclusiveness required that only inhabitants of Tyre take part in the ceremony.

> It was this ceremony, and the importance it held for the people, which would bring about Tyre's destruction and the slaughter or enslavement of the populace. In 332 BCE, Alexander the Great arrived at the city, fresh from the subjugation of Sidon, and demanded Tyre's surrender. Following Sidon's lead, the Tyrians acknowledged Alexander's greatness and presented him with gifts. All seemed to be going well and, pleased with

> their submission, Alexander said he would present a sacrifice in honor of their god in the Temple of Melqart. The Tyrians could not allow this as it would be sacrilegious for a foreigner to present a sacrifice in the holy home of their god and even more so as the ceremony of the *egersis* was close at hand. The historian Worthington presents what followed: "Azemilk, King of Tyre, proposed a compromise. Tyre would become Alexander's ally, but he should sacrifice on the mainland at Old Tyre, opposite the island. An angry Alexander sent envoys to say this was unacceptable and that the Tyrians had to surrender. They murdered the envoys and threw them off their walls" (105). Alexander then ordered the siege of Tyre. (Mark, "Tyre")

After a siege of seven months, Alexander destroyed the walls of Tyre and took the city. Tyre's 30,000 inhabitants were either massacred or sold into slavery. Alexander destroyed the city as a consequence of their defiance of him.

23:18 And her merchandise and her hire shall be holiness to the Lord: it shall not be treasured nor laid up; for her merchandise shall be for them that dwell before the Lord, to eat sufficiently, and for durable clothing.

Like the world, after her time of judgment, her trade will revive, her business prosperity will return, and she will dedicate her gains in merchandise as holy to Jehovah. The time is yet to come, and Tyre is a symbol of the wealthy nations of the world who, in the last days, will bring gifts, money, and honor to the Lord and His people (See Isaiah 60:5-7; Psalms 45:12; Haggai 2:8).

Summary Review of Chapters 13–23

Chapters 13–23 were mostly addressed to other nations but Isaiah taught and emphasized principles, blessings and warnings to the people and leaders of these nations that would give them hope and lead them closer to God. His purpose was to teach that truth applies to all of the world. Turning to God gives hope and peace—regardless of where you live. Isaiah compared nations and their leaders to events that will happen in the last days. Some of the doctrines that were taught in these chapters were:

Israel is redeemed through Jehovah's gracious compassion (13:11; 14:1–2).

Moab bases her appeal to Zion for shelter and that "a throne shall be established in loving kindness" (16:4–5).

The Philistines are not allowed to rally themselves with Judah against Assyria, because Jerusalem is already inviolable through faith in Jehovah (14:32).

The allied forces of Damascus and Israel had failed because they forsook the God of their salvation for idols (17:10).

Ethiopia is converted to Jehovah through seeing God's hand in history (18:7).

Egypt is won to Jehovah's worship through divine discipline (19:22).

Edom's fickle cry for light in the night (21:11–12) is not deep or sincere enough to secure her from rejoicing over Judah's calamities, and therefore not sufficient to avert her deserved doom (34:10).

Careless, godless abandon on the part of people in imminent peril of siege is a sin (22:14).

A man's pride, even of one who is a high officer of state, "shall bring him low" (22:16, 19).

The profits derived from merchandise are no better morally than the hire of a harlot unless consecrated to the service of Jehovah (23:18) (see Robinson, *The Book of Isaiah in Fifteen Studies*, 95–96).

ISAIAH CHAPTER 24

A Promise That the Dead Will Be Visited—after Many Days

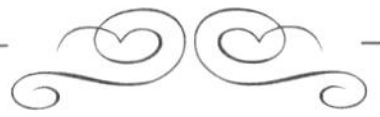

CHAPTERS 24–27 FOLLOW THE MESSAGES OF DOOM PRONOUNCED UPON the surrounding nations and are closely associated with them. They appear to be one continuous revelation, probably divided into chapters sometime after Isaiah's day. The central theme of these chapters is the destruction and the establishment of a city. These chapters taken together form a chiasmas as seen below.

Al The Lord's harvest from a destroyed world (24:1–13)
 Destruction (24:1–12)
 Gleanings (24:13)
  B[1] The song of the world remnant (24:14–16a)
   C[1] The sinful world overthrown (24:16b–20)
    D[1] The waiting world (24:21–23)
     E[1] The song of the ruined city (25:1–5)
      F MOUNT ZION (25:6–42)
     E[2] The song of the strong city (26:1–6)
    D[2] The waiting people of God (26:7–21)
   C[2] Spiritual forces of evil overthrown (27:1)
  B[2] The song of the remnant of the people (27:2–6)
A[2] The Lord's harvest from a destroyed people (27:7–13)

Destruction (7–11)
Gleanings (12–13) (Motyer, 194–195)

Chapters 24 and 25 are prophetic in nature. Chapter 24 indicates that the whole earth is defiled and will be burned. This chapter also describes the Lord's people and how He will be glorified in Zion (isles of the sea) as well as by the people of Judah in Jerusalem. Chapter 25 follows this thought and teaches that the Lord will be exalted in Mount Zion. In Isaiah chapters 24 and 25, one sees a pattern that is very common in Isaiah's writings; Isaiah often delivers a pronouncement of serious warnings mingled with a note of optimism (as in chapter 24) and then follows it with a prophecy of joyful promises, concluding with a somber tone of caution (as in chapter 25). Chapter 26 speaks of a song that will be sung in the land of Judah followed by Chapter 27 speaking of Jacob taking root and the blossoming of Israel.

The first six verses of this chapter speak of a general apostasy and judgment that could be compared to any time period. The judgment is on its way and will level all classes of society. The reason for this is given in verse 5, "because they have transgressed the laws, violated the statutes, [and] broken the everlasting covenant." Even "the earth" becomes polluted by Israel's sins and it shares their guilt. As a result the earth will be "burned, and few men left" (vs. 6).

24:1 Behold, the Lord maketh the earth empty, and maketh it waste, and turneth it upside down, and scattereth abroad the inhabitants thereof.

empty (Heb. *baqaq*)—to devastate.
waste (Heb. *balaq*)—to lay waste.

There will come a day of judgment when the earth will be devastated and emptied of wickedness. The Lord said: "For a desolating scourge shall go forth among the inhabitants of the earth, and shall continue to be poured out from time to time, if they repent not, until the earth is empty, and the inhabitants thereof are consumed away and utterly destroyed by the brightness of my coming" (D&C 5:19). The earth is compared to a container that is turned "upside down." Similar imagery was used in the Lord's declaration, "I will wipe Jerusalem as a man wipeth a dish, wiping it, and turning it upside down" (2 Kgs. 21:13). The Lord will cleanse the earth of the wicked as one turns a bowl upside down and empties, or pours out, the filth. A similar promise was made by Malachi when he wrote if God did not send us Elijah the prophet, then He must "come and smite the whole earth with a curse" (Malachi 4:6). Moroni reworded that, and he said if Elijah the prophet does not come, the whole earth would be utterly wasted at the coming of the Lord (see JS—H 1:39).

24:2 And it shall be, as with the people, so with the priest; as with the servant, so with his master; as with the maid, so with her mistress; as with the buyer, so with the seller; as with the lender, so with the borrower; as with the taker of usury, so with the giver of usury to him.

Isaiah lists twelve groups (people, priests, servants, masters, and others) who represent all levels of society. They come in six pairs (servant - master, etc.) and indicates that the inhabitants of the land will be scattered, regardless of their status or position.

In the April 1971 general conference, President Spencer W. Kimball identified the "priest" spoken of in verse 2 to "denote all religious leaders of any faith. . . . From among the discordant voices we are shocked at those of many priests who encourage the defilement of men and wink at the eroding trends and who deny the omniscience of God. Certainly these men should be holding firm, yet some yield to popular clamor" (Kimball, "Voices of the Past, of the Present, of the Future").

24:3 The land shall be utterly emptied, and utterly spoiled: for the Lord hath spoken this word.

Utterly emptied—completely laid waste.
Utterly spoiled—completely plundered.

In biblical Hebrew, the repetition of a word, for example, "empty, empty" in verse 3, makes the word comparative ("more empty") or superlative ("most empty"). By repeating "empty" three times in verses 1 and 3, Isaiah stresses his point—the earth will be extremely, or completely emptied or laid waste. Elder Marion G. Romney quoted verse 3 as evidence that Isaiah envisioned our day and foresaw the burning of the earth as described in verse 6 (see Romney, in Conference Report, April 1968, 113).

24:4 The earth mourneth and fadeth away, the world languisheth and fadeth away, the haughty people of the earth do languish.

Languisheth (Heb. *amal*)—to be weak, exhausted, or to droop.

Fadeth (Heb. *nâbêl*)—to wither.

The earth itself mourns because of the wickedness of its inhabitants. In Moses 7:48, the earth seeks rest "from the filthiness" that is on it. This wickedness causes the earth to mourn, to be exhausted, and to wither away. Specifically, the sin of pride causes the people to do the same—to be spiritually weak, and exhausted. President Joseph Fielding Smith noted that our generation is heading for the destruction spoken of in verses 4 and 6 (see *Doctrine of Salvation*, 3:316).

24:5 The earth also is defiled under the inhabitants thereof; because they have transgressed the laws, changed the ordinance, broken the everlasting covenant.

Defiled (Heb. *chânêph*)—to pollute, profane or make godless.

The earth itself become defiled as a result of the wickedness of its inhabitants. The Prophet Joseph Smith said that verse 5 refers to the Gentiles' breaking the covenant when he stated:

> Thus after this chosen family had rejected Christ and His proposals, the heralds of salvation said to them, "Lo we turn unto the Gentiles"; and the Gentiles received the covenant, and were grafted in from whence the chosen family were broken off; but the Gentiles have not continued in the goodness of God, but have departed from the faith that was once delivered to the Saints, and have broken the covenant in which their fathers were established (see Isaiah 24:5); and have become high-minded, and have not feared; therefore, but few of them will be gathered with the chosen family. Have not the pride, high-mindedness, and unbelief of the Gentiles, provoked the Holy One of Israel to withdraw His Holy Spirit from them, and send forth His judgments to scourge them for their wickedness? This is certainly the case (*Teachings of Presidents: Joseph Smith*, 15).

The Lord repeated the message of verse 5 in Doctrine and Covenants 1:15. Elder Rudger Clawson quoted verse 5 as a warning against administering in the priesthood without authority (see Clawson, in Conference Report, April 1914, 22–23). Elder George F. Richards stated that the unauthorized changing of the ordinance of baptism from immersion to sprinkling was a fulfillment of Isaiah 24:5 (see Richards, in Conference Report, April 1930, 76). President Joseph Fielding Smith pointed to the need for a restoration of the everlasting covenant which Isaiah said was broken (see Smith, *Doctrines of Salvation*, 1:168). Elder LeGrand Richard cited verses 5 and 6 as a prophecy of the nearly one thousand churches in modern America who are following their own wisdom and not the precepts of God (see Richards, "The Things of God and Man")

The Prophet Joseph Smith said of the ordinances: "If there is no change of ordinances, there is no change of Priesthood. Wherever the ordinances of the Gospel are administered, there is the Priesthood" (Smith, *Teachings of the Prophet Joseph Smith*, 158).

24:6 Therefore hath the curse devoured the earth, and they that dwell therein are desolate: therefore the inhabitants of the earth are burned, and few men left.

Desolate (Heb. *'âsham*)—to be held guilty.

The result of this, or any apostasy is that the earth is cursed and its inhabitants are guilty of their sins. At the coming of Christ, a part of the punishment of those alive will be that they will be burned. President Joseph Fielding Smith used verse 6 as evidence that only telestial beings will be burned at the Second Coming of Christ (see *Doctrines of Salvation*, 3:62).

Sorrow of the Wicked over Their Destruction

Verses 7 through 12 describe the sorrow of the wicked over their destruction and can be compared to the second coming of Christ. Just as their sin had consequences for them, and the earth, now their sin removes their joy (vs. 7), dissipates their satisfaction and hence reduces their joy further (vs. 8–9), produces a desolation on their cities (vs. 10), and in the end leaves them with no joy (vs. 11) and no security (vs. 12).

24:7 The new wine mourneth, the vine languisheth, all the merry-hearted do sigh.

What is "new wine"? It is grape juice that has been fermented and is alcoholic (see Acts 2:13–15). It is a lower quality wine (see Luke 5:39). Isaiah is painting a picture of little time being spent on quality (old wine), hope for the future (a vine weakened or perishing), or in doing anything that would make your heart glad. The party is over. Even those who by nature are happy are now despondent and depressed.

24:8 The mirth of tabrets ceaseth, the noise of them that rejoice endeth, the joy of the harp ceaseth.

The sounds of gaiety and the free abundance of wine are gone. The party lifestyle of the world ends.

24:9 They shall not drink wine with a song; strong drink shall be bitter to them that drink it.

Even when they drink, there is no joy in it. There is no satisfaction in what they drink as there is no satisfaction in sin.

24:10 The city of confusion is broken down: every house is shut up, that no man may come in.

Confusion (Heb. *tôhûw*)—formless, confusion, unreality, a place of chaos, wasteland.

The city described here is just like the earth as described in Genesis 1:2—"without form (*tôhûw*—pronounced to'-hoo) and void." It serves no purpose and has no life in it. It is only a place of confusion, chaos, and a place where reality does not exist. It is a city of *tôhûw*. It has no meaning nor stability within its walls. "The city of *tôhûw* lives without the ordering, life-giving hand of God, opting for a life on its own, within itself, depending on itself. Consequently, it is unstable and without purpose, spinning on the wheel but having dismissed the potter, its ever-changing shapes and fashions not dictated by purpose but by whimsy. Life is simply one thing after another" (Motyer, 201). Today's city of *tôhûw* exists in every nation and does not see reality as God does, but produces their own reality, a reality in which their wickedness will only result in confusion, anxiety, and fear. Their fear is manifest by barring the entrance to every house so that no other wicked person may enter. The wicked fear the wicked because they see their desires as being similar to their own. Their intentions are evil and will only produce a spiritual and emotional wasteland.

24:11 There is a crying for wine in the streets; all joy is darkened, the mirth of the land is gone.

This verse corresponds to verses 7–9. In those verses they drank new wine, but it did not help them. Alcohol or stimulants will not assist in bringing joy. Wickedness never brings joy. When righteousness is gone, joy is extinguished. They have shut themselves up in their houses for protection and they realize that there is no security or joy in having wicked neighbors in a wicked city.

24:12 In the city is left desolation, and the gate is smitten with destruction.

Left (Heb. *shâ'ar*)—remains, left behind.

Desolation (Heb. *shammâh*)—astonished, wasted, horrified.

The literal translation of this verse is "Astonishment is left behind in the city, and to ruination the gate is crushed." Nothing is left for the wicked except their astonishment and their wickedness.

24:13 When thus it shall be in the midst of the land among the people, there shall be as the shaking of an olive tree, and as the gleaning grapes when the vintage is done.

Isaiah now turns to a message of hope in verses 13–15. There is to be a group in the midst of the land (the earth) who shall sing unto the Lord and glorify Him. He further identifies the place as "in the fires . . . in the isles of the sea" (v. 15). A marginal note in the KJV suggests the word "valleys" instead of "fires." Isaiah consistently uses the term "isles of the sea," undoubtedly with reference to America. Similarly, the Book of Mormon prophet Jacob spoke of the Nephites' being on "an isle of the sea" (2 Nephi 10:20). Thus Isaiah seems to be describing the Latter-day Saints, who will be singing and glorifying God in the day of the earth's turmoil and devastation.

Jewish tradition applies the "gleanings" to the remnants of Israel among the Gentiles (see Slotki, 112). To glean a crop refers to the gathering anything little by little (or slowly) after the reapers have harvested a crop. Latter-day Saints recognize that remnants of Israel will be among the Lord's "gleanings" of the olive trees, but that other people ("gleaning grapes") will also become part of God's harvest in the last days.

24:14 They shall lift up their voice, they shall sing for the majesty of the Lord, they shall cry aloud from the sea.

The "they" in this verse refers to the people in verse 13 who have been carefully gleaned, or gathered, and are a part of God's latter-day harvest. These sweet grapes will sing in praise of the Lord and what He has done for them.

24:15 Wherefore glorify ye the Lord in the fires, even the name of the Lord God of Israel in the isles of the sea.

The "gleaned saints" will glorify the Lord even when they have been "in the fires." "In the fires" refers to the fires of affliction. When we come to see the difficulties of our lives in the same way that God sees them, ". . . we will see that our trials were calculated to cause us to turn to our Heavenly Father for strength and support. Any affliction or suffering we are called upon to bear may be directed to give us experience, refinement, and perfection" (Stapley, "The Blessings of Righteous Obedience"). Affliction gives us earned empathy for others and this will be seen in the next verse. These Saints will be in the "isles of the sea," or in Zion.

24:16 From the uttermost part of the earth have we heard songs, even glory to the righteous. But I said, My leanness, my leanness, woe unto me! the treacherous dealers have dealt treacherously; yea, the treacherous dealers have dealt very treacherously.

The prophet fancies he hears songs of deliverance. The righteous sing with a common theme—glory to the Righteous One. It is doubtful that they are singing about themselves, but are singing to God. But these songs are premature; more judgment must follow (see Robinson, *The Book of Isaiah in Fifteen Sutdies*, p. 100). Isaiah writes of his "leanness," which is similar to what he expresses when he was called as a prophet in Isaiah 6:5. He is feeling the betrayal and condemnation that others are feeling as deeply as they are feeling it. He has earned empathy in his earlier affliction and now exercises it in a hope of future mercy for others.

The last part of this verse could be translated "For betrayers betray: with betrayal betrayers betray." The false promises of the world have betrayed the inhabitants of the earth. Satan will betray all he is able to in the most treacherous way possible for him.

24:17 Fear, and the pit, and the snare, are upon thee, O inhabitant of the earth.

The pit in this verse represents those who die and are sent to hell (see Rev. 20:2–3, Isaiah 14:15). Judgments have come to the inhabitants of the earth, and they fear death because they have been snared by Satan's temptations and have been caught up in their sins. They will join Satan in *Sh*^{e}*'ôwl* or Hades (see Isaiah 14:9).

24:18 And it shall come to pass, that he who fleeth from the noise of the fear shall fall into the pit; and he that cometh up out of the midst of the pit shall be taken in the snare: for the windows from on high are open, and the foundations of the earth do shake.

Noise (Heb. *qôwl*)—voice, sound or noise.

Windows (Heb. *'□rubbâh*)—windows or "flood gates" as used in Gen 7:11, 8:2; 2 Kings 7:19 and Mal 3:10.

It seems that we can find the voice of fear in this world. The voice of fear temporarily raises the ratings of the radio/TV/podcast, etc. host. Fear is an easier language to master and most of the time is used to manipulate others to fall into the pit of hell. It does not matter the political or ideological preference, those who use fear often lead people into a snare. The person who comes out of the pit in Revelation 9:11 is called Abaddon ("to perish") or Apollyon ("the destroyer"). Regardless of the name given to Satan, his fear leads to snares. His fear leads to the pit of hell. It is also important to note that those who are wicked will go from one snare to another.

The "windows" from on high are often translated as flood gates. Just as in the time of Noah, a judgment is coming on the wicked. The final judgments of fire on the apostate world are compared to the ancient deluge. A "universal catastrophe is about to burst in on every side like a terrible flood" (Robinson, *The Book of Isaiah in Fifteen Studies*, p. 100).

Conditions before the Second Coming of the Lord

The remainer of the chapter describes "events and conditions as they will be just before or in conjunction with the Second Coming of the Lord. A more penetrating description of these same events is found in Doctrine and Covenants 88:86–94 (*Old Testament Student Manual*, 162).

24:19 The earth is utterly broken down, the earth is clean dissolved, the earth is moved exceedingly.

24:20 The earth shall reel to and fro like a drunkard, and shall be removed like a cottage; and the transgression thereof shall be heavy upon it; and it shall fall, and not rise again.

Verses 19–20 describe the catastrophic events associated with the Lord's Second Coming. The Savior quoted part of verse 20 in two revelations given to Joseph Smith (see D&C 49:23; 88:87 as quoted below). The Prophet Joseph Smith taught that the events spoken of in verse 20 were soon to occur as the Second Coming rapidly approached (see *Teachings of Presidents: Joseph Smith*, 29, 71).

> Wherefore, be not deceived, but continue in steadfastness, looking forth for the heavens to be shaken, and the earth to tremble and to reel to and fro as a drunken man, and for the valleys to be exalted, and for the mountains to be made low, and for the rough places to become smooth—and all this when the angel shall sound his trumpet. (D&C 49:23)

> For not many days hence and the earth shall tremble and reel to and fro as a drunken man; and the sun shall hide his face, and shall refuse to give light; and the moon shall be bathed in blood; and the stars shall become exceedingly angry, and shall cast themselves down as a fig that falleth from off a fig tree. (D&C 88:87)

24:21 And it shall come to pass in that day, that the Lord shall punish the host of the high ones that are on high, and the kings of the earth upon the earth.

24:22 And they shall be gathered together, as prisoners are gathered in the pit, and shall be shut up in the prison, and after many days shall they be visited.

High ones (Heb. *mârôwm*)—haughty, proud.
On high—identical to "high ones."
Prison (Heb. *maçgêr*)—dungeon.
Pit/prison—these terms refer to spirit prison (Isaiah 14:15, 19; Rev. 19:19 20:3)

The "high ones" and the "kings of the earth" have been identified by President Joseph Fielding Smith as some of those who live in the latter days but do not keep the law, and who will therefore be shut up in the spirit prison (see *Doctrines of Salvation*, 2:155). Joseph Smith taught that we will find ". . . that God will deal with all the human family equally, and that as the antediluvians had their day of visitation (1 Pet. 3:19 20), so will those characters referred to by Isaiah have their time of visitation and deliverance, after having been many days in prison. . . . They will be visited by this priesthood and come out of their prison, upon the same principle as those who were disobedient in the days of Noah were visited by our Savior" (Jackson, 49–50). Isaiah assures us that the dead who have been gathered together as prisoners in a pit will be visited after many days.

24:23 Then the moon shall be confounded, and the sun ashamed, when the Lord of hosts shall reign in mount Zion, and in Jerusalem, and before his ancients gloriously.

The long-awaited day will come when the Lord Jesus Christ will reign. He will reign in mount Zion (location of the temple), and will do so from Jerusalem. He will also reign over the ancients who have passed on the other side of the veil. Christ reigns and rules over all.

ISAIAH CHAPTER 25

The Lord God Will Wipe Away Tears from All the Faces

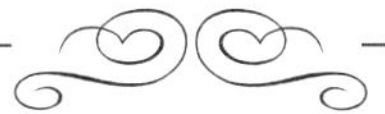

In chapter 24, Isaiah wrote on how the whole earth will become defiled and will be burned at the Second Coming of Christ. Chapter 25 is also prophetic in nature. The first five verses of the chapter are a song of gratitude for deliverance of a ruined city (Jerusalem) after having gone through "much tribulation." The remainder of the chapter focuses on Mount Zion. It is a chapter dealing with joyful promises to the faithful who live the last days.

Joy in the Lord

Those who survived the judgments and the destructions upon the earth as described in Isaiah 24 will praise the Lord. Isaiah preserves the words of a hymn of praise in the first five verses of this chapter. The hymn includes words that bring us great comfort: Jehovah is our "strength" and our "refuge from the storm"; he is our "shadow from the heat." It is a hymn of thanksgiving to Jehovah for deliverance from the Assyrians and symbolically from the evils of the last days. It is a hymn that celebrates the triumph over the wicked.

25:1 O Lord, thou art my God; I will exalt thee, I will praise thy name; for thou hast done wonderful things; thy counsels of old are faithfulness and truth.

Praise (Heb. *yâdâh*)—to give thanks to.
Wonderful (Heb. *pele'*)—something of an extraordinary nature.
Truth (Heb. *'ômen*)—faithful. This is the only time in the bible where this Hebrew word is used.

A personal knowledge of and relationship with God starts Isaiah's hymn of praise. He gives thanks to God and exclaims God has done many things of an extraordinary nature. Planned is a noun ("plans," *'esôt*) that is related to the verb which supplies "Counsellor" in Isaiah 9:6. Isaiah links the planning of a council with the counsels that have been given long ago. Isaiah wants us to understand that the Lord's counsels of old are a part of His "pre-planning of his acts long ago" (Motyer, 208). Isaiah will refer to this again in Isaiah 42:9 and 46:10.

A better way to translate the latter part of this verse would be "Thou hast accomplished wonders, plans formed long ago, with perfect faithfulness." Literally the plans were made with "faithful faithfulness." The repetition of the word "faithful" suggests a totality and/or perfection in God's plans and in His execution of them (see Motyer, 208).

25:2 For thou hast made of a city an heap; of a defenced city a ruin: a palace of strangers to be no city; it shall never be built.

Made (Heb. *sûwm*)—transform.
Built (Heb. *bânâh*)—to build or to rebuild.

The city referred to is Babylon. It has become a "heap" and a "ruin." In its days Babylon was regarded as a palace on account of its splendor. Many of its inhabitants were considered "strangers" or foreigners, whose capital pre-eminently Babylon was, the metropolis of the pagan world. There were "Aliens from the commonwealth of Israel and strangers from the covenants of promise, having no hope" (Eph. 2:12) because they were without God.

Again Isaiah testifies that Babylon will never be rebuilt (see Isa. 13:19–20). The greatest city in the world in Isaiah's day will completely disappear and be left desolate. Similarly, the spiritual Babylon that exists around us today will one day be transformed into a heap and a ruin. A forgotten monument to a people who forgot God.

25:3 Therefore shall the strong people glorify thee, the city of the terrible nations shall fear thee.

Terrible (Heb. *'ârîyts*)—fearful, powerful, or tyrannical.

As a result of Babylon becoming a ruined city as spoken of in verse 2, "the strong people" will glorify the same person who caused Babylon to be destroyed—they will glorify God. The organization (or city) that is composed of the terrible and mighty nations will still fear the awesome power of God. This city is the same city referred to in Isaiah 24:10 and is a city of confusion and meaninglessness. A city that has a structure but does not reference God. It is one city comprised of "the terrible nations." The Hebrew word for terrible (*'ârîyts*) has a connotation of the unsparing use of power or strength against others. In our day, spiritual Babylon does not have a city center where you can physically go and say, "this is the center of spiritual Babylon." Instead, its location is anywhere in the world where people serve Satan.

25:4 For thou hast been a strength to the poor, a strength to the needy in his distress, a refuge from the storm, a shadow from the heat, when the blast of the terrible ones is as a storm against the wall.

God is a strength to those in need. He provides strength in our most difficult days and a protection from the storms of our lives. He is like a place of shade for a traveler in the heat of the day. Isaiah uses a phrase "as a storm" and this refers to "a tempest of rain," or a winter flood. Its waters rush against the wall weakening its foundations and its blast may cause the collapse the structure.

25:5 Thou shalt bring down the noise of strangers, as the heat in a dry place; even the heat with the shadow of a cloud: the branch of the terrible ones shall be brought low.

Branch (Heb. *zâmîyr*)—a twig that has been pruned.

This verse could be translated: "As the heat of a dry land is brought down by the shadow of a cloud, so thou shalt bring down the tumult (a shout of victory) of foreigners (or those who are hostile to the Lord's people); and as the heat by the shadow of the cloud is brought low, so the branch (the offspring) of the terrible ones shall be brought low."

Just like the heat of the day saps the energy and vitality of a desert inhabitant, so will the Lord prune those inhabitants of the city of confusion.

They will wither as they are humbled by God. All of this will occur at the Second Coming of Christ.

THE LORD'S FEAST ON MOUNT ZION

After the coming of Christ, all nations will be invited to a wonderful feast on Mount Zion, as described in verses 6–8. During the feast, people will celebrate (verse 6) as God removes their spiritual blindness (verse 7) and comes as the conqueror of that which causes sorrow, and as a result He will wipe away our tears (verse 8) at this great celebration.

25:6 And in this mountain shall the Lord of hosts make unto all people a feast of fat things, a feast of wines on the lees, of fat things full of marrow, of wines on the lees well refined.

Fat things (Heb. *shemen*)—figurative of richness, delicacies.
"Full of marrow"—the choicest dainties (Ps 63:5).

The "feast of fat things" refers to serving fat, full-flavored meat, available only to royalty and to the wealthy and made even richer by the addition of bone marrow (see Keil, 439).

"Wine on the lees" is a substance described by the Hebrew word *Shmareem*, which signifies the jellies or preserves that were highly esteemed in the royal feasts of Eastern countries. These wines were prepared from lees (dregs) after the fermentation process was complete, and of grape skins, which preserved the wine and maintained remarkable color and flavor—truly a prized addition to the feast. Sometimes the rich juices of the lees were strained and served to accompany a feast; but strained or not, the preservative quality of the lees kept the juices from turning to a strong vinegar (See Fallows, *Bible Encyclopedia*, s.v. "wine," 1724; Gesenius, *Hebrew and English Lexicon of the Old Testament*, 1036–37; Keil, 439; *Encyclopedia Judaica*, 6:1418).

The great feast of the Lord in the Millennium will invite all to "Come unto Christ" and celebrate with Him. It will be a time of joy and happiness. This verse in Isaiah was also given to the prophet Joseph Smith and to the early Saints in 1831. At this time some of the Saints had gone to Jackson County Missouri to help establish Zion. The Lord prophesied that the Saints of this time period would be able to "lay the foundation" (D&C

58:7) and would testify that it will be established, but that Zion would not be established in all of her glory until "after much tribulation" (D&C 58:4). After this time of tribulation, this great feast Isaiah refers to would be held. After this verse is quoted, the Lord teaches that this feast will fulfill the words of the prophets. Preparation for this feast will begin with a spiritual "supper" at a temple where all will be invited to worthily attend and after this, the great feast of the marriage of the Lamb (Second Coming) would occur. The Lord said:

> And also that a feast of fat things might be prepared for the poor; yea, a feast of fat things, of wine on the lees well refined, that the earth may know that the mouths of the prophets shall not fail;
>
> Yea, a supper of the house of the Lord, well prepared, unto which all nations shall be invited.
>
> First, the rich and the learned, the wise and the noble;
>
> And after that cometh the day of my power; then shall the poor, the lame, and the blind, and the deaf, come in unto the marriage of the Lamb, and partake of the supper of the Lord, prepared for the great day to come.
>
> Behold, I, the Lord, have spoken it. (D&C 58:8–12)

25:7 And he will destroy in this mountain the face of the covering cast over all people, and the veil that is spread over all nations.

The "veil that is spread over all nations" is undoubtedly the veil of darkness, ignorance, and unbelief. It will be destroyed by the Lord's pouring out of knowledge upon the heads of the Latter-day Saints, and all others who will hearken in the dispensation. Also those who will live during the Millennium with Christ will be taught:

> God shall give unto you knowledge by his Holy Spirit, yea, by the unspeakable gift of the Holy Ghost, that has not been revealed since the world was until now; (D&C 121:26).

25:8 He will swallow up death in victory; and the Lord God will wipe away tears from off all faces; and the rebuke of his people shall he take away from off all the earth: for the Lord hath spoken it.

Paul quotes this passage to the Corinthians and says that when the resurrection takes place, this saying will be brought to pass (see 1 Corinthians 15:54). The "wiping away of the tears" refers to the effects of the Atonement (see Revelation 7:17; 21:4). The "rebuke of his people" represents the continual trials and afflictions which the Savior will cause to cease among Israel.

This verse also gives us a very personal glimpse into the relationship that God's people will have with Him after the Second Coming. The relationship will be as close as a family member and very trusting. There are very few people who we will allow to wipe a tear off of our cheek. We may let someone see us cry, but we are often reserved and guarded when this occurs. We would need to trust and love someone and be very familiar with them to allow them this intimate privilege. Such will be our relationship—intimate, loving, trusting, and close—with the Savior after this coming to the earth.

25:9 And it shall be said in that day, Lo, this is our God; we have waited for him, and he will save us: this is the Lord; we have waited for him, we will be glad and rejoice in his salvation.

Verses 9–12 almost come across as a hymn dealing with the day after Christ comes in glory. "Jehovah's people will rejoice that in the midst of desolating calamities which are safely past, they waited patiently for Jehovah's salvation and, in consequence, now enjoy peace and rest; whereas Moab and all other enemies of Israel are described as suffering untold anguish and desolation" (Robinson, *The Book of Isaiah in Fifteen Studies*, p. 101).

Elder Robert D. Hales of the Quorum of the Twelve Apostles shared the following account of how President David O. McKay had to wait upon the Lord:

> As a young man, President David O. McKay prayed for a witness of the truthfulness of the gospel. Many years later, while he was serving his mission in Scotland, that witness finally came. Later he wrote, "It was an assurance to me that sincere prayer is answered 'sometime, somewhere.'"

> We may not know when or how the Lord's answers will be given, but in His time and His way, I testify, His answers will come. For some answers we may have to wait until the hereafter. This may be true for some promises in our patriarchal blessings and for some blessings for family members. Let us not give up on the Lord. His blessings are eternal, not temporary. (Hales, "Waiting upon the Lord: Thy Will Be Done")

25:10 For in this mountain shall the hand of the Lord rest, and Moab shall be trodden down under him, even as straw is trodden down for the dunghill.

Moab symbolizes the wicked, proud, and arrogant (see Jer. 48:27–32) who are destroyed at the Second Coming. They are "for the dunghill" or the wicked are considered to be "in the water of the dung heap." This was the place where straw was trodden into make it manure (see Psalms 83:10).

25:11 And he shall spread forth his hands in the midst of them, as he that swimmeth spreadeth forth his hands to swim: and he shall bring down their pride together with the spoils of their hands.

In Isaiah chapter 15 and 16, Moab was seen as a nation that only relied on itself. It would not join with God but desired to make its own destiny and its own path through life. Now Isaiah compares this same self-assured confidence in their own abilities to a swimmer who powers through the waters on their own accord. They only rely on their own strength and their own pride. But just as in chapters 15 and 16, the neglect of and rejection of God leads to drowning in sin. We are more dependent on God than a swimmer is on their hands, feet, and limbs.

25:12 And the fortress of the high fort of thy walls shall he bring down, lay low, and bring to the ground, even to the dust.

Isaiah uses repetitive language in this verse to emphasize the destruction of the proud. He uses "bring down," "lay low," "bring down to the ground," and "to the dust."

ISAIAH CHAPTER 26

The Promise of Perfect Peace

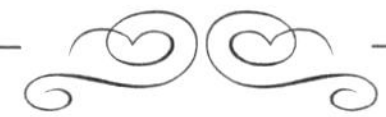

Chapters 24 and 25 prophesied of the Second Coming of Christ and of His reign in Mount Zion. Chapter 26 follows these events and is a song of hope that will be sung in the land of Judah after the Second Coming of Christ.

26:1 In that day shall this song be sung in the land of Judah; We have a strong city; salvation will God appoint for walls and bulwarks.

The song consists of four verses that are each three lines long. The first verse is the second half of verse 1 and focuses on a city's true strength. Verse 2 centers on the requirements for entrance into this city. Verse 3 indicates the perfect peace that exists in the city while the last verse of the song (verse 4) encourages the faithful in the city to trust God.

A strong city is literally "a city of strength." The strength of this city surrounds it like walls and bulwarks would surround a well defended city. The true strength of this city comes from the salvation emanating from God. Any city's strength is not the result of their walls or their missile defense systems. A city's true strength and its greatest defense is provided by the spiritual walls of Jehovah's salvation.

26:2 Open ye the gates, that the righteous nation which keepeth the truth may enter in.

Truth (Heb. *'êmûwn*)—Faithful, established, faith, truth. Note that this is the only time in the King James Version of the bible where this word is translated as "truth." Most of the time it is translated as "faithful" or "established."

The gates of this city are to be opened to the faithful. The noun for "truth" would be better translated as faithful and is plural in Hebrew. This suggests an amplitude, or higher level of faithfulness, in those who enter this city of Zion. Those who live there are described as being righteous and faithful.

26:3 Thou wilt keep him in perfect peace, whose mind is stayed on thee: because he trusteth in thee.

Keep (Heb. *shâmar*)—to hedge about, to guard, protect, attend to.
Perfect peace (Heb. *shâlôwm shâlôwm*)—lit. "peace peace," true peace, peace amplified, perfect peace.
Mind (Heb. *yêtser*)—purpose, imagination, mind-set.

Perfect peace is the result of those whose mindset is focused on God. Their way of looking at the world is through the lens of faith. Another way of translating this verse would be "Thou [the Lord] keeps in true peace those whose total way of looking at things is focused on thee: because they trust in thee."

26:4 Trust ye in the Lord for ever: for in the Lord Jehovah is everlasting strength:

Strength (Heb. *tsûwr*)—rock.

Those who find perfect peace have trusted the Lord. He becomes "an everlasting rock" to them. This imagery recalls the rock of Horeb (Exodus 17:6) and how Christ is the rock of our salvation. The faithful build and pattern their lives on the rock of Christ.

26:5 For he bringeth down them that dwell on high; the lofty city, he layeth it low; he layeth it low, even to the ground; he bringeth it even to the dust.

The lofty city probably referred to Babylon at first, the city of worldliness. But it is also called the "city of confusion" in Isaiah 24:10 and is "the city of the terrible nations" (Isaiah 25:3). This city of the prideful is symbolic of the world organized without God. Isaiah prophecies the city's destruction three times in this verse. Isaiah states that "he layeth it low" (twice) and "bringeth it" low—even to the dust. The use of the same idea three times implies a completeness or totality of this action.

26:6 The foot shall tread it down, even the feet of the poor, and the steps of the needy.

Poor (Heb. *'ânîy*)—depressed, in mind or circumstances: afflicted, humble, lowly, needy, poor.

The "it" referred to in this verse is the lofty city. Those who will "tread" or trample this city are described as being "needy," "afflicted," or "poor." They are the Lord's people who will be given this victory not because of any contribution that they have made, but because the Lord makes them victors with Him.

26:7 The way of the just is uprightness: thou, most upright, dost weigh the path of the just.

This verse is (lit.) "The path belonging to the righteous is altogether right: Upright One, you smooth the track for the righteous" (Motyer, 215). The pathway for the righteous is a planned path. It is smooth, "altogether right" or straight, and leads us to be righteous, right with God, and just. It leads us to share in His righteousness and become more like God.

26:8 Yea, in the way of thy judgments, O Lord, have we waited for thee; the desire of our soul is to thy name, and to the remembrance of thee.

As the faithful traverse God's planned path, they must wait for the judgments of God to come to pass. This patience develops righteousness and refines the Saint. It purifies the desire of their souls (heart and mind, body and spirit) to take God's name upon them. Saints who wait patiently for Christ are willing to take the name of Christ as their own.

> Willingness to take upon us the name of Jesus Christ can therefore be understood as willingness to take upon us the authority of Jesus Christ. According to this meaning, by partaking of the sacrament we witness our willingness to participate in the sacred ordinances of the temple and to receive the highest blessings available through the name and by the authority of the Savior when he chooses to confer them upon us. (Oaks, "Taking upon Us the Name of Jesus Christ")

26:9 With my soul have I desired thee in the night; yea, with my spirit within me will I seek thee early: for when thy judgments are in the earth, the inhabitants of the world will learn righteousness.

The soul is made up with the spirit and the body of a person (Doctrine and Covenants 88:15). With his spirit (often symbolized by our hearts) and with his body (a symbol of our actions), the soul of the righteous desires to be like Christ. The desire starts out early in the morning and lasts into the night. The repetition of this idea in this verse suggests the faithful's total intention and willingness to follow the Savior in their lives.

The promise made in this verse is to all of the world that if they want to "learn righteousness," they simply start with a desire to follow Christ. We must be consistent in our righteous desires and exercise our patience as we act and become more like Christ. In a way this verse could be seen as a warning to the righteous of our day. We must be looking for His Second Coming and we must also get our life in harmony with God.

26:10 Let favour be shewed to the wicked, yet will he not learn righteousness: in the land of uprightness will he deal unjustly, and will not behold the majesty of the Lord.

As we strive to help all of those around us to "learn righteousness," we must not become overwhelmed at the greatness of the task ahead of us. There are many of the inhabitants of the earth who will accept the gospel when it is shared with them and they are ". . . only kept from the truth because they know not where to find it" (D&C 123:12). There are a group of these inhabitants who are wicked and even though we show great "favour" to them as we teach them the gospel, the wicked will "not learn righteousness."

As long as they choose to be wicked, they are incapable of feeling the Spirit of God. Without the Holy Ghost, there can never be a lasting conversion to the gospel of Christ. Our eternal hope is that they will exercise faith in Christ and repent so that they one day can behold the majesty of the Lord.

26:11 Lord, when thy hand is lifted up, they will not see: but they shall see, and be ashamed for their envy at the people; yea, the fire of thine enemies shall devour them.

The phrase "they shall see" is better translated as "let them see." Isaiah is reflecting on the day when the Lord lifts up His hand in power against His adversities. Even though the wicked will refuse to see God's hand in what occurs, Isaiah pleads for God to "let them see." Ignorance of God's influence in the world will not help the wicked at all. Becoming aware of God's hand in our lives leads to an understanding of His will for us.

Fire is a symbol of active divine holiness (Motyer, 216). The influence of God will either entice the wicked to repent and be cleansed from sin, or it will devour them at the Second Coming of Christ.

26:12 Lord, thou wilt ordain peace for us: for thou also hast wrought all our works in us.

Ordain (Heb. *shâphath*)—to locate, establish, bring, ordain, set on.

Peace is the result of personal righteousness (see Isaiah 32:17). Peace is established, brought to our minds and hearts or ordained by God. We see this more clearly if we rephrase the second part of this verse as "indeed all of our works thou hast done for us." God brings the righteous peace—a perfect peace (26:3) in this life and in the life to come.

26:13 O LORD our God, other lords beside thee have had dominion over us: but by thee only will we make mention of thy name.

The other Lords that have had dominion over Israel could include rulers of this world such as Pharaoh, Nebuchadnezzar or heathen kings (see 2 Chron. 12:8, 28:5–6). It could also refer to other spiritual Lords like idols, lusts, etc. (see Rom. 6:16–18).

26:14 They are dead, they shall not live; they are deceased, they shall not rise: therefore hast thou visited and destroyed them, and made all their memory to perish.

All of the other Lords referred to in verse 13 are dead. The effect of their captivity has ended. Even the memory of the captivity is gone through the power of the Lord.

26:15 Thou hast increased the nation, O Lord, thou hast increased the nation: thou art glorified: thou hadst removed it far unto all the ends of the earth.

In verses 15–19 Isaiah speaks of the Millennium and the process of gathering all of the righteous to the end of the earth. He testifies of the prayer of the righteous during their distress (vs. 16) and how they did not have the power to save themselves (vs. 17–18). He then writes about the resurrection (vs. 19).

26:16 Lord, in trouble have they visited thee, they poured out a prayer when thy chastening was upon them.

A prayer (Heb. *lachash*)—"a whispered prayer"

One of the great problems recorded in scripture is man's indifference to God in times of prosperity. Too often man forgets his Creator, but in times of trouble they again remember their God and turn to Him for mercy and help in their afflictions. In the day of their affliction, they can merely whisper a prayer to God. Does this imply that they hope God hears their prayer, but they don't have any confidence that God will hear it? Iniquity separates us from God. Isaiah explained that "But your iniquities have separated between you and your God, and your sins have hid his face from you, that he will not hear" (Isaiah 59:2). Righteousness always inspires confidence in God and that your prayers are heard and answered. Wickedness always moves us away from God.

26:17 Like as a woman with child, that draweth near the time of her delivery, is in pain, and crieth out in her pangs; so have we been in thy sight, O Lord.

In typical fashion, Israel turned unto the Lord for help only when they were in great pain. In the same way a woman struggling to give birth is delivered of pain only when her child is born, so Israel will be free of pain when the Lord restores Zion once again (see vs. 16–18).

The Savior used the same analogy of a woman delivering a child, but did not relate it to the text of Isaiah (see John 16:21). Isaiah spoke of the delivery of Judah as a nation, while the Savior referred to the sorrow the disciples would experience over His death, which sorrow would be replaced with joy when He was resurrected.

26:18 We have been with child, we have been in pain, we have as it were brought forth wind; we have not wrought any deliverance in the earth; neither have the inhabitants of the world fallen.

The analogy of a woman delivering a child continues in this verse. For a wicked nation, they will go through a very painful experience, but they will gave birth to wind or in other words, they will be nothing from their travail.

26:19 Thy dead men shall live, together with my dead body shall they arise. Awake and sing, ye that dwell in dust: for thy dew is as the dew of herbs, and the earth shall cast out the dead.

"Thy dead" refers to the dead who you are concerned about. This is the first clear statement in the Old Testament of the resurrection of those we care about. They will be resurrected along with "my dead body"—the body of the prophet Isaiah. You could also interpret the "my" as referring to the Lord Jesus Christ. Through Christ, all are made alive in the resurrection. This verse is a clear statement of the fact of resurrection, the Lord's and our own.

This verse also calls for singing and rejoicing. The resurrection is like the dew is to herbs. Dew descends and refreshes. The resurrection will come from God and refresh our bodies. Isaiah referred to this imagery earlier in Isaiah 18:4 and implied that the effect of a cloud of dew was a rich and plentiful harvest.

26:20 Come, my people, enter thou into thy chambers, and shut thy doors about thee: hide thyself as it were for a little moment, until the indignation be overpast.

26:21 For, behold, the Lord cometh out of his place to punish the inhabitants of the earth for their iniquity: the earth also shall disclose her blood, and shall no more cover her slain.

Isaiah opened the song in verse 2 with "Open ye the gates." Isaiah matches a closing to this chapter with "Shut the Gates." In doing this he invites us to remember a scene from the Exodus. In Exodus 12, Israel went into their homes and shut the door, and the Lord destroyed the firstborn of Egyptians. Joseph Smith used this passage to show that Judah would obtain deliverance at Jerusalem (see *TPJS*, p. 17). The context shows that the verses refer to the time when Judah will be secluded in Jerusalem and the arm of the Lord will fall upon the nations, as foretold by the Savior and repeated to the Prophet Joseph Smith (see D&C 45:16, 43–47).

> The prophet exhorts his own people, his disciples, to continue a little longer in the solitude of prayer, till God's wrath is overpast. They are to be saved, but the land as a whole is incapable of salvation. Yet in that day (27:1) the agents of destruction shall themselves be destroyed: viz., "the swift serpent," Assyria; "the crooked serpent," Babylonia; and the sea "monster," Egypt. (Robinson, *The Book of Isaiah in Fifteen Studies*, p. 103).

President Charles W. Penrose applied Isaiah 26:20–21 to the Latter-day Saints living in seclusion in the mountains of Zion when he said:

> We are to be saviors of men, too, in sending or carrying the gospel to every nation, kindred and tongue and people. That is imposed upon us; that is required of us. We are here on the earth with a mission to perform. Every Latter-day Saint, every man and woman and boy and girl born in the covenant or who has received it, is under obligations to do all that is possible for the sending forth of the word of the Lord to all the nations of the earth. A good many of my brethren here on this stand and around have been out to the world, and we have done our part as far as we could in sounding a warning to the nations of the earth. We have traveled extensively among the nations that are now at war. We have preached and lifted up our voices and warned them of troubles and judgments to come, and now these things are upon them. We see the fulfillment of the words

of the Lord; and while we do not rejoice in human suffering, we cannot help rejoicing in the fact that the Lord made known to us, years and years ago, that these things would come, and showed us how we might escape and help others to escape them. I remember the words of Isaiah, the prophet, which we have often quoted, where he says unto Zion: . . . (Isa. 26:20–21)

These things have been literally fulfilled in our time and our experience; and how thankful we ought to be that we are here in these chambers of the mountains, that Zion, bringing good tidings, has come up into the high mountain as Isaiah predicted, that we are here dwelling in quiet places and peaceable resting places just as Isaiah saw that we would in the latter days, (chap. 32) and that in the midst of the troubles and dangers that are abroad in the world, we have the consolation of having done our duty and warned the inhabitants of the earth of judgments to come. And the Lord said that after our testimony would come the testimony of earthquakes and of the waves of the sea heaving themselves beyond their bounds, of floods and fire and flame and the sword and wars and rumors of wars and earthquakes in divers places, and these are but 'the beginnings of sorrows' for the latter days. Now, we have done a great deal in warning the inhabitants of the earth concerning this, and those who have gone forth weeping sometimes, have come back bearing precious seeds and planted them right here in the chambers of these mountains, and we are surrounded by peace and good-will and kindness of heart among the ranks of the Latter-day Saints. (Penrose, in Conference Report, April 1918, 17–18)

ISAIAH CHAPTER 27

We Are Gathered "One by One"

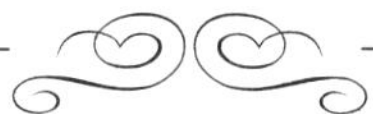

THIS CHAPTER FOCUSES ON THE SECOND COMING OF CHRIST. ISAIAH builds on this theme throughout the chapter and emphasizes that when Christ comes again, the righteous will be gathered to the temple. This is a wonderful conclusion to the topics discussed in chapters 24–26 which contained prophecies of the Second Coming of Christ and of His reign on Mount Zion.

27:1 In that day the Lord with his sore and great and strong sword shall punish leviathan the piercing serpent, even leviathan that crooked serpent; and he shall slay the dragon that is in the sea.

Sore (Heb. *qâsheh*)—fierce, intense, severe, hard.
Crooked (Heb. *'□qallâthôwn*)—tortuous.
Dragon (Heb. *tannîyn*)—a land or sea monster.

In the day of the Second Coming of Christ, He will come with a sword. Isaiah describes the sword with three words—sore (fierce, severe, unsparing), great (enough for any task), and strong (powerful enough for any foe). This matches the three words used in this verse to describe His foe—piercing serpent, crooked serpent, and dragon (a monster). A leviathan was a serpent (especially the crocodile or some other large sea monster) and represented the forces of chaos. It was a symbol of the ancient city of Babylon and associated with spiritual Babylon in the Book of Revelation.

In scripture, both the dragon and the serpent are symbols for Satan (see Revelation 12:9). The sword of God will be used to defeat the enemy Satan and all that he stands for. In Satan there is only a promise of hell and death. In 2 Nephi 9:10–14, Jacob says that awful monster, death and hell, will be overcome and destroyed. Therefore the destruction of the leviathan is destroying death and hell.

The Lord's Vineyard Is His People and They Will Fill the World

27:2 In that day sing ye unto her, A vineyard of red wine.

Why are you are going to sing? Christ has destroyed the things we fear the most—death and hell. Now we sing of a vineyard of red wine. The vineyard represents God's people and the red wine is a symbol of the Savior's atoning blood and comes from a productive vineyard. It is His vineyard and He is in charge of it.

27:3 I the Lord do keep it; I will water it every moment: lest any hurt it, I will keep it night and day.

Keep (Heb. *nâtsar*)—to guard, watch over.

The Lord Himself is mindful of His vineyard. He watches over it and protects it. We can have confidence that when we are in need, God will be watching over us and will provide what is needed ("the water") in "every moment" when it is needed—both day and night.

27:4 Fury is not in me: who would set the briers and thorns against me in battle? I would go through them, I would burn them together.

As God watches over His vineyard, we can see Him looking for weeds (briers and thorns) that may start to grow. It is as if He is challenging a weed to grow so that He can quickly destroy it. The destruction of the weed, or wickedness from His people, is not because He is mad or angry. It comes from love and a desire to make His vineyard (people) become as productive as possible.

27:5 Or let him take hold of my strength, that he may make peace with me; and he shall make peace with me.

The "him" referred to in this verse is a reference to the figurative weed (briers and thorns) of the last verse. This is an invitation to all to "take hold" of the horns of the temple altar and gain asylum in God's mercy (see I Kings 1:50; 2:28). It is an invitation to come unto Christ and join His strength. As the weed joins itself to the strength of God, it is transformed figuratively into a productive member of the vineyard and God will give them peace as a full and equal member of a productive vineyard.

27:6 He shall cause them that come of Jacob to take root: Israel shall blossom and bud, and fill the face of the world with fruit.

Come (Heb. *bôw'*)—to go in, enter, come in.

God will cause that those who enter into Jacob (Israel) will grow (take root). They will become productive (blossom and bud) in the vineyard of the Lord. It is this covenant Israel that will spread and fill the world with their labor—the fruit of the Tree of Life. This is also what Alma taught at the end of Alma 32. The tree that righteous Israel becomes produces fruit leading to "everlasting life" (verse 41). The fruit "is most precious, which is sweet above all that is sweet, and which is white above all that is white, yea, and pure above all that is pure;" (verse 42). This fruit is identified by Nephi as the fruit of the Tree of Life (see 1 Nephi 8:10–12, 11:8, 9, 22–23; 15:36).

27:7 Hath he smitten him, as he smote those that smote him? or is he slain according to the slaughter of them that are slain by him?

Isaiah asks if God had smote Israel to the same extent as He smote their conquerors. Did Israel suffer the causalities to the same extent as those God destroyed? Jehovah's chastisements of Israel were light compared with the judgments of Jehovah upon other nations.

27:8 In measure, when it shooteth forth, thou wilt debate with it: he stayeth his rough wind in the day of the east wind.

Debate (Heb. *rîyb*)—to plead, strive, contend.

When the time comes for "it," or Israel, to be like a vine and shoot forth (spread or expand), God will plead its cause. The East wind can be a violent wind but is limited in its duration. God limits the duration of Israel's days of trials as He limits the rough winds.

27:9 By this therefore shall the iniquity of Jacob be purged; and this is all the fruit to take away his sin; when he maketh all the stones of the altar as chalkstones that are beaten in sunder, the groves and images shall not stand up.

> Purged (Heb. *kâphar*)—to cover, make atonement for.
> Sin (Heb. *chaṭṭâ'âh*)—an offence (sometimes habitual sinfulness).
> Beaten in sunder—broken in pieces or pulverized.

Jacob needed to renounce its sins and forsake his idolatry. Forgiveness is always possible through the Atonement. In this verse, the Hebrew word *Kaphar* is translated as "purged." In other places in the Old Testament the word is translated as "atonement" or "covering." In other words, the iniquity of Jacob will be atoned for by Christ. The entire fruit of Christ's Atonement is to take away sins. Isaiah indicates that once Christ has made a full atonement, the altar of the temple will no longer be needed and will be pulverized. Literally the rocks will be like pulverized limestone.

27:10 Yet the defenced city shall be desolate, and the habitation forsaken, and left like a wilderness: there shall the calf feed, and there shall he lie down, and consume the branches thereof.

The "defenced city" refers to Jerusalem. Jerusalem will be destroyed and is compared to an area where a calf feeds. The calf eats the bark off of the branches and brakes them off of the tree. The calf leaves the tree broken and exposed to the elements. And as it will be seen in the next verse, this will cause the remaining branches to wither, dry out and cast in the fire.

27:11 When the boughs thereof are withered, they shall be broken off: the women come, and set them on fire: for it is a people of no understanding: therefore he that made them will not have mercy on them, and he that formed them will shew them no favour.

"When the boughs are withered" refers to the tribes of Israel becoming wicked. When they are wicked, they will be "broken off" (scattered) and then cast into the fire (judged). The wicked are a group who do not have an "understanding" of that which matters most—the gospel of Jesus Christ. As a result, the Creator will not have mercy on them or favor them.

27:12 And it shall come to pass in that day, that the Lord shall beat off from the channel of the river unto the stream of Egypt, and ye shall be gathered one by one, O ye children of Israel.

Beat (Heb. *châbaṭ*)—to beat off, thresh, an act associated with the harvest of olives.

"In that day" refers to the last days preparatory to the coming of Christ. The "channel of the river" refers to the Euphrates River. The area between the Euphrates and Egypt's "stream" (Nile) contains much of the Middle East. This prophecy reminds us that in our day, Jehovah spares no pains to gather "one by one" the remnant of His people from Assyria and Egypt.

27:13 And it shall come to pass in that day, that the great trumpet shall be blown, and they shall come which were ready to perish in the land of Assyria, and the outcasts in the land of Egypt, and shall worship the Lord in the holy mount at Jerusalem.

The Jubilee trumpet in Leviticus 25:9 was blown on the Day of Atonement and was to be sounded throughout the land. The Great Day of Atonement is the day the "outcasts" or exiles will return to Jerusalem to worship the Lord who will have returned to rule and reign for one thousand years. The Day of Atonement saves those who were about "ready to perish" in an increasingly wicked world. The Great Day of the Lord may be dreadful for the wicked, but it will also gather the righteous to the temple. It is very interesting to note that the righteous end up in the temple. If our focus is on the temple, we will be ready to meet the Lord at His coming.

ISAIAH CHAPTER 28

A Pattern for Acquiring Spiritual Knowledge

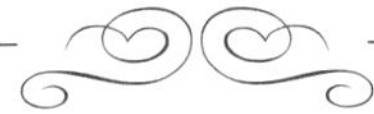

In chapters 13–27 Isaiah's visions centered on God's implementation of His divine purposes. Chapters 28–35 focus on the testimony of the reality of God's power. God's purpose is to encourage, edify, and bring all of His sons and daughters back into His presence. It is by God's power that this will be accomplished.

Chapter 28 starts this focus by testifying that Christ is our cornerstone and that the coming forth of the Book of Mormon (chapter 29) sets us on the foundation of Christ. The defense, preservation, and purification of Israel is testified of in chapters 30–33 as a preparation for the Second Coming of Christ. Chapter 34 and 35 testify of the Second Coming and how Zion prepares a people for this great event.

Starting in chapter 28 there are six "woes" mentioned. "Woe" in Hebrew is '*hôwy*' which is a word of summons or a greeting such as "Ho!" or "Alas!" The six woes of summoning or greeting are directed at:

1st Woe 28:1—"the crown of the pride, to the drunkards of Ephraim."
2nd Woe 29:1—"Ariel."
3rd Woe 29:15—those "that seek deep to hide their counsel from the Lord."
4th Woe 30:1—"the rebellious children, saith the Lord, that take counsel, but not of me."

5th Woe 31:1—"them that go down to Egypt for help."
6th Woe 33:1—"thou that spoilest and thou wast not spoiled."

28:1 Woe to the crown of pride, to the drunkards of Ephraim, whose glorious beauty is a fading flower, which are on the head of the fat valleys of them that are overcome with wine!

Overcome (Heb. *hâlam*)—smite, stricken, hammered down.

The "crown of pride" refers to Samaria, the capital of Ephraim and more specifically the drunkards of Ephraim. Like a drunk person, they are irrationally rushing toward to their own destruction. The first woe is given to this prideful people. Ephraim at the time was the leading tribe of the northern ten tribes of Israel and in Isaiah's day, they were about to be captured by Assyria in 722 BC. Their "fading" beauty indicates that their drunken party is almost over. Their pride has led them to their destruction.

28:2 Behold, the Lord hath a mighty and strong one, which as a tempest of hail and a destroying storm, as a flood of mighty waters overflowing, shall cast down to the earth with the hand.

Mighty (Heb. *châzâq*)—Powerful, power in relation to the task to be accomplished.
Strong (Heb. *'ammîyts*)—Strength (in the abstract) that resides in the instrument or agent.

The Lord could have named Assyria as the "mighty and strong" nation, but He doesn't. His emphasis is not on the name of a nation, but on the principles being taught by these events. When a nation is wicked, God often sends "a tempest", and/or "a flood of mighty waters" to humble them. Whatever or whoever is the agent, they will be strong enough to accomplish God's will. They will be powerful enough to accomplish the task that God wants them to complete. In this case, Assyria will be the tempest and storm that will slam into Ephraim and cast her down.

In fulfillment of this prophecy, in 724 BC, Shalmaneser, King of Assyria, besieged Samaria. After a three-year siege, Sargon II will complete the task and carry the ten tribes into captivity.

28:3 The crown of pride, the drunkards of Ephraim, shall be trodden under feet:

Isaiah emphasizes that any nation that is prideful must choose to repent and become humble, or they will be compelled to be humble. The phrase "trodden under feet" indicates a future period of subjugation and enslavement (see 1 Cor. 15:24–25; D&C 49:6; 76:61, 106).

28:4 And the glorious beauty, which is on the head of the fat valley, shall be a fading flower, and as the hasty fruit before the summer; which when he that looketh upon it seeth, while it is yet in his hand he eateth it up.

Hasty fruit (Heb. *bikkûwr*)—first fruits, the first of the crops and fruit that ripened, was gathered, and offered to God according to the ritual of Pentecost

Figs usually ripened in August; but a few earlier ones ripened in June and were regarded as a delicacy (see Jer. 24:2; Hos 9:10; Mic 7:1). As easily as an early ripe fig is singled out, picked, and eaten by a passerby (see Nahum 3:12), so will Assyria consume Samaria.

28:5 In that day shall the Lord of hosts be for a crown of glory, and for a diadem of beauty, unto the residue of his people,

This verse introduces hope into the conversation. Earlier in verse 1, the words "crown" (of pride) and "beauty" (fading) were used for a people running to their own doom. Now these two words are used again in association with what God can provide—a "crown of glory" and a "diadem of beauty." The crown is given to those who will be a king and diadems are given as a symbol of those who have overcome and won a great victory. With the Lord, we will be given a "crown of life" in God's kingdom (see Rev. 2:10) and will share Christ's victory over sin and death.

28:6 And for a spirit of judgment to him that sitteth in judgment, and for strength to them that turn the battle to the gate.

Gate (Heb. *sha'ar*)—gate, entrance, symbolic of the defense of a city.

In Isaiah 4:4, the "spirit of judgment" aided in the purging of wickedness out of Jerusalem and its people. The spirit of judgment involves justice and mercy. "It is 'a right judgment in all things'" (see Motyer, 80–81). A "righteous judgment" (John 7:24; 2 Thessalonians 1:5; Romans 2:5; Alma 41:14) brings strength to those who are defenders of righteousness.

28:7 But they also have erred through wine, and through strong drink are out of the way; the priest and the prophet have erred through strong drink, they are swallowed up of wine, they are out of the way through strong drink; they err in vision, they stumble in judgment.

Erred (Heb. *shâgâh*)—to be led astray, stumbled.
Swallowed (Heb. *bâla'*)—engulfed, swallowed.

Isaiah sees the current religious and political leaders as being "led by," influenced "through," and "engulfed" in the influence of wine and strong drink. They have succumbed to their indulgences in alcohol. This indulgence in alcohol has been spiritually devastating and resulting in them being "out of the way" (misled into forbidden paths), having "erred" (stumbled in their decisions), having "erred in vision" (lost the ability to receive revelation and thereby rely on their own vision) and have "stumbled in judgment" (of others). Their indulgence has prevented them from fulfilling their roles as leaders and are as spiritually perceptive as a drunk.

28:8 For all tables are full of vomit and filthiness, so that there is no place clean.

The result of a leader's indulgence in alcohol is vivid. It stinks like vomit. It creates filth where you would least like their filth to be. The result is a spiritually unclean individual, and the effect reaches every part of their homes and society.

28:9 Whom shall he teach knowledge? and whom shall he make to understand doctrine? them that are weaned from the milk, and drawn from the breasts.

Isaiah asks the question: "Whom shall he teach knowledge? and whom shall he make to understand doctrine?" Then he answers it himself. The young.

The principle of revelation taught here through the analogy of a baby's being fed on milk before taking solid foods was also taught by Paul (see 1 Corinthians 3:1–2; Hebrews 5:11–14), by Peter (see 1 Peter 2:2), and by the Prophet Joseph Smith (see D&C 19:21–22). One must learn basic principles before he is ready to understand the mysteries of God. One must learn righteous instructions in their youth. After you learn about righteousness, you naturally are attracted to righteousness. You learn about it and then you act in faith on what you learned. The youth then will share the knowledge and their understanding of doctrine to others.

28:10 For precept must be upon precept, precept upon precept; line upon line, line upon line; here a little, and there a little:

Precept (Heb. *tsav*)—command, ordinance.
Line (Heb. *qav*)—cord, line, measuring-line.

The word "precept" comes from the Latin word *praecipere* meaning "to warn or instruct." The Webster's 1828 dictionary defined "precept": "In a general sense, any commandment or order intended as an authoritative rule of action; but applied particularly to commands respecting moral conduct." A precept is simply a general or basic command or ordinance intended to regulate behavior or thought.

Starting with a general command/ordinance, you add another general or basic command/ordinance. They must build on each other. Isaiah then adds "line upon line." Isaiah is using the imagery of builders—the plumb and the line that were used to lay stones. These building stones built homes and the temple. The House of God would have started with the cornerstone and then using the line and the plumb you would fit stone next to stone and stone upon stone.

We individually are built the same way as the temple. We start with the cornerstone (see verse 16) Jesus Christ and use Him as our guide. We build on Christ one basic principle at a time—"here a little, there a little." We add one ordinance onto another ordinance. Each one is designed to bind us closer to God. It takes a long time to build a temple and it takes a long time to build our temples in Christ. The prophet Joseph Smith compared this building process to climbing a ladder. He said: "When you climb up a ladder, you must begin at the bottom, and ascend step by step, until you arrive at the top; and so it is with the principles of the gospel—you must begin with the first, and go on until you learn all the principles of exaltation" (*Teachings of Presidents: Joseph Smith*, 348).

Elder David A. Bednar of the Quorum of the Twelve Apostles clarified the Lord's pattern for giving us spiritual knowledge:

> I believe many of us unknowingly accept a faulty assumption about the Lord's pattern. And this faulty assumption then produces erroneous expectations about how we receive spiritual knowledge. And that faulty assumption and our misinformed expectations ultimately hinder our ability to recognize and respond to the promptings of the Holy Ghost. Let me suggest that many of us typically assume we will receive *an* answer or *a* prompting to our earnest prayers and pleadings. And we also frequently expect that such an answer or a prompting will come immediately and *all at once*. Thus, we tend to believe the Lord will give us A BIG ANSWER QUICKLY AND ALL AT ONE TIME. However, the pattern repeatedly described in the scriptures suggests we receive "line upon line, precept upon precept," or in other words, *many small answers over a period of time*. Recognizing and understanding this pattern is an important key to obtaining inspiration and help from the Holy Ghost. (Bednar, "Line upon Line, Precept upon Precept," emphasis in original)

28:11 For with stammering lips and another tongue will he speak to this people.

"Stammering lips and another tongue" indicates that the Lord will teach "this people" (the drunkards) with a language that they cannot understand. God teaches by the Spirit. Revelation from God is only understood by those who are willing and prepared to listen to Him.

28:12 To whom he said, This is the rest wherewith ye may cause the weary to rest; and this is the refreshing: yet they would not hear.

Would (Heb. *'âbâh*)—willing to.

God has made promises to the faithful to provide for their rest. The weary are those who are at the end of a long journey or difficult toil. God's rest refreshes our bodies and spirits. Even though we have this promise, they (those whom Isaiah is speaking to) are not willing to even listen to His message. The next two verses will remind them again that Jehovah will soon speak to them by the Assyrians.

28:13 But the word of the Lord was unto them precept upon precept, precept upon precept; line upon line, line upon line; here a little, and there a little; that they might go, and fall backward, and be broken, and snared, and taken.

God's word was a command and an ordinance, each building on each other, so that their temple of faith was built on the cornerstone of Christ. For them, God's word sounded like a babbling fool in another language. Instead of listening and thereby producing a temple of faith, they could only mock it, and, as a result, the rulers at Jerusalem would be taken captive by Assyria.

28:14 Wherefore hear the word of the Lord, ye scornful men, that rule this people which is in Jerusalem.

28:15 Because ye have said, We have made a covenant with death, and with hell are we at agreement; when the overflowing scourge shall pass through, it shall not come unto us: for we have made lies our refuge, and under falsehood have we hid ourselves:

"Covenant with death"—a covenant with Egypt to fight Assyria.

In what way had Judah "made a covenant with death, and with hell"? They had "deliberately entered into a covenant to serve, in return for protection, a god or gods other than their own. Death, *maweth*, is here the god of the underworld, Sheol or hell. It was customary for the prophets to speak of the alien deities as lies and falsehood (compare Amos 2:4; Jer. 10:14). Israel made a covenant with death because that is what 'the wages of sin' are—death (Romans 6;23)" (*Old Testament Student Manual*, 163).

In Isaiah 28:15, 18–19, Isaiah mentions the "overflowing scourge" twice and may indicate two different time periods. The Lord has sent and will yet send many scourges upon the earth. In March 1829 the Lord said: "For a desolating scourge shall go forth among the inhabitants of the earth, and shall continue to be poured out from time to time, if they repent not, until the earth is empty, and the inhabitants thereof are consumed away and utterly destroyed by the brightness of my coming" (D&C 5:19).

The Prophet Joseph Smith identified one of these scourges when he said: "The servants of God will not have gone over the nations of the Gentiles, with a warning voice, until the destroying angel will commence to waste the inhabitants of the earth, and as the prophet [Isaiah] hath said, 'It shall be a vexation to hear the report" (*Teachings of Presidents: Joseph Smith*, 87). Similarly, the Lord told Joseph: "And there shall be men standing in that generation that shall not pass until they shall see an overflowing scourge; for a desolating sickness shall cover the land" (D&C 45:31). "The Lord's scourge shall pass over by night and by day, and the report thereof shall vex all people; yea, it shall not be stayed until the Lord come" (D&C 97:23).

In speaking of this scourge, the Prophet Joseph Smith added:

> And now I am prepared to say by the authority of Jesus Christ, that not many years shall pass away before the United States shall present such a scene of bloodshed as has not a parallel in the history of our nation; pestilence, hail, famine, and earthquake will sweep the wicked of this generation from off the face of the land, to open and prepare the way for the return of the lost tribes of Israel from the north country. . . .[T]herefore I declare unto you the warning which the Lord has commanded me to declare unto this generation, remembering that the eyes of my Maker are upon me, and that to Him I am accountable for every word I say wishing nothing worse to my fellow-men than their eternal salvation; therefore, "Fear God. and give glory to Him, for the hour of His judgment is come." Repent yc, repent ye, and embrace the everlasting covenant, and flee to Zion, before the overflowing scourge overtake you, for there are those now living upon the earth whose eyes shall not be closed in death until they see all these things, which I have spoken, fulfilled. Remember these things; call upon the Lord while He is near, and seek Him

> while He may be found, is the exhortation of your unworthy servant. (Smith, *History of the Church*, 272)

28:16 Therefore thus saith the Lord God, Behold, I lay in Zion for a foundation a stone, a tried stone, a precious corner stone, a sure foundation: he that believeth shall not make haste.

> "A 'stone in Zion' could be 'a stone, namely Zion. . . . A 'tested stone' is either one 'which has undergone tests', or 'which imposes tests' by offering opportunities either to build upon it or to turn to another foundation. 'Precious' signifies the intrinsic value of it, the privilege of the way of faith. 'Sure foundation' is '(well)-founded foundation" (Motyer, 233).

The tried and precious cornerstone is Jesus Christ Himself. Elder Bruce R. McConkie wrote:

> One of Isaiah's great Messianic prophecies was that the promised Messiah would be "for a stone of stumbling and for a rock of offence to both the houses if Israel, for a gin and for a snare to the inhabitants of Jerusalem. And many among them shall stumble, and fall, and be broken, and be snared, and be taken." (Isaiah 8:14–15) Both Paul (Rom. 9:33) and Peter (1 Peter 2:7–8) record the fulfilment of this prophecy. (*Mormon Doctrine*, 657)

Jacob referred to this figure when he said that "by the stumbling of the Jews they will reject the stone upon which they might build and have safe foundation" (Jacob 4:15). The prophecy that the stone would be rejected by the Jews is also found in Psalm 118:22 and is quoted by the Savior in the New Testament (see Matthew 21:42). Paul also used the same imagery when he said that foundation of The Church of Jesus Christ was apostles and prophets, with Christ Himself being the chief cornerstone (see Ephesians 2:19–20).

28:17 Judgment also will I lay to the line, and righteousness to the plummet: and the hail shall sweep away the refuge of lies, and the waters shall overflow the hiding place.

"The line"—the measuring-line of the plummet.

"Plummet"—An instrument used by carpenters, masons, etc. in adjusting to a perpendicular line in connection with a square."

"Judgment also will I lay to the line, and righteousness to the plummet" alludes to the building trades and continues the imagery found in 28:16. Stonemasons use a measuring line and plumb bob (plummet) to ensure a proper fit in the structure. A builder uses a plumb bob to find a straight vertical line. The plumb bob is a heavy weight attached to a cord which, when dropped, falls perpendicular to its beginning point. Thus the builder knows he has a straight line. With righteousness and justice as His measuring tools, the Savior starts with the chief cornerstone (Himself) and lays out a perfect and firmly built house. If the stones do not measure up to these standards, they will be set aside (1:21). A firmly established building with righteous dwellers will survive sweeping hail and overflowing waters, especially one reared through the "covenant with death" (Isaiah 28:18).

28:18 And your covenant with death shall be disannulled, and your agreement with hell shall not stand; when the overflowing scourge shall pass through, then ye shall be trodden down by it.

Disannulled (Heb. *kaphar*)—to cover, make an atonement, reconciliation.

Their signed treaty with Egypt to fight Assyria (see 28:15) will prove meaningless. When the time of their distress comes, they will feel the full effects of the event. This verse also has a very significant second meaning. Isaiah uses the Hebrew word for atonement in this verse to testify that the effects of death and hell will not stand. Through Christ's Atonement, the effects of death and hell are disannulled (covered, atoned for) and will not stand.

28:19 From the time that it goeth forth it shall take you: for morning by morning shall it pass over, by day and by night: and it shall be a vexation only to understand the report.

The scourge mentioned in the previous verse will "pass over" them like an overflowing river. Its destruction will be continuous both day and night and it will be difficult to simply understand the devastations that are given in a report.

28:20 For the bed is shorter than that a man can stretch himself on it: and the covering narrower than that he can wrap himself in it.

The word "for" could be translated as "because." This verse explains why the continuous devastation occurred in verse 19. In the same way that a small bed is too short for a tall person, or a small blanket does not adequately provide warmth and comfort to an adult, the protection the wicked have sought in a security without God will be wholly inadequate.

The imagery of the bed and the inadequate covers is more easily understood than the imagery of the plummet. Obviously, if one is not covered by the atoning blood of Jesus Christ, he will find himself like a man in a bed too short for him with a blanket that is too small to cover him. No matter how appealing sin may look at first, it can never satisfy man's inner needs. The sinful man will be ever like the man in a short bed with inadequate covers. He will twist and turn and constantly seek comfort, but he cannot find it. The Atonement of Christ for sin covers, or is efficacious for, only those who trust in God with all their hearts and keep His holy commandments.

28:21 For the Lord shall rise up as in mount Perazim, he shall be wroth as in the valley of Gibeon, that he may do his work, his strange work; and bring to pass his act, his strange act.

Strange (Heb. *nokriy*)—unknown, unfamiliar (fig.)

This verse also begins with the word "for" and adds a second reason for the devastation in verse 19. The background for mount Perazim is found in 2 Samuel 5:17–21. It is a place where God inspired David to rise up and conquer Israel's enemies. Their enemies came again against David at the valley of Gibeon. Once again David sought the Lord and he was told to *bestir* (make physical or mental effort) himself and conquer Israel's enemies.

God inspires us to rise up and make physical or mental efforts to conquer all enemies of righteousness. To assist us, God gives us a "work" or an "act" that may appear strange to us. The "strange act" referred to in this verse is identified in the Doctrine and Covenants as the restoration of the gospel in the latter days and its going forth through the Spirit of the Lord (see D&C 95:4; 101:95). The Lord probably calls His work a strange act because the world does not usually rely upon the Spirit to prove or understand things. Oliver Cowdery said, "the angel Moroni told Joseph Smith that this strange act would bring about a marvelous work and a wonder, and that the scripture in Isaiah was about to be fulfilled" (see *Messenger and Advocate*, Feb. 1835, p. 79). This verse shows a chronological link between chapters 28 and 29 of Isaiah.

28:22 Now therefore be ye not mockers, lest your bands be made strong: for I have heard from the Lord God of hosts a consumption, even determined upon the whole earth.

Consumption (Heb. *kalah*)—complete destruction.

"O, beware, my Lord, of jealousy; It is the green-ey'd monster, which doth mock the meat it feeds on" (William Shakespeare, *Othello*). Those who mock lack understanding and are not able to comprehend the significance of greatness. Mocking makes the bands of ignorance and spiritual indifference stronger with each taunt. For them, God has decreed a complete destruction—wherever they are on the earth.

Parables of Sowing and Reaping

These two parables are based on the work of the farmer and the reaper. The farmer plows, plants, and harvests each item in its own way and according to its own time. The reaper threshes the different kinds of grain with different methods. Isaiah teaches in the next few verses that the Lord has planted His people at different times in various places and the Lord will gather His people and thresh out the wicked according to appointed times of the harvest.

28:23 Give ye ear, and hear my voice; hearken, and hear my speech.

With each "woe" mentioned in chapters 28–34 there is a corresponding promise. The first promise is found in Isaiah 28:23–29. The reaping and thrashing of the world (as with the example of how land is worked over by a farmer.) In other words, God will properly and fairly deal with the wicked, according to their actions, thoughts, and desires.

28:24 Doth the plowman plow all day to sow? doth he open and break the clods of his ground?

How long does a farmer plow his field? Only the time it takes to get it ready to sow. The Lord is the plowman who, like the farmer, performs all His work in its proper order and has specific results in mind.

28:25 When he hath made plain the face thereof, doth he not cast abroad the fitches, and scatter the cummin, and cast in the principal wheat and the appointed barley and the rie in their place?

Plain (Heb. *shavah*)—smooth.
The face (Heb. *paniym*)—surface.
Fitches—dill.
Principal wheat—plant the wheat in rows.

Fitches are a very fragile plant—the plant grows and develops with little pods which contain seeds. Cummin "seeds are often used as a spice in the East, both bruised to mix with bread, and also boiled in the various messes and stews which compose an Oriental banquet. It is also used medicinally as a stimulant (Tristram). In Egypt and Syria, black cummin is sprinkled thickly over flat cakes of the country before they are baked and are hot to the taste" (Slotki, 132–133).

In this verse, three verbs teach us of the careful action of God. "Cast abroad" (sow), "scatter," and "cast in" (plant) indicate that God knows what to do with each seed that He plants. He knows how to plant faith in the heart of each of His daughters and sons.

28:26 For his God doth instruct him to discretion, and doth teach him.

Discretion (Heb. *mishpat*)—judgment, ordinances.

The seeds that are planted by God in our hearts and minds instruct us in His ways. They literally lead to ordinances and prepare us for judgment (the threshing in the next verse). The seeds of faith in Christ will always teach, prepare, and enable us to come closer to God.

28:27 For the fitches are not threshed with a threshing instrument, neither is a cart wheel turned about upon the cummin; but the fitches are beaten out with a staff, and the cummin with a rod.

Threshing instruments were used by the more affluent in Isaiah's day. The poor would thresh their corn by allowing the oxen or horses walk on it and their sharp hoofs threshed the corn. These animals would not be yoked to any implement, but simply driven wildly over the sheaves strewn upon the threshing floor. If you are a little more affluent, you will use a threshing sledge that would be drug by an animal. On the bottom of this sledge are rocks and iron that separates the kernels from the husks.

How do you thresh fitches and cummin? Fitches and cummin bear small, delicate seeds. If a threshing machine or cartwheel were used to thresh them, they would be completely destroyed or lost. You start by cutting the branches off the stocks and then holding them upside down and smacking a stick against the branch while the seeds fall out. Therefore, the "fitches are beaten out with a staff, and the cummin with a rod" to loosen and separate the seeds. Neither can bear the heavy cylinder of the corn-threshing instrument, or the feet of oxen; but while the fitches can be easily separated from its slight case by a slender rod, the harder pod of the cummin requires to be beaten with a stouter staff in order to dislodge the seed.

Isaiah's message seems to be this: The Lord uses different means to separate the righteous from the unrighteous and to punish or chastise the unrighteous. Some he crushes with a threshing instrument or cartwheel; others he beats with a rod or staff.

28:28 Bread corn is bruised; because he will not ever be threshing it, nor break it with the wheel of his cart, nor bruise it with his horsemen.

Bruised (Heb. *daqaq*)—threshed.

Anciently, after the bread corn was spread upon the threshing floor, a threshing instrument or cartwheel was rolled over it, bruising but not crushing the kernels. The farmer did not spend too much time threshing ("he will not ever be threshing"), lest the wheel of the cart or the horsemen crush the kernels.

28:29 This also cometh forth from the Lord of hosts, which is wonderful in counsel, and excellent in working.

> However, Jehovah's judgments upon them will not be arbitrary. The methods employed by peasants in agriculture are a parable of God's purpose in disciplining. For example, the husbandman does not plow and harrow his fields the whole year round; he plows and harrows that he may also sow and reap. So God will not punish his people forever; a glorious future awaits the redeemed. The husbandman does not thresh all kinds of grain with equal severity; no more will God discipline his people beyond their deserts. (Robinson, *The Book of Isaiah in Fifteen Studies*, p. 109–110)

The farmer does not plow and harrow his fields the whole year round. He plows to prepare to plant. He plants to have a harvest. Isaiah endeavored to show how the Lord tenderly and lovingly worked with ancient Israel and works with each of us today. The Lord softens the soil of our hearts and minds so that the seeds of faith are sown. At an appointed time, God requires a harvest and separates the seed from the chaff. To harvest the righteousness within us, sometimes God uses a staff of disappointment to separate us from an unrighteous act. Other times He may use the rod of adversity to help us get rid of an unrighteous habit. Addictions may need to be separated from our lives with the wheel of the cart or a threshing instrument of severe trials and God's discipline. The Lord loves His children and is always trying to get our attention to help us become the most productive persons that we may be.

It should always be remembered why Jehovah from time to time punishes His children, individually and collectively. He does it ". . . in order that He may be able to bless. He sifts, but He does not destroy. He does not thresh His own people, but He knocks them; and even when He threshes, they may console themselves in the face of the approaching period of judgment, that they are never crushed or injured" (*Old Testament Student Manual*, 163–164).

ISAIAH CHAPTER 29

A Great and Marvelous Work

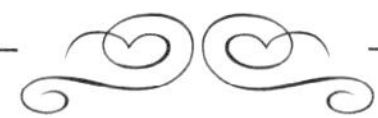

THIS CHAPTER COMPARES THE DISTRESSES OF JERUSALEM TO THE DIFFICULTIES of the people of the Book of Mormon. There are few in the world other than members of The Church of Jesus Christ of Latter-day Saints who understand this chapter. As Elder LeGrand Richards explained:

> If you will read that thoughtfully, you will know that he not only saw the destruction of Jerusalem, but he saw the destruction of another great center like unto Jerusalem. Then he adds:
>
> "And thou shalt be brought down and shalt speak out of the ground, and thy speech shall be low out of the dust, and thy voice shall be, as of one that hath a familiar spirit, out of the ground, and thy speech shall whisper out of the dust."
>
> Nobody in this world could explain that intelligently or know what people Isaiah saw like unto Jerusalem without the Book of Mormon. (Richards, in Conference Report, April 1963, 118)

29:1 Woe to Ariel, to Ariel, the city where David dwelt! add ye year to year; let them kill sacrifices.

"Ariel" means "altar of God," or "hearth of God," which is in David's city—Jerusalem. The phrase "add ye year to year" can simply mean "in another year" or "in many years." Jerusalem's woe will come, and in the next verse this woe will be compared to another nation's difficulties.

29:2 Yet I will distress Ariel, and there shall be heaviness and sorrow: and it shall be unto me as Ariel.

Difficult days are ahead for Jerusalem. Isaiah compares these difficulties to another nation.

29:3 And I will camp against thee round about, and will lay siege against thee with a mount, and I will raise forts against thee.

29:4 And thou shalt be brought down, and shalt speak out of the ground, and thy speech shall be low out of the dust, and thy voice shall be, as of one that hath a familiar spirit, out of the ground, and thy speech shall whisper out of the dust.

Familiar spirit (Heb. *bwa ˇowb*)—from the root "*ba ab*" meaning father or ancestor.

The phrase "familiar spirit" refers to a ghost or spirit. Jews will bear testimony of their offenses and the resulting punishment, as will the Jaredites and Nephites, who speak "out of the ground," as it were, through their written records.

> Isaiah described the spirit of the Book of Mormon as "familiar." It resonates with people who know the Old Testament, especially those who are conversant with its Hebrew language. The Book of Mormon is rich with Hebraisms—traditions, symbolisms, idioms, and literary forms. It is familiar because more than 80 percent of its pages came from Old Testament times. (Nelson, "The Exodus Repeated")

Nephi adds a few words before and after he quotes verses three and four when he wrote:

> But behold, I prophesy unto you concerning the last days; concerning the days when the Lord God shall bring these things forth unto the children of men.

> After my seed and the seed of my brethren shall have dwindled in unbelief, and shall have been smitten by the Gentiles; yea, after the Lord God shall have camped against them round about, and shall have laid siege against them with a mount, and raised forts against them; and after they shall have been brought down low in the dust, even that they are not, yet the words of the righteous shall be written, and the prayers of the faithful shall be heard, and all those who have dwindled in unbelief shall not be forgotten.
>
> For those who shall be destroyed shall speak unto them out of the ground, and their speech shall be low out of the dust, and their voice shall be as one that hath a familiar spirit; for the Lord God will give unto him power, that he may whisper concerning them, even as it were out of the ground; and their speech shall whisper out of the dust. (2 Nephi 26:14–16)

Elder McConkie explained these verses spoke of the Nephites and it is they that "'shalt be brought down, and shalt speak out of the ground, and thy speech shall be low out of the dust, and thy voice shall be, as of one that hath a familiar spirit, out of the ground, and thy speech shall whisper out of the dust.' Where else in all history are there two better examples of peoples who were brought down and utterly destroyed than the Jaredites and Nephites? And whose voices, being stilled in death, yet speak from their graves for all to hear? Does not their united voice have a familiar spirit? Is it not whispering out of the ground the same prophetic message that is now and always has been the burden of the living prophets? Does not the Book of Mormon proclaim a familiar message, one already written in the Bible?" (McConkie, *A New Witness for the Articles of Faith*, 432).

29:5 Moreover the multitude of thy strangers shall be like small dust, and the multitude of the terrible ones shall be as chaff that passeth away: yea, it shall be at an instant suddenly.

Nephi adds a few words before and added some commentary on verse 5 when he wrote:

> For thus saith the Lord God: They shall write the things which shall be done among them, and they shall be written and sealed

> up in a book, and those who have dwindled in unbelief shall not have them, for they seek to destroy the things of God.
>
> Wherefore, as those who have been destroyed have been destroyed speedily; and the multitude of their terrible ones shall be as chaff that passeth away—yea, thus saith the Lord God: It shall be at an instant, suddenly— (2 Nephi 26:17–18).

From the Book of Mormon we see how quickly the Nephite nation was destroyed. It took just one battle. After that battle the Lamanites hunted down any of the remaining Nephites who believed in Christ and would not deny Him. The majority of the Nephite nation, at least as portrayed to us in the record that speaks from the ground, came to an end in an instant, suddenly. In comparison, John the revelator also portrays the end of the world "in one day shall it be destroyed" (Rev. 18:8).

29:6 Thou shalt be visited of the Lord of hosts with thunder, and with earthquake, and great noise, with storm and tempest, and the flame of devouring fire.

Nephi said that those who were not destroyed but who dwindled in unbelief would be smitten by the Gentiles (see 2 Nephi 26:19). Nephi then described in great detail the conditions which would exist among the Gentiles in the last days, causing the Lord to visit them with thunder, earthquakes, and so forth (see 2 Nephi 26:20–27:2).

Elder LeGrand Richards taught that verse 6 also could be compared to the destruction of the Nephites at the coming of Christ, as described in 3 Nephi chapter 8 (see "Value of the Holy Scriptures," 123). The thunder and the tempest and the earthquake and the destruction of the Nephites and Lamanites serves as a parallel to the coming destruction preceding the Second Coming of Christ to the world.

29:7 And the multitude of all the nations that fight against Ariel, even all that fight against her and her munition, and that distress her, shall be as a dream of a night vision.

29:8 It shall even be as when an hungry man dreameth, and, behold, he eateth; but he awaketh, and his soul is empty: or as when a thirsty man dreameth, and, behold, he drinketh; but he awaketh, and, behold, he is faint, and his soul hath appetite: so shall the multitude of all the nations be, that fight against mount Zion.

> And all the nations that fight against Zion, and that distress her, shall be as a dream of a night vision; yea, it shall be unto them, even as unto a hungry man which dreameth, and behold he eateth but he awaketh and his soul is empty; or like unto a thirsty man which dreameth, and behold he drinketh but he awaketh and behold he is faint, and his soul hath appetite; yea, even so shall the multitude of all the nations be that fight against Mount Zion. (2 Nephi 27:3)

Verses 7 and 8 describe the spiritual famine that will exist in the latter days (see Amos 8:11–12).

Woe to the Spiritually Blind

Verses 9–13 condemn all those who are spiritually blinded because of their false worship. These verses also contain the second woe mentioned in chapters 28–34. Woe unto all who are spiritually blinded because of their false worship. Orson Pratt has interpreted verse 1 to mean that the Jews continued to "kill sacrifices" after the day of sacrifices had been done away with, and that they added "year to year" in their futile observance of the Law of Moses.

29:9 Stay yourselves, and wonder; cry ye out, and cry: they are drunken, but not with wine; they stagger, but not with strong drink.

Stay (Heb. *mâhahh*)—to question or hesitate, i.e. (by implication) to be reluctant or to delay.

Wonder (Heb. *tâmahh*)—to be in consternation—be amazed, be astonished.

> For behold, all ye that doeth iniquity, stay yourselves and wonder, for ye shall cry out, and cry; yea, ye shall be drunken but not with wine, ye shall stagger but not with strong drink. (2 Nephi 27:4)

Those who sin should question themselves why they are sinning. Their sins lead to a loss of control of themselves. They are not thinking clearly, logically, or intelligently. They should hesitate to sin because of what it does to them and their relationship with God. By implication they should be reluctant to engage in sin at all. We all sin and the advice for us today is to "stay yourselves." We should question why we want to look like and act like a spiritual drunk. We should hesitate before we act on a temptation and wonder (be astonished or amazed) that we are considering sinning.

29:10 For the Lord hath poured out upon you the spirit of deep sleep, and hath closed your eyes: the prophets and your rulers, the seers hath he covered.

Covered (Heb. *kâçâh*)—to cover, conceal, or hide.

Verse 10 is also describing the spiritual famine that will exist in the latter days (see Isaiah 29:8). It will be a time when the prophets and seers will have been hidden from the world so that they cannot see them. It will be a time of spiritual slumber—even a deep spiritual sleep. Nephi adds a small commentary on this verse when he writes:

> . . . For behold, ye have closed your eyes, and ye have rejected the prophets; and your rulers, and the seers hath he covered because of your iniquity.
>
> And it shall come to pass that the Lord God shall bring forth unto you the words of a book, and they shall be the words of them which have slumbered. (2 Nephi 27:5–6)

29:11 And the vision of all is become unto you as the words of a book that is sealed, which men deliver to one that is learned, saying, Read this, I pray thee: and he saith, I cannot; for it is sealed:

29:12 And the book is delivered to him that is not learned, saying, Read this, I pray thee: and he saith, I am not learned.

Book (Hab. *cêpher*)—it is interesting to note that Strong's Concordance defines this word as properly meaning "writing (the art or

> a document)" and by implication a book, scroll, bill, letter, or evidence of learning.

> Isaiah uses the word book twenty times in this section to refer to the gold plates. This book contains "revelation from God" and is a record of the Jaredite and Nephite nations, those "who have slumbered in the dust" (JST 29:14). It is a "sealed book," parts of which are kept from the wicked but which will come forth in the Lord's time to be read "by the power of Christ" (JST 29:16). After Joseph Smith has completed his translation of a portion of the sealed book, he will return it to God, who will "preserve" the record until he sees fit to bring it forth (JST 29:24). (Parry, *Understanding Isaiah*, 263)

The book that comes forth is simply referred to as the "vision of all." It has everything in it. We don't know until we get to the brother of Jared's description of what he put in there, it is a vision of the beginning of the world to the end thereof. So Isaiah really did mean it is vision of all. We just don't have all the Book of Mormon yet; therefore, we don't have the full revelation, any more than we have the full revelation of Christ.

Elder Orson Pratt described how these two verses were literally fulfilled when he said:

> [Soon after Joseph received the plates] a certain portion of the characters on these plates were copied off by the Prophet, and the manuscript sent, by the hands of Martin Harris, a farmer who lived in that neighborhood, to the city of New York, to show them to the learned, to see if they could translate them. Among those to whom they were presented was Professor Anthon—a man noted for his learning in languages—but he could not translate them. You may here inquire, what was the particular character in which these plates were written? They inform us that they wrote in two separate characters. Some of their plates were written in Hebrew and some in the Egyptian; but both the Hebrew and the Egyptian, after they came from Jerusalem, were reformed by them. I mean the alphabets were altered or changed.

If they had not done this by design, we know that in the course of a thousand years languages will greatly change, and sometimes new characters will be added to alphabets. We know that none of them, at the present time, are precisely as they were anciently; they have been added to from time to time. The Hebrew, on the eastern continent, had the points representing the vowels added to it after the Nephites left Jerusalem; and no doubt the Egyptian, understood when they left, has been greatly changed since. They wrote, therefore, in the reformed Egyptian—a language that the learned Professor Anthon did not understand. He requested Martin Harris, however, to bring the plates to him, telling him, if he would, that he could perhaps assist him in the translation.

Joseph translated the few characters that were sent to Professor Anthon, and when the translation and the original were shown to him and he had compared them, he expressed the opinion that the translation was correct, and he gave a paper to that effect to Martin Harris. As Mr. Harris was leaving the room, Mr. Anthon said, "How did this young lad obtain the plates?" Said Martin Harris, "He obtained them by the ministration of an holy angel." Professor Anthon immediately requested him to return the paper that he had given him, and as soon as Mr. Harris had done so, he tore it to pieces, saying, "Angels do not appear in our day" (*Journal of Discourses*, 15:185).

The Lord had shown Martin Harris that he must go to New York City with some of the characters, so we proceeded to copy some of them. And he took his journey to the eastern cities and to the learned, saying, "Read this, I pray thee." And the learned said, "I cannot," but if he would bring the plates they would read it. But the Lord had forbidden it. And he returned to me and gave them to me to translate, and I said, "I cannot, for I am not learned." But the Lord had prepared spectacles for to read the book, therefore I commenced translating the characters, and thus the prophecy of Isaiah was fulfilled. (Jackson, *Joseph Smith's Commentary on the Bible,* 50)

29:13 Wherefore the Lord said, Forasmuch as this people draw near me with their mouth, and with their lips do honour me, but have removed their heart far from me, and their fear toward me is taught by the precept of men:

The Savior called the scribes and Pharisees "hypocrites," saying that Isaiah had prophesied of them and then quoted this verse (see Matthew 15:7–9; Mark 7:6–7). This might lead some to believe that the prophecy was limited to the time of the Savior, and that it was fulfilled. But the fact that He quoted only verse 13, and not verse 14 with it, indicates the Savior was saying that the Pharisees were the kind of people Isaiah prophesied of—not that they were the fulfillment of His prophecy.

This verse also describes the spiritual condition of the world at the time of the restoration of the gospel. When God the Father and Jesus Christ appeared to Joseph Smith in 1820, Christ described the churches of Joseph's day. He said "that all their creeds were an abomination in his sight; that those professors were all corrupt; that: 'they draw near to me with their lips, but their hearts are far from me, they teach for doctrines the commandments of men, having a form of godliness, but they deny the power thereof'" (Joseph Smith—History 1:19).

The "marvellous work and a wonder" in verse 14 is associated with the Lord's setting His hand the second time to recover His people (see Isaiah 11:11) in 2 Nephi 25:17 and 29:1. According to 2 Nephi 25:18, this marvelous work would be accomplished through the bringing forth of the Lord's words, specified as the words of Nephi's seed (the Book of Mormon) in 2 Nephi 29:2. This is also confirmed by the Savior's words to the Nephites after His resurrection (see 3 Nephi 21:1–9).

29:14 Therefore, behold, I will proceed to do a marvellous work among this people, even a marvellous work and a wonder: for the wisdom of their wise men shall perish, and the understanding of their prudent men shall be hid.

Proceed (Heb. *yâçaph*)—pronounced yaw-saf' or we would say Joseph. This verse could be translated "Therefore, behold, I will [that] Joseph do a marvelous work among this people . . ."

> When Isaiah promised that the Lord would "set up an ensign for the nations" and gather the dispersed of Israel, the ensign, the standard, the divine flag around which all men should rally was to be the holy gospel. (Isa. 5:26; 11:12.) When the Lord said, as Isaiah records, "Forasmuch as this people draw near me with their mouth, and with their lips do honour me, but have removed their heart far from me, and their fear toward me is taught by the precept of men: Therefore, behold, I will proceed to do a marvellous work among this people, even a marvellous work and a wonder: for the wisdom of their wise men shall perish, and the understanding of their prudent men shall be hid" (Isa. 29:13-14)—when these divine words were uttered, they had reference to the restoration of the gospel in our day. And some of these very words were quoted by the Son of God in the First Vision. (JS-H 1:19.) Many latter-day revelations identify the marvelous work here named as the restored gospel. (McConkie, *Millennial Messiah*, 106)

This verse is a sweet promise that a loving Father in Heaven will work to pull Israel out of their spiritual stupor (29:9). To do this, He will do a "marvelous work and a wonder" among His people. He will bring forth the Book of Mormon. There are several times where God references Isaiah's prophecy when He spoke with Joseph Smith. A few of them are:

"Now behold, a marvelous work is about to come forth among the children of men" (D&C 4:1).

"A great and marvelous work is about to come forth unto the children of men" (D&C 6:1).

"A great and marvelous work is about to come forth among the children of men" (D&C 11:1).

"A great and marvelous work is about to come forth unto the children of men" (D&C 12:1).

"A great and marvelous work is about to come forth among the children of men" (D&C 14:1).

"And by your hands I will work a marvelous work among the children of men, unto the convincing of many of their sins, that they may come unto repentance, and that they may come unto the kingdom of my Father" (D&C 18:44).

"And their wisdom shall be great, and their understanding reach to heaven; and before them the wisdom of the wise shall perish, and the understanding of the prudent shall come to naught" (D&C 76:9).

It is interesting to note that in 1818, Martin was instructed by the Spirit not to join any church until the words of Isaiah were fulfilled in Isaiah 29:13–14.

This verse contains the second promise mentioned in chapters 28–34. A loving Father in Heaven in His attempt to pull Israel out of their spiritual stupor, will do a "marvelous work and a wonder" among His people. He will bring forth the Book of Mormon.

29:15 Woe unto them that seek deep to hide their counsel from the Lord, and their works are in the dark, and they say, Who seeth us? and who knoweth us?

Verses 15–16 contain the third woe mentioned in chapters 28–34. Woe (or misery) to them that seek to hide their thoughts, their works, and their deeds from the Lord. They try to dictate to their Creator how they feel life should be, even though they know not the Creator. They only worship His creation. It appears the Jews were trying at Isaiah's time to secretly hide their secret governmental trade from the Lord. This may indeed refer to the secret government action with Egypt when they proposed to break trade agreements with Assyria by not paying them their annual tribute tax any longer.

29:16 Surely your turning of things upside down shall be esteemed as the potter's clay: for shall the work say of him that made it, He made me not? or shall the thing framed say of him that framed it, He had no understanding?

Isaiah is asking, "Can clay make itself into something?" Likewise, can we make ourselves into something without God? Those who think that lasting and eternal success can be divorced from God have "no understanding."

29:17 Is it not yet a very little while, and Lebanon shall be turned into a fruitful field, and the fruitful field shall be esteemed as a forest?

Verses 17–24 contain Isaiah's third promise mentioned in chapters 28–34. Even to such God will continue to reveal Himself in wisdom and instruction. The promise is one of a future tense. Before the Lord will turn the world into a fruitful field, the Book of Mormon had to come forth first.

Earlier in the chapter, Isaiah foretold "of an ancient record that would come out of the ground in the latter days, in a time preceding the restoration of Palestine as a fruitful field. This record would be in the form of a book, he said, having to do with a people who had been destroyed suddenly" (Petersen, "The Angel Moroni Came!").

Orson Pratt in speaking of verse 17 commented:

> This book could not mean the New Testament, for when that was written it was about the time that Lebanon was to be forsaken by the Jews and become a desolation, a forest, or wilderness for many generations. "Upon the land of my people shall come up thorns and briers." (Isaiah 27:13) Hence the land of Palestine, which includes Lebanon, was, when the New Testament was written, about to be cursed. But immediately after the unlearned should read the book, "Lebanon shall be turned into a fruitful field, and the fruitful field shall be esteemed as the forest." The book, therefore, that Isaiah prophesies of, is to come forth just before the great day of the restoration of Israel to their own lands; at which time Lebanon and all the land of Canaan is again to be blessed, while the fruitful field occupied by the nations of the Gentiles, "will be esteemed as a forest;" the multitude of the nations of the Gentiles are to perish, and their lands which are now like a fruitful field, are to be left desolate of inhabitants and become as Lebanon has been for many generations past; while Lebanon shall again be occupied by Israel, and be turned into a fruitful field. These great events could not take place until the Lord should first bring forth a book out of the ground" (Pratt, 276–277).

Orson Pratt also stated that ". . . Mr. Smith did not know anything about this prophecy at that time, for he was unacquainted with the contents of the Bible; he was brought up to work. This part of the prophecy was fulfilled to the very letter; the 'words of the book,' not the book itself, were sent to the learned. If Mr. Smith had sent the plates to New York the terms of this prophecy would not have been fulfilled" (*Journal of Discourses*, 2:288).

Elder Mark E. Petersen stated in another way when he said:

> Not only did the prophets predict its appearance, but Isaiah set a limit on the time of its publication. That time limit was related to the period when fertility would return to Palestine. Isaiah said that the book would come forth first, and then added that in "a very little while . . . Lebanon shall be turned into a fruitful field, and the fruitful field shall be esteemed as a forest." (in Conference Report, October 1965, 61)

President Joseph Fielding Smith spoke of Great Britain's role in this:

> The British government changed all this, when they obtained the mandate. You see, the mandate of Palestine was given to Great Britain. That nation and other nations spent millions of pounds in rehabilitating that land. The Sea of Galilee is now a great reservoir, and the flood waters from the various streams are being diverted into it.
>
> Canals have been built for irrigation, and the Jordan has been changed from its natural channel into channels or into canals on each side of the original stream. These irrigate some seven million acres, which could not be under cultivation otherwise. Hydro-electric stations have been built on these streams. One power plant is located about eight miles below the lake of Galilee, where there is a similar dam to the Hoover Dam. This contains about 10 billion cubic feet of water for irrigation and power purposes. Passing through the turbines, most of the water is returned to the Jordan. The power plants are ample for a territory the size of Vermont. The Palestine Electric Corporation supplies electric power and light for all Palestine, except Jerusalem and its vicinity. (*Doctrines of Salvation*, 3:259–260)

The growth in the fruitfulness of this land has been incredible. For example, in 1929–30, the value of fruit exported from Jerusalem was at 1.5 million dollars. By 1937 it had increased to 20 million. In 2020, the value of exported fruit is estimated to be 49 billion dollars (see TrendEconomy).

Anyone who studies this chapter of Isaiah should realize that the time limit for the fulfillment of this verse has expired. This new volume of scripture must have come forth before now or Isaiah was not a true prophet, for Palestine is fruitful again.

Where is that book? You can read that book of scripture today and it is known as The Book of Mormon. It is another testament of Christ.

29:18 And in that day shall the deaf hear the words of the book, and the eyes of the blind shall see out of obscurity, and out of darkness.

The Book of Mormon will help those who are spiritually deaf to hear the word of God. Elder Bruce R. McConkie defined spiritual deafness as "the state of those who are lacking in spirituality, whose spiritual ears are not attuned to the whisperings of the still small voice of the Spirit. Spiritual blindness is the identifying mark which singles out those who are unable to see the hand of God manifest in the affairs of men. Such have 'unbelief and blindness of heart' (D&C 58:15)" (*Mormon Doctrine*, 184).

Elder Orson Pratt also saw a literal fulfillment of Isaiah's prophecy in the physically deaf being restored to hearing: "Those who were so deaf that they could not hear the loudest sound, have had their ears opened to hear the glorious and most precious words of the Book of Mormon, and it has been done by the power of God and not of man" (Pratt, 177). Elder LeGrand Richards noted that the Book of Mormon has been printed in braille so that the physically blind would be able to know its message (see LeGrand, "Value of the Holy Scriptures").

29:19 The meek also shall increase their joy in the Lord, and the poor among men shall rejoice in the Holy One of Israel.

Poor (Heb. *'ebyôwn*)—a person in want, needy, poor.

Because of the book mentioned in verse 19, the joy of the meek increases. The meek of the earth will recognize the book for what it really is—the work of the Lord. The Book of Mormon will give those in need for increased spirituality a reason to rejoice.

29:20 For the terrible one is brought to nought, and the scorner is consumed, and all that watch for iniquity are cut off:

29:21 That make a man an offender for a word, and lay a snare for him that reproveth in the gate, and turn aside the just for a thing of nought.

At the other end of the spiritual spectrum of the meek are the terrible, the scorner, and those that look for opportunities to sin. This type of people looks for ways to offend the righteous and lay traps for them. Joseph Smith, in writing of the persecution he and other Saints had suffered in Missouri, referred to verse 21 when he said: "We refer you to Isaiah, who considers those who make a man an offender for a word, and lay a snare for him that reproveth in the gate. We believe that the old Prophet verily told the truth: and we have no retraction to make. We have reproved in the gate, and men have laid snares for us. We have spoken the words and men have made us offensive" (*Teachings of Presidents: Joseph Smith*, 124).

29:22 Therefore thus saith the Lord, who redeemed Abraham, concerning the house of Jacob, Jacob shall not now be ashamed, neither shall his face now wax pale.

Elder Orson Pratt quoted this verse and taught that Isaiah referred to the restoration of the house of Jacob that will come through the Book of Mormon. He said:

> The house of Jacob has been made ashamed, and his face has waxed pale, ever since he was driven away from Lebanon or Canaan, but the Lord has now brought forth out of the ground a book which shall, accompanied by His power, restore the tribes of Jacob from the four quarters of the globe, and establish them in the land of Palestine and Lebanon forever; and His holy name they shall no more profane, but shall be a righteous people throughout all their generations, while the earth shall stand, and they shall possess their promised land again in eternity, never more to pass away; therefore, they shall never again be made ashamed. It is in vain for the Gentiles to seek the conversion of Jacob, and to bring about their great redemption, only in the way that the Lord God of Israel hath predicted and appointed: they may call meetings and conventions to convert the Jews, but let them know assuredly that the book spoken of by Isaiah is to accomplish the salvation of the house of Jacob,

> and bring about the restoration of all Israel, while the Gentiles who will not receive sit and be numbered and identified with the house of Jacob, must surely perish, yea, and they shall be utterly wasted with storm and tempest, with earthquakes and famine, with the flame of devouring fire, and their fruitful lands shall be esteemed as a forest, while Jacob shall dwell in safety forever. (Pratt, 278; see also 2 Nephi 25:17–18; 29:1–2)

29:23 But when he seeth his children, the work of mine hands, in the midst of him, they shall sanctify my name, and sanctify the Holy One of Jacob, and shall fear the God of Israel.

This is a prophecy of the effect the Book of Mormon will have on the descendants of Jacob. The verse starts out that when he (Jacob) will see his descendants, he will see that they are now in God's hands. God will be in the midst of them and they will praise Him and sanctify God's name. They will show their respect (fear) for Him.

29:24 They also that erred in spirit shall come to understanding, and they that murmured shall learn doctrine.

Elder Orson Pratt explained what Isaiah meant by the phrase "they also that erred in spirit shall come to understanding" when he wrote:

> Oh, how my heart has been pained within me when I have seen the blindness of the Christian world, and I knew that many of them were sincere! I knew they desired to know the truth, but they scarcely knew whether to turn to the right or to the left, so great were the errors that were taught in their midst, and so strong the traditions which they had imbibed, the fear of the Lord being taught them by the precepts of men instead of by inspiration and the power of the Holy Ghost.
>
> . . . But those who have read this book will bear me record that their minds have been forever set at rest in regard to doctrine, so far as the ordinances of the kingdom of God are concerned. Those who erred, and did not know whether sprinkling, pouring or immersion was the true method of baptism, now

> know? Why? Because the Book of Mormon reveals the mode as it was given to the ancient Nephites on this continent. So in regard to every other principle of the doctrine of Christ—it is set forth in such great plainness that it is impossible for any two persons to form different ideas in relation to it, after reading the Book of Mormon. (*Journal of Discourses*, 15:188–189; *Old Testament Student Manual*, 166).

President Ezra Taft Benson has stated, "The Book of Mormon is the great standard we are to use" (Benson, "The Book of Mormon Is the Word of God"). The Book of Mormon is the great restorer of doctrine to our days and is the "keystone" of our religion. Truly Isaiah saw our day and coming forth of the Book of Mormon.

ISAIAH CHAPTER 30

Turning to God Leads to Rest and Confidence

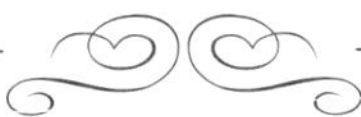

Many of us who dwell in Zion repeat the transgressions of some of our ancient Israelite ancestors: We reject our living prophets, or we accept only a portion of their counsel; we forget to pray to our Father, or we pray insincerely or irregularly; we trust in our arms and armies for protection rather than in our God, as our ancestors trusted anciently in Egypt's horses, chariots, and armies; and we despise God's word, or find the gospel too hard to accept. This trust in worldly affairs and the lack of trust in God is the topic of the first seventeen verses of this chapter.

In verses 18–26, Isaiah describes the fulfillment of all of God's promises to His faithful. Isaiah testifies that the Lord hears and answers our prayers, He provides blessings and guidance, and we can enjoy the bounties of the land.

There are four major topics in chapters 30 and 31 and those topics are:

Dependence upon Egypt will result in disappointment. Isaiah uses five examples to illustrate this theme. Those five examples are found in 30:1–5, 6–7, 12–14, 16–17; 31:1–3.

As the children of Israel reject God's word they will be punished, and as they return to the Lord, they will be blessed.

Blessings will be given to righteous Israel in the latter days.

Judgment will come upon the wicked world.

30:1 Woe to the rebellious children, saith the Lord, that take counsel, but not of me; and that cover with a covering, but not of my spirit, that they may add sin to sin:

Israel and Judah had been cautioned by the Lord not to put their trust in other nations. But they turned to Egypt for protection from the Assyrians. They would not listen to the counsel of God given by Isaiah, nor would they listen to "my spirit" or the Holy Ghost. They would only listen to the council of themselves. "The covering" mentioned in this verse refers to Egypt. Israel sought protection from a source other than God and that simply added one more sin to their growing list of sins.

This verse begins the fourth woe (verses 1–10) mentioned by Isaiah in chapters 28–34. Woe to the rebellious children who make friends with God's enemies. (For example: Israel makes an alliance with Egypt for protection against Assyria). These rebellious children rejecting the counsel of God's prophets. They try to silence the voice of prophecy and demand that the prophets and seers preach not that which is right but, false doctrine which will support their wickedness.

30:2 That walk to go down into Egypt, and have not asked at my mouth; to strengthen themselves in the strength of Pharaoh, and to trust in the shadow of Egypt!

Egypt becomes a symbol of a fallen and sinful world. Israel is choosing to "go down into" the world. The Lord wanted a complete severance of Israel from the worldliness of Egypt at the Exodus. They were never to go back. There is no strength in Pharaoh, nor can Israel trust in Egypt to protect them.

Notice the exodus images in this verse. Pharaoh in Egyptian means "king" (Josephus, 8.6,2). The word "Phra" or "the sun," was the hieroglyphic symbol and title of the king. He was their light and was their god. Like Israel, we are not to walk by the light of a false god. There is no strength in false worship. There can never be trust in the false promises of the world.

30:3 Therefore shall the strength of Pharaoh be your shame, and the trust in the shadow of Egypt your confusion.

What Israel has sought with an alliance with Egypt will not happen. There will be no added strength or protection. The only results will be shame and confusion. The words "shame" (*bôsheth*) and "confusion" (*k^{e}limmâh*) are synonymous. "They place more emphasis on 'reaping shame,' the objective disappointment of hope, than on 'feeling embarrassed,' though the latter is never absent" (Motyer, 246). In the end, any alliance with worldliness will diminish our hope and will result in confusion.

30:4 For his princes were at Zoan, and his ambassadors came to Hanes.

Zoan = "place of departure." It was an ancient city of lower Egypt called Tanis by the Greeks; located on the eastern bank of the Tanitic branch of the Nile.

Hanes = "grace has fled." It was west of the Nile, in central Egypt.

The reference to Zoan and Hanes refers to a united Egypt that at the time was under the control of a strong Ethiopian dynasty. "Isaiah's point is that though to the outward eye Egypt may now appear strong there will be no result except disappointment" (Motyer, 246).

30:5 They were all ashamed of a people that could not profit them, nor be an help nor profit, but a shame, and also a reproach.

Jeremiah had a similar message when he wrote: "Why gaddest thou about so much to change thy way? thou also shalt be ashamed of Egypt, as thou wast ashamed of Assyria" (Jeremiah 2:36). Neither will be able to help or profit Israel. Both will bring embarrassment.

30:6 The burden of the beasts of the south: into the land of trouble and anguish, from whence come the young and old lion, the viper and fiery flying serpent, they will carry their riches upon the shoulders of young asses, and their treasures upon the bunches of camels, to a people that shall not profit them.

"The burden of the beasts of the south" is a message of doom for those of Judah who traveled with loads of gifts on animals toward Egypt. Israel exaggerates Egypt's resources to be able to help them in time of war and danger. In the subtle imagery of this verse, Isaiah is simply reversing Exodus and putting Israel back into captivity, saying if you go with Egypt, they cannot deliver you. They represent bondage. Isaiah also notes that one way back into bondage, Israel will be afflicted with "the viper and fiery flying serpent." The fiery flying serpents are the same creatures that plagued the Israelites as they escaped Egypt and its armies (see Num. 21:4–6; Deut. 8:15).

30:7 For the Egyptians shall help in vain, and to no purpose: therefore have I cried concerning this, Their strength is to sit still.

"To sit still"—"do nothing for you."

Egypt will do nothing to help Israel. Their promised help is "in vain," has "no purpose," and will do nothing for Israel. The Book of Mormon prophet Jacob similarly admonished his brethren to "seek not to counsel the Lord, but to take counsel from his hand" (Jacob 4:10). President Joseph Fielding Smith used the first seventeen verses of this chapter as an example of the Lord's sending the prophets to warn Israel and Judah before they were scattered and taken captive (see *Doctrines of Salvation*, 3:4). Their rejection of prophets' council will bring their demise.

Israel's Refusal to Listen to Prophets Will Now Have Consequences

The next few verses show that "the action of Judah in relation to Egypt is only a symptom; the cause is fundamental refusal to hear the Lord's word" (Motyer, 247).

30:8 Now go, write it before them in a table, and note it in a book, that it may be for the time to come for ever and ever:

The historical warning in the first seven verses becomes a record for the future as Isaiah is commanded to it. Isaiah wrote the prophecy in a table (tablet) and in a book (scroll) and suggests that there was both a public and a private record. Isaiah emphasizes the need for this prophecy, and what it teaches us to be recorded for the future.

30:9 That this is a rebellious people, lying children, children that will not hear the law of the Lord:

Elder Marion D. Hanks spoke of verses 9–10 when he said:

> To recreant Israel God said, ". . . this is a rebellious people, lying children, children that will not hear the law of the Lord: Which say to the seers, See not; and to the prophets, Prophesy not unto us right things, speak unto us smooth things, prophesy deceits" (Isa. 30:9–10).
>
> . . . Some of us may be less happy than we should be or could be because of arrogance or pride. We think we are sufficient unto ourselves. We think we do not need God or his Christ. We may be, as President Joseph F. Smith once wrote, lazy, or "among the proud and self-vaunting, who read by the lamp of their own conceit, interpret by rules of their own contriving . . . become a law unto themselves, and so pose as the sole judges of their own doings." (Hanks, "Joy through Christ")

More recently, Elder Jeffery R. Holland said:

> Unfortunately, messengers of divinely mandated commandments are often no more popular today than they were anciently. . . .
>
> Sadly enough, . . . it is a characteristic of our age that if people want any gods at all, they want them to be gods who do not demand much, comfortable gods, smooth gods who not only don't rock the boat but don't even row it, gods who pat us on the head, make us giggle, then tell us to run along and pick marigolds. (Holland, "The Cost—and Blessings—of Discipleship")

30:10 Which say to the seers, See not; and to the prophets, Prophesy not unto us right things, speak unto us smooth things, prophesy deceits:

Samuel the Lamanite said something very similar to the Nephites when he said, ". . . [I]f a prophet come among you and declareth unto you the word of the Lord, which testifieth of your sins and iniquities, ye are angry with him, and cast him out. . . . But behold, if a man shall come among you and shall say: Do this, and there is no iniquity; do that and ye shall not suffer;

. . . do whatsoever your heart desireth— . . . because he speaketh flattering words unto you, and he saith that all is well, then ye will not find fault with him" (Hel. 13:26–28).

30:11 Get you out of the way, turn aside out of the path, cause the Holy One of Israel to cease from before us.

The wicked are essentially saying that God's holiness is what troubles sinners. This is very cynical, very sarcastic. For Israel, when life starts getting tough, instead of dealing with life the way the Lord asks us to deal with it, many people revert to the ways of the world. They want to leave the path of God and do it the way the world does it. So that Israel becomes a personification of every person under pressure who reverts to the ways of the world when things are tough.

30:12 Wherefore thus saith the Holy One of Israel, Because ye despise this word, and trust in oppression and perverseness, and stay thereon:

For the phrase "trust in oppression and perverseness," the Jerusalem Bible reads, "you . . . prefer to trust in wile and guile and rely on these."

Because of their rejection of God's word through Isaiah, and Israel's trust in the arm of flesh (Egypt), their pending destruction will surely come.

30:13 Therefore this iniquity shall be to you as a breach ready to fall, swelling out in a high wall, whose breaking cometh suddenly at an instant.

Isaiah compares Judah's iniquity to a large crack in the outside wall that protects Jerusalem. The crack expands, weakening the wall until it suddenly crumbles. Similarly, Judah's inhabitants have been weakened through sin; their iniquity increases like the crack in the wall until the nation is destroyed because its enemies are able to enter through the breach. This excellent description illustrates the effect of sin on all of us. Even a little sin, not repented of, can be like a crack in a wall, which can grow larger and larger until it leads to our spiritual destruction.

30:14 And he shall break it as the breaking of the potters' vessel that is broken in pieces; he shall not spare: so that there shall not be found in the bursting of it a sherd to take fire from the hearth, or to take water withal out of the pit.

Isaiah likens the fall of Judah to a shattered clay vessel that can no longer serve its original purpose. Not a single shard (a fragment of the shattered vessel) is large enough to serve as a scoop "to take fire from the hearth" or "to take water" from a pool of water. Similarly, Judah's inhabitants are not suitable to serve as God's holy people.

30:15 For thus saith the Lord God, the Holy One of Israel; In returning and rest shall ye be saved; in quietness and in confidence shall be your strength: and ye would not.

There is no word for "repentance" in Hebrew. The word used most of the time was "return." He is saying—repent and "rest" on (or rely on) the Lord. When you repent, there needs to be a quietness and confidence in God's strength. Trust in His power to help you to return to Him. Repentance leads to rest and confidence in the presence of God.

30:16 But ye said, No; for we will flee upon horses; therefore shall ye flee: and, We will ride upon the swift; therefore shall they that pursue you be swift.

Most of the horses were purchased from Egypt during Isaiah's day. Perhaps Israel is hoping to increase their number of horses as they ally with Egypt. Isaiah indicates that Israel is going to need horses, but not for an attack. They will need them to flee!

30:17 One thousand shall flee at the rebuke of one; at the rebuke of five shall ye flee: till ye be left as a beacon upon the top of a mountain, and as an ensign on an hill.

The promise given in Deuteronomy 32:30 is now reversed. The only thing that will be left is a beacon on a mountain and an ensign on a hill. Where there had once been a multitude living in a city, only a small remnant would be left. Although only a few of Judah's population would remain, they will still act as an ensign and beacon.

Future Events: Millennium and Judgment

The next few verses emphasize wonderful things that await the righteous. We wait for and long for the coming of Christ and His reign on earth for a thousand years. We wait for the promised blessings associated with that event.

30:18 And therefore will the Lord wait, that he may be gracious unto you, and therefore will he be exalted, that he may have mercy upon you: for the Lord is a God of judgment: blessed are all they that wait for him.

Wait (Heb. *châkâh*)—to long for.

Exalted (Heb. *rûwm*)—to rise or rise up.

Judgment (Heb. *mishpâṭ*)—Justice, making the right decision at the right time.

The Hebrew reading of this verse indicates that the Lord is longing to be gracious and show mercy on Israel. But this blessing will not come immediately, but in due time. When the time is right, He will be gracious and merciful to you. God always administers the perfect decision with the perfect timing. We, however, are asked sometimes to wait. We wait for the promised blessings that will come. Blessings will come for those who long for Him.

30:19 For the people shall dwell in Zion at Jerusalem: thou shalt weep no more: he will be very gracious unto thee at the voice of thy cry; when he shall hear it, he will answer thee.

Another promise for the righteous who dwell in Zion is that they will no longer have cause to weep. This is a reference to the millennial reign of Christ, when the influence of sin will be no more and death as we know it will be a thing of the past (see Isaiah 25:8). There will be no more need for tears. God does hear our prayers. He is responsive to our cries. He gives answers to our questions and concerns.

30:20 And though the Lord give you the bread of adversity, and the water of affliction, yet shall not thy teachers be removed into a corner any more, but thine eyes shall see thy teachers:

Teachers (Heb. *châkâh*)—to direct, teach, or instruct. While translating this to be teachers works, the Hebrew is singular and would be better translated as "Thy Teacher" and refers to Christ.

In life we have periods of adversity and affliction. Like bread and water, adversity and affliction may be common to us during periods of our life. Thy can be exhaustive teachers sent to us by the Master Teacher. We are tried and tested as He was tried and tested. Using the symbols of the sacrament (bread and water), Isaiah teaches that when we take them inside of us, both have the potential to make us more like Him. There is a great promise that we will see what our "teachers" have taught us. Let us always use our adversity and afflictions as steppingstones toward Christ and not stumbling blocks.

30:21 And thine ears shall hear a word behind thee, saying, This is the way, walk ye in it, when ye turn to the right hand, and when ye turn to the left.

Picture somebody walking through a gauntlet with a voice behind them telling them which way to go to avoid any traps or snares. This is the fourth promise mentioned by Isaiah in chapters 28–34. God is promising to us that there is someone who can do this for us today. The Holy Ghost will speak truth in our ears and say whether to go to the right or to the left, "This is the way, walk ye in it."

30:22 Ye shall defile also the covering of thy graven images of silver, and the ornament of thy molten images of gold: thou shalt cast them away as a menstruous cloth; thou shalt say unto it, Get thee hence.

Instead of idols and graven images defiling individual members of Israel, Israel will now cast away her idols as one throws away a menstruous cloth. According to the Law of Moses, a menstruous cloth defiled anyone who touched it, making him or her ritually unclean (see Lev. 15:19–30). Similarly, anyone who touched an idol was religiously unclean. Israel will tell her idols, "Get thee hence."

30:23 Then shall he give the rain of thy seed, that thou shalt sow the ground withal; and bread of the increase of the earth, and it shall be fat and plenteous: in that day shall thy cattle feed in large pastures.

Verse 22 speaks of a disrespect for God and Israel's change of heart. The result will be astounding. God will restore great temporal blessings. The earth "shall be fat and plenteous: in that day shall thy cattle feed in large pastures."

30:24 The oxen likewise and the young asses that ear the ground shall eat clean provender, which hath been winnowed with the shovel and with the fan.

Provender (Heb. *b*^{e}*lîyl*)—fodder, corn.

To "ear the ground" is to work the soil. Because of the plenty that will abound, the animals are now given the same food that the people were eating in the days of Isaiah. The implication is that the food that the people will be eating will be so much better and will come as a blessing from the Lord.

30:25 And there shall be upon every high mountain, and upon every high hill, rivers and streams of waters in the day of the great slaughter, when the towers fall.

The phrase "in the day" provides a great contrast between a great day of blessings and a day of slaughter. It is the same day—the Second Coming of Christ. For the righteous, they will be provided great spiritual blessings, an abundance of the "living waters" of Christ. For the wicked, it will be similar to the day when Assyria was destroyed.

30:26 Moreover the light of the moon shall be as the light of the sun, and the light of the sun shall be sevenfold, as the light of seven days, in the day that the Lord bindeth up the breach of his people, and healeth the stroke of their wound.

At the coming of Christ and during His reign in the Millennium, the light of the gospel will shine triumphant. The Lord will bind "up the breach" that had developed between Him and His people. He will heal "the stroke of their wound" by the Atonement. Jesus Christ will make us "at one" with God and heals us spiritually, emotionally, temporally, and physically.

30:27 Behold, the name of the Lord cometh from far, burning with his anger, and the burden thereof is heavy: his lips are full of indignation, and his tongue as a devouring fire:

30:28 And his breath, as an overflowing stream, shall reach to the midst of the neck, to sift the nations with the sieve of vanity: and there shall be a bridle in the jaws of the people, causing them to err.

Isaiah describes God's countenance with the four terms "nose," "lips," "tongue," and "breath," connecting each with His anger and power to destroy. He will use a "sieve of vanity" or a winnowing fan of destruction. As a beast of burden is held in its path by the bridle it wears, so will the wicked be restrained, unable to escape God's judgments.

30:29 Ye shall have a song, as in the night when a holy solemnity is kept; and gladness of heart, as when one goeth with a pipe to come into the mountain of the Lord, to the mighty One of Israel.

In contrast to verse 28, the righteous will have a song of hope and gratitude. The "holy solemnity" refers to the Passover (Ex. 12:42) when Israel went up to Jerusalem (the mountain of the Lord or Zion). There were joyous feasts where Israel went with music and gladness (see Deut. 16:16; Ezra 2:65; Ps. 122:1–14). This verse is probably not referring to one specific feast or event but indicating that any time the righteous return to the mountain of the Lord that there will be gladness in their heart and songs of joy will be sung spontaneously.

30:30 And the Lord shall cause his glorious voice to be heard, and shall shew the lighting down of his arm, with the indignation of his anger, and with the flame of a devouring fire, with scattering, and tempest, and hailstones.

Once again Isaiah provides a contrast. For the wicked, there will be no joyful singing. The arm is a symbol of power and the wicked will come to know how powerful God really is. They will experience fire, tempests, and hailstones like Egypt did in Exodus chapter 9.

30:31 For through the voice of the Lord shall the Assyrian be beaten down, which smote with a rod.

Just like the Assyrians who carried away the ten tribes into captivity were eventually "beaten down," so will the wicked be humbled and smitten.

30:32 And in every place where the grounded staff shall pass, which the Lord shall lay upon him, it shall be with tabrets and harps: and in battles of shaking will he fight with it.

The NIV presents this verse quite differently: "Every stroke the Lord lays on them with his punishing rod will be to the music of tambourines and harps, as he fights them in battle with the blows of his arm."

30:33 For Tophet is ordained of old; yea, for the king it is prepared; he hath made it deep and large: the pile thereof is fire and much wood; the breath of the Lord, like a stream of brimstone, doth kindle it.

Tophet = "place of fire"

Right outside of the city of Jerusalem in the Trophetan valley. Ancient Israel had a place established where they worshiped their false gods and burnt sacrifices to them including on occasions their children (see Jer. 25:35, 2 Kings 21:6). The Lord is saying, we're going to have another sacrifice in Tophet so go get ready for it. Pack the valley full of wood and when the Assyrians come, God's breath will kindle the fire, and nothing will be able to extinguish it. In comparison to the Assyrian army, the army of Satan will be defeated and there is nothing that they can do to prevent this from happening. It has been "ordained of old."

ISAIAH CHAPTER 31

Turn to God and Be Saved

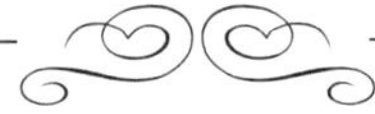

This chapter may be divided into two parts. The first part is in verses 1–3 where Isaiah prophesies woe unto all who rely on the arm of flesh rather than on God. The second part lies in the remaining verses (4–9) and foretells that if Zion will cast away our wickedness as one casts away false gods, then the Lord will defend her. He will be like a mighty lion, "roaring on his prey" (31:4), or like a bird, flying protectively over her nestlings to preserve them. He will also use His mighty sword to protect Zion.

31:1 Woe to them that go down to Egypt for help; and stay on horses, and trust in chariots, because they are many; and in horsemen, because they are very strong; but they look not unto the Holy One of Israel, neither seek the Lord!

This is the fifth woe mention in chapters 28–34. Woe unto those who depend on help from the arm of flesh and blood (such as Israel on Egypt and their horses, chariots, and horseman) rather than upon the spirit of the living God.

The horses in this verse represent brute strength, the chariots represent military strength, and the horsemen represent the strength of a well-trained personnel. Woe, or misery, will come to those who spiritually "go down" to rely on anything other than God. You cannot depend on your own strength, the collective strength of a nation's military, or the combined strength of well-trained servants of sin.

Strength comes in looking to God. There is only an illusion of strength in everything else.

31:2 Yet he also is wise, and will bring evil, and will not call back his words: but will arise against the house of the evildoers, and against the help of them that work iniquity.

The wise in this verse likely refers to the leaders of Israel who are wise in their own eyes. They have ignored what the Lord has said to them, and the consequences of this choice. However, the Lord lets us all know that He "will not call back his words." He will not change what He has said. The phrase "the help of them that work iniquity" refers to those who help others to do evil. The "them" likely refers to Egypt who was allied with the house of evildoers, or Israel.

31:3 Now the Egyptians are men, and not God; and their horses flesh, and not spirit. When the Lord shall stretch out his hand, both he that helpeth shall fall, and he that is holpen shall fall down, and they all shall fail together.

Israel was so blinded by fear and unbelief that they chose Egyptian chariots as allies against the Assyrian cavalry. They chose to trust men and brute strength instead of God and the Spirit. The result will be simple—failure.

31:4 For thus hath the Lord spoken unto me, Like as the lion and the young lion roaring on his prey, when a multitude of shepherds is called forth against him, he will not be afraid of their voice, nor abase himself for the noise of them: so shall the Lord of hosts come down to fight for mount Zion, and for the hill thereof.

"Abase himself"—to be disheartened or frightened.

This verse contains a simple promise. If Israel will turn from their wicked ways, then the Lord will fight the battles of Zion. If they repent, God will fight Assyria for them. They don't need Egypt's help. A little noise coming up against God is meaningless when God is on your side.

This is the fifth promise that Isaiah mentions in chapters 28–34. If Israel will turn from their wicked ways, the Lord will fight the battles of Zion so they can dwell in peace.

31:5 As birds flying, so will the Lord of hosts defend Jerusalem; defending also he will deliver it; and passing over he will preserve it.

Not only can God be compared to a powerful young lion (verse 4), but He can also be compared to a protecting bird that sores overhead watching and waiting for an opportunity to defend us. As God defends us, He will deliver us from our enemies. Like a bird, He will quickly pass over what does not matter in our lives to preserve us in our time of need.

31:6 Turn ye unto him from whom the children of Israel have deeply revolted.

> Only the Lord can save Israel. Isaiah said, "Turn ye unto him from whom the children of Israel have deeply revolted," and "then shall the Assyrian fall with the sword, not of a mighty man," but of the Lord. The "Egyptian" and the "Assyrian" of the latter days may be those in whom a modern people trust rather than in the Lord. (*Old Testament Student Manual*, 166)

31:7 For in that day every man shall cast away his idols of silver, and his idols of gold, which your own hands have made unto you for a sin.

Idol (Heb. 'ĕ*lîyl*)—of nought, good for nothing, worthless.

The phrase "in that day" refers to the coming of Christ and His millennial reign. In context of the previous verses, this is a reminder that God will fight our battles like a lion and watch over us like a bird. It is our responsibility to be vigilant and ready for His coming day. It will be a day when every idol will be "cast away." It will be a day when the worthless god of atheism will be fully recognized and abandoned.

31:8 Then shall the Assyrian fall with the sword, not of a mighty man; and the sword, not of a mean man, shall devour him: but he shall flee from the sword, and his young men shall be discomfited.

Discomfited (Heb. *maç*)—to be subject to slavery; literally, "shall be liable to tribute."

Isaiah returns to the pressing matter of the present. Assyria will come, and Assyria will fall but not because of the power of an army or weapons. "Not of a mighty man . . . not of a mean man" indicates that no man will be responsible for Assyria's demise. Assyria will flee and then become subject to tribute or slavery to another kingdom.

31:9 And he shall pass over to his strong hold for fear, and his princes shall be afraid of the ensign, saith the Lord, whose fire is in Zion, and his furnace in Jerusalem.

The Assyrians (the wicked) will flee to their own fortresses because of their fear of the Lord and His power to destroy. The phrases "fire is in Zion" and "furnace in Jerusalem" find a counterpart in 33:14, where it is written that the righteous will dwell with the devouring fire and everlasting burnings. Both are references to the future promise that the righteous will dwell with Christ in His kingdom.

Concluding Thought Questions

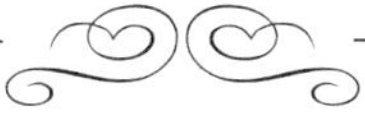

When Christ spoke to the Nephites, He said: "And now, behold, I say unto you, that ye ought to search these things. Yea, a commandment I give unto you that ye search these things diligently; for great are the words of Isaiah" (3 Nephi 23:1). As you read these words, I would hope that your study of Isaiah's words has given you greater peace in your hearts and a brighter hope for a better day. Please consider writing down some 'take-aways' from your study as you ponder these questions:

What did you learn from Isaiah that was "great" for you?

What did you learn from Isaiah that brought you closer to Christ?

What do you never want to forget that you learned from the book of Isaiah?

Bibliography

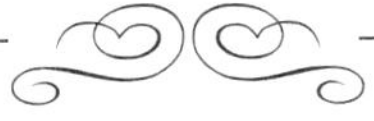

Ballard, Melvin J., *Melvin J. Ballard, Crusader for Righteousness*, Salt Lake City, UT: Bookcraft, 1966.

Bednar, David A., "Line upon Line, Precept upon Precept," *New Era*, September 2010, 3–4.

Benson, Ezra Taft, "The Book of Mormon Is the Word of God," April 1975 general conference.

Benson, Ezra Taft, "The Book of Mormon—Keystone of Our Religion," October 1986 general conference.

Benson, Ezra Taft, "Cleansing the Inner Vessel," April 1986 general conference.

Benson, Ezra Taft, "Flooding the Earth with the Book of Mormon," October 1988 general conference.

Benson, Ezra Taft, *This Nation Shall Endure*, Salt Lake City, UT: Deseret Book Company, 1979.

Bright, William P., *A History of Israel*, United Kingdom: Presbyterian Publishing Corporation, 2000.

Calvin, John, *Commentary on Isaiah*, Ravenio Books, 2012.

Calvin, John, "Calvin's Commentary on the Bible," 1840–57, *https://biblehub.com/commentaries/calvin/isaiah/4.htm.*

Carlin, Dan, *The End is Always Near: Apocalyptic Moments, from the Bronze Age Collapse to Nuclear Near Misses,* HarperCollins, 2019.

Carter, Kate B., *Our Pioneer Heritage*, Salt Lake City, UT: Daughters of Utah Pioneers, https://www.familysearch.org/search/catalog/161828?availability=Family%20History%20Library.

Clark, James R., *Messages of the First Presidency*, vol. 6, United States: Bookcraft, 1966.

Clawson, Rudger, in Conference Report, April 1914, 22–23.

Coltrin, Zebedee, "Statement of Zebedee Coltrin," *Minutes*, 3 October 1883, Salt Lake School of Prophets, Salt Lake City, Utah: LDS Church Archives.

Cowdery, Oliver, "Letter IV," *LDS Messenger and Advocate,* Feb. 1835, 1:77–80, *https://contentdm.lib.byu.edu/digital/collection/NCMP1820-1846/id/7058.*

Critchlow, William J., Jr., in Conference Report, October 1967, 85

Durant, Will, *Our Oriental Heritage*, United States: MJF Books, 1997.

Eyring, Henry B. "Come unto Christ," Brigham Young University devotional, 29 October 1989, speeches.byu.edu.

Faust, James E., "Brigham Young: A Bold Prophet," Brigham Young University devotional, 21 August 2001, speeches.byu.edu.

Faust, James E., "The Lord's Day," October 1991 general conference.

Faust, James E., "Opening the Windows of Heaven," October 1998 general conference.

Hales, Robert D., "Making Righteous Choices at the Crossroads of Life," October 1988 general conference.

Hales, Robert D., "Waiting upon the Lord: Thy Will be Done," October 2011 general conference.

Hanks, Marion D., "Joy through Christ," April 1972 general conference.

Hinckley, Gordon B., "An Ensign to the Nations," October 1989 general conference.

Hinckley, Gordon B., "To All the World a Testimony," April 2000 general conference.

Hinckley, Gordon B., "Walking in the Light of the Lord," October 1998 general conference.

Holland, Jeffrey R., "The Cost—and Blessings—of Discipleship," April 2014 general conference.

Holland, Jeffrey R., "Of Souls, Symbols, and Sacraments," Brigham Young University devotional, 12 January 1988.

Jackson, Kent P., *Joseph Smith's Commentary on the Bible*, Salt Lake City, UT: Deseret Book Company, 2006.

Jamieson, Robert, A.R. Faussett, and David Brown, *Commentary on the Whole Bible*, Harrington, DE: Delmarva Publications, 2013.

Jones, Spencer V., "Overcoming the Stench of Sin," April 2003 general conference.

Josephus, Flavius, *Antiquities of the Jews*, CreateSpace Independent Publishing Platform, 2013.

Journal of Discourses. 26 vols. London: Latter-day Saints Book Depot, 1855-86.

Keil, Carl Friedrich and Franz Delitzsch, *Biblical Commentary on the Old Testament*, United Kingdom: T. & T. Clark, 1866.

Kimball, Spencer W., Conference Report, October 1962.

Kimball, Spencer W., Conference Report, April 1979, 7.

Kimball, Spencer W. "Like All the Nations," *Church News*, 15 October 1960, 14.

Kimball, Spencer W., "Voices of the Past, of the Present, of the Future," April 1971 general conference.

Lee, Harold B., in Conference Report, October 1949, 56.

Lee, Harold B., "The Way to Eternal Life," *Ensign*, Nov. 1971, 15.

Lee, Harold B., "Watch, That Ye May Be Ready," October 1971 general conference.

Ludlow, Daniel H., *A Companion to your Study of the Old Testament*, Salt Lake City, UT: Deseret Book Company, 1981.

Ludlow, Victor L., *Isaiah: Prophet, Seer, and Poet*, Salt Lake City, Utah: Deseret Book Company, 1982.

Lundwall, N.B., *Faith Like the Ancients*, Privately Printed, 1997.

Mark, Joshua J., "Tyre," *World History Encyclopedia*, 2 September 2009, http://www.ancient.eu/Tyre.

McConkie, Bruce R., *A New Witness for the Articles of Faith*, Salt Lake City, UT: Deseret Book Company, 1985.

McConkie, Bruce R., *Doctrinal New Testament Commentary,* Salt Lake City, UT: Deseret Book Company, 1972.

McConkie, Bruce R., *The Millennial Messiah: The Second Coming of the Son of Man*, Salt Lake City, UT: Deseret Book Company, 1982.

McConkie, Bruce R., *The Mortal Messiah: From Bethlehem to Calvary*, Salt Lake City, Utah: Deseret Book Company, 1980.

McConkie, Bruce R., *Mormon Doctrine*, Salt Lake City, Utah: Bookcraft, 1966.

McConkie, Bruce R., "The Mystery of Mormonism," October 1979 general conference.

McConkie, Bruce R., "Ten Keys to Understanding Isaiah," *Ensign*, October 1973, 82.

McConkie, Bruce R., "This Final Glorious Gospel Dispensation," *Ensign*, April 1980, 22.

Messenger and Advocate, Apr. 1835, 110, *https://www.josephsmithpapers.org/paper-summary/history-1834-1836/79.*

Miller, Fred P., "Commentary on Isaiah," *MoellerHaus Publisher*, 1999, http://www.moellerhaus.com/isaiahdi.htm.

Miller, Jerry L. and Robert L. Miller, *Isaiah in the Book of Mormon: A Guide to Spiritual Growth,* Salt Lake City, UT: 2001.

Morris, Henry M., *The Biblical Basis for Modern Science*, United States: Baker Book House, 1984.

Moyter, J. Alec, (1993), *The Prophecy of Isaiah: An Introduction and Commentary,* Downers Grove, IL: InterVarsity Press, 1993.

Nelson, Russell M., "The Exodus Repeated," CES Fireside for Young Adults, 7 September 1997, speeches.byu.edu.

Nyman, Monte S., *Great Are the Words of Isaiah*, Salt Lake City: Bookcraft, 1980.

Nyman, Monte S., *Isaiah and the Prophets: Inspired Voices from the Old Testament,* Religious Studies Center, Brigham Young University, 1984.

Nyman, Monte S. "Restoring 'Plain and Precious Parts': The Role of Latter-day Scriptures in Helping Us Understand the Bible," *Ensign*, Dec. 1981, 21.

Oaks, Dallin H., "Taking upon Us the Name of Jesus Christ," April 1985 general conference.

Old Testament Student Manual 1 Kings–Malachi, 3rd Edition, Salt Lake City, UT: The Church of Jesus Christ of Latter-day Saints, 2003.

Packer, Boyd K., "The Balm of Gilead," *Ensign,* October 1987.

Parry, Donald W., Jay A. Parry, and Tina M. Peterson, *Understanding Isaiah*, Salt Lake City, Utah: Deseret Book Company, 1998.

Penrose, Charles W., in Conference Report, April 1918, 17–18.

Penrose, Charles W., "The Second Advent," *Millennial Star,* 10 September 1859, 583.

Penrose, Charles W., "Who and What Are the Angels?", *Improvement Era*, August 1912, 950–951.

Petersen, Mark E., "A Man Must Be Called of God," Brigham Young University devotional, 30 September 1979.

Petersen, Mark E., "The Angel Moroni Came!", October 1983 general conference.

Petersen, Mark E., in Conference Report, October 1965, 61.

Pratt, Orson, *Orson Pratt's Works: On the Doctrines of the Gospel,* Salt Lake City, UT: Deseret News Press, 1945.

Pritchard, James B., *Ancient Near Eastern Texts Relating to the Old Testament with Supplement*, United States: Princeton University Press, 2016.

Revell, Chelsea and Rabbi Yonatan Neril, "Trees and Humans in the Holy Land," *Interfaith Center for Sustainable Development*, 24 January 2016, https://www.interfaithsustain.com/trees-and-humans-in-the-holy-land-2/.

Richards, George F., in Conference Report, April 1930, 76.

Richards, LeGrand, in Conference Report, April 1963, 118.

Richards, LeGrand, *A Marvelous Work and a Wonder,* Salt Lake City, UT: Deseret Book Company, 1990.

Richards, LeGrand, "The Things of God and Man," October 1977 general conference.

Richards, LeGrand, "Value of the Holy Scriptures," April 1976 general conference.

Robinson, George L., *The Book of Isaiah In Fifteen Studies,* New York: Young Men's Christian Association Press, 1910.

Romney, Marion G., in Conference Report, April 1968, 113.

Slotki, Israel W., *Isaiah: Hebrew Text and English Translation with an Introduction and Commentary by the Rev. Dr. I.W. Slotki*, United Kingdom: Soncino Press, 1949.

Smith, Gary V., *The American New Commentary*, Volume 15A Isaiah 1–39, (United States: Broadman & Holman, 2007).

Smith, Joseph F., "*Doctrines of Salvation*" Deseret Book Company, Salt Lake City, 1955

Smith, Joseph F., "Fruits of the Spirit," *Improvement Era*, July 1899, 699–700.

Smith, Joseph Fielding, *Answers to Gospel Questions*, 5 volumes, Salt Lake City, UT: Deseret Book Company, 1957–1966.

Smith, Joseph Fielding, in Conference Report, April 1966, 14.

Smith, Joseph Fielding, *Doctrines of Salvation: Sermons and Writings*, vol. 3, United States: Bookcraft, 1973.

Smith, Joseph Fielding, *The Progress of Man*, Salt Lake City, Utah: Deseret News Press, 1952.

Smith, Joseph Fielding, *The Signs of the Times,* Salt Lake City, UT: Deseret Book, 1970.

Smith, Joseph Jr., *History of The Church of Jesus Christ of Latter-day Saints.* Edited by B. H. Roberts. 7 vols., 2d ed. rev. Salt Lake City: The Church of Jesus Christ of Latter-day Saints, 1932–51.

Stapley, Delbert L., "The Blessings of Righteous Obedience," October 1977 general conference.

Steele, Valerie, *Encyclopedia of Clothing and Fashion*, volume 1, Germany: Charles Scribner's Sons, 2006.

The Teachings of Presidents of the Church: Spencer W. Kimball, Salt Lake City, UT: The Church of Jesus Christ of Latter-day Saints, 2006.

The Teachings of Presidents of the Church: Joseph Smith, Salt Lake City, UT: The Church of Jesus Christ of Latter-day Saints, 2011.

Talmage, James E., *The Articles of Faith: Being a Consideration of the Principal Doctrines of The Church of Jesus Christ of Latter-day Saints*, Salt Lake City, Utah: Deseret Book Company, 1988.

Tanner, N. Eldon, "Why Is My Boy Wandering Tonight?", October 1974 general conference.

Taylor, John, *The Government of God,* United Kingdom: S.W. Richards, 1852.

Taylor, John, "The Government of God," *Ensign,* August 1971.

TrendEconomy, "Annual International Trade Statistics by Country," *TrendEconomy.com,* 5 April 2021, https://trendeconomy.com/data/h2/Israel/08.

Tristram, Henry Baker, *The Land of Israel: A Journal of Travels in Palestine, Undertaken with Special Reference to Its Physical Character*, Society for Promoting Christian Knowledge, 1865.

Whitney, Orson F., in Conference Report, April 1919, 70.

Widtsoe, John A. (1960), *Evidences and Reconciliations*, Bookcraft, Salt Lake City UT.

Widstoe, John A. *Improvement Era*, April 1944, 225.

Widstoe, John A. *Rational Theology: As Taught by the Church of Jesus Christ of Latter-day Saints*, Salt Lake City, UT: Deseret News, 1915.

Wirthlin, Joseph B., "Seeking the Good," April 1992 general conference.

Williams, Clyde J., "A Shield against Evil," *Ensign*, January 1996, 28.

Woodruff, Wilford, *Collected Discourses: 1886–1889*, compiled by Brian H. Stuy, United States: B.H.S. Publishers, 1989.

Woodruff, Wilford, *Journal of Wilford Woodruff*, 15 June 1878, Historical Department, The Church of Jesus Christ of Latter-day Saints, Salt Lake City.

Young, Brigham, as reported in Brown, James S., *Life of a Pioneer: Being the Autobiography of James S. Brown*, Czechia: Charles River Editors, 2019, 122–123. As quoted in Hinckley, Bryant S., *The Faith of Our Pioneer Fathers,* Salt Lake City, UT: Deseret Book Company, 1956, 13.

Young, Edward J., *Book of Isaiah*, United States: William B. Eerdmans Publishing Company, 1992.

Notes

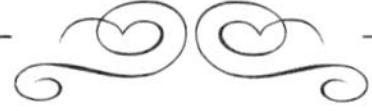

Notes

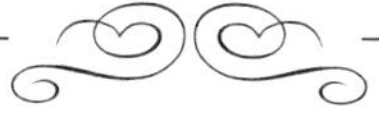

Notes

Notes

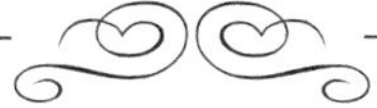

Notes

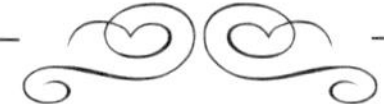

About the Author

Robert Miller's love for Isaiah started early when he and his father worked to coauthor a book on Isaiah's teachings in the Book of Mormon. His research has expanded and Robert now shares the results in videos, blogs, and as a teacher. He has taught youth and adults the words of prophets for 27 years. He and his wife are happy parents of five children.

Scan to visit

www.brotherrmiller.wordpress.com